W9-CTY-381

Long Way Home

Journeys of a Chinese Montanan

To Don,

Enjoy my Book

Flora Wong

By FLORA WONG with Tom Decker

Long Way Home

Journeys of a Chinese Montanan

The views expressed by the author/publisher in this book do not necessarily represent the view of, nor should be attributed to, Sweetgrass Books. Sweetgrass Books is not responsible for the content of the author/publisher's work.

ISBN 10: 1-59152-083-5
ISBN 13: 978-1-59152-083-2

Published by Wing Shing Company

© 2011 by Wing Shing Company

All rights reserved. This book may not be reproduced in whole or in part by any means (with the exception of short quotes for the purpose of review) without the permission of the publisher.

For more information, visit www.longwayhomebook.com

You may order extra copies of this book by calling Farcountry Press toll free at (800) 821-3874.

Produced by Sweetgrass Books
PO Box 5630, Helena, MT 59604; (800) 821-3874;

sweetgrassbooks
a division of Farcountry Press
www.sweetgrassbooks.com.

Printed in the United States.

16 15 14 13 12 11   1 2 3 4 5

Dedicated to the memories of my husband, Charlie Wong, my parents, Chen Sun Ho and Lee Sing Kim, and my sister Joyce. Many years ago, I lost these vital family members, but their inspiration lives on. They have given me the best of traditions, both American and Chinese.

Table of Contents

Acknowledgments

This story is not a detailing of my entire life. Instead, I have chosen to share select moments of significance in my life.

What you will also find are key people in these stories, all of whom have helped me in my life. Examples, counsel and advice from Mother and Father; my husband, Charlie; my sisters and brothers and a number of friends have been of great benefit to me all my years. My children, too, have provided wonderful inspiration.

For their encouragement in writing this story and for their support over many years, I thank my sisters, Edith Chong, Florence Woo, Maymie Ho and Dorothy Wong, as well as brothers Kenneth and Robert Lee, along with Robert's wife, Pearly.

I am most grateful to Amy Yang for her friendship, her wonderful advice and her willingness to talk about our pasts.

I am indebted to Beverly Conner, professor of English at the University of Puget Sound; Suzanne Barnett, a China historian now retired from the University of Puget Sound; and Robert Swartout, Carroll College history department chair and professor of history. All reviewed early drafts of my story and made helpful suggestions. My sincere gratitude also goes out to my children, Bess Wong, Gloria Wong, Thel Wong, Poy Wong and Nancy Wong. They took time to share stories, read drafts of my book and make many clarifications and corrections. In 1995, Bess organized, recorded and transcribed interviews with me and my sisters. These documents were essential in telling my story.

Patty Dean provided a wealth of historical connections and ideas on Helena and the Chinese community, so I am in her debt.

To Tom Decker, who patiently helped me put this book together, I also want to say thank you.

Editor's Note

Family and place names are given as Flora Wong remembers them, but other family members have differing recollections. For instance, the village name of Lin Fong Lei is Flora's Anglicized version of the name she knew in China. Others in the family write it as Lin Fong Leh or Lin Fong Lai.

Even the spelling of Flora's mother's name is subject to question. Flora's memory is Chen Sun Ho, but other versions include Chan Sun Ho or Chen Chee.

The surname Wong itself is subject to various spellings. Common versions include Huang, Hwang, Wang and Wone, while Vietnamese alternatives include Bong, Huynh and Hoang. When Charles Wong entered the United States in 1922, he used yet another spelling of Wong, which was Houang. By a 2009 estimate, more than thirty-nine million people in the world have the Wong surname, so different forms of the name flourish.

Names and spelling discrepancies continue within the family. Growing up, Poy and Nancy Wong believed their names were Poy Yin Wong and Nancy Fae Wong. At high school graduation, they found their birth certificates showed different middle names: Poy Neal Wong and Nancy Flora Wong.

To provide context, the book contains brief histories of Japan's invasion of China, World War II, China's civil war between the Nationalists and the Communists and land reform in China. Several college professors reviewed early drafts of the book and offered corrections and clarifications. I was guided by their thoughtful comments. For any discrepancies or errors that escaped attention, I take full responsibility.

Tom Decker

Concise History of China

1931   **September:** Japan invades Manchuria in northern China

1934   **October:** Long March of Chinese Communists to escape Nationalist armies begins in Jiangxi in southeast China

1935   **January:** Mao Zedong gains control of Chinese Communist Party

       October: Long March ends in Shaanxi in northwest China

1937   **July:** Japan invades China, Marco Polo Bridge incident

       September: Nationalist-Communist Parties form united front against Japan

       December: Rape of Nanking massacre begins

1945   **August:** Japan surrenders at end of World War II

1949   **January:** In full-scale civil war, Tientsin and Peking surrender to Communists

       April: Nanking and Shanghai surrender to Communists

       October 1: Mao Zedong proclaims formation of People's Republic of China (PRC)

       October: Nationalist government moves from Guangzhou to Chongqing ahead of advancing Communist Army

       December: Nationalists lose mainland and cross to Taiwan, Chiang Kai-shek declares formation of Republic of China on island

1950   **February:** China signs thirty-year Sino-Soviet treaty with USSR

       October: China joins fight in Korea

       June: Communist Party approves land reform policies

1958   China begins Great Leap Forward reforms

Lee Family History

1878 **May:** Lee Sing Kim, Flora's father, born

1903 **January:** Chen Sun Ho, Flora's Mother, born

1906 **February:** Charles Wong, Flora's future husband, born

1928 **October:** Flora Lee born in Boston

1936 Lee Family moves from Boston to Lin Fong Lei

1938 Flora's brothers and sister, Robert, Kenneth and Edith, return to the U.S.

1947 **January:** Flora Lee and Charles Wong marry

1948 **December:** Flora and sister Joyce depart China for U.S.

1949 Sisters Florence, Maymie and Dorothy escape ahead of Communist takeover

CHAPTER ONE

To China

MY FATHER ALWAYS TOLD US that we would live in China. My family lived in Boston then, where Father ran a small store in the city's Chinatown.

When I grew older, Mother and my older sisters told me how Father became full of life when he talked of returning to live in his home village along the southern coast of China. Usually reserved and calm, he became spirited as he painted a picture of village life. Even his expressions were lively as he described how we would spend our time outside in the warm sun. How we would enjoy a simple life in a village filled with people we knew. How we would be close to family and ancestors. Best of all, my father described scenes of a farm with a large house and rice fields reaching up to the hills. We would have animals to tend. We would leave Boston's crowds behind.

Most of his talk of China, of course, was adult discussion. I was only six or so when he first described his plans to move our family to his homeland. He was matter-of-fact about the topic, and Mother seemed to approve. As I remember it, I wasn't in a rush to leave Boston, the only home I knew. To a little girl, my father's tales of his past in China made little impression.

But when Father spoke, I just knew to stay quiet and listen.

Born May 15, 1878, in China, my father was named Lee Sing Kim. Lee was a very common name, particularly in Guangdong Province. As evidence of the importance of family to the Chinese, the surname was listed first; so the name Lee came ahead of my father's given name Sing Kim.

My father had little formal education, but he toiled long hours to earn money and succeed. To his children, he ruled the house. The revered head of our close-knit family, Father received the deference expected in a Chinese family. Beyond this respect, he inspired a bit of fear in his children, particularly the younger ones. I don't believe he set out to be a daunting figure, but as children we regarded him as distant and unapproachable, something of a mystery. I came to admire him for his bold approach to life, his attention to our family and his dedication to his work—attributes I recognized in him later in China.

If Mother and Father felt any misgivings about our move to China, I don't recall hearing them say a word. Most likely, they had no doubts. In most ways, my father and mother were very much alike. Their marriage combined traits of thrift, ingenuity and a certain toughness. Living in China, I am sure they agreed, would be better than living in Boston—better for family and better for economic reasons. In large measure, their decision also reflected the desire for the familiar setting of their native land. In the end, my parents were willing to risk a long, disruptive voyage, betting all their American savings on the land and family they once knew in China.

In our family, of course, the children followed Father's word without question. As one of the youngest family members, I remember feeling only a sense of excitement as our adventure unfolded.

Remembering my father, I can picture his kind face and gentle way of speaking to his children. In a family filled with young daughters, he was devoted but distant and strict. We often did not see or hear him. Some nights, as we sat close together around the dinner table, he might talk with each of us in turn. But he was gone from the house many days and nights as he tended to his store or socialized with other Chinese men in our Boston neighborhood. At home, he kept his thoughts to himself. In many respects, my father was like most Chinese men: formal and resolute in the face of any adversity.

Father was the oldest of three boys. When his two brothers died young, Father took on the responsibilities of caring for and leading his extended family, including his nephew, who became like a son. Confronted with the duties of household head at a young age, he developed a sharp sense of self-reliance and decisiveness.

Father married his first wife, Lai, in China. They had three children. Son number one, whose name I never learned, died very young. Within a year or so, son number two, Lee Shi Kong, was born. Next came a daughter, Lee Fong. When Father came to the United States, Lai and the two children stayed behind in China, a common occurrence among many Chinese families at the time.

Details about how Father entered the United States are unclear. One family account indicates he was actually born in Portland, Oregon, but that may have been part of an invented story to help him gain entry to the country. While I can't be sure, he probably came to America to find work and send money back to his family in China. Later on, he would have figured, he could return to his village to enjoy a comfortable life. For many, many years, men from Father's region in Guangdong Province took this path, a pattern set for others to follow. The men came to America for work. They corresponded with family, dispatched money home and maintained long-distance relationships. Eventually, some returned to their Chinese homes; others remained in America, earning money to send back to China.

I don't know when Father arrived in the United States, but shortly after he left China, Lai died. What became of his children remains unknown. After Lai's death, my father followed another Chinese custom. He contacted a matchmaker in his home village to help him find another wife. In another rural town close to my father's home, the matchmaker found my mother, Chen Sun Ho. The middle child in a large family with many brothers and sisters from his home region, she met my father's standards for a new wife. Although they had never met, he arranged for her passage by ship to Boston, and they were married in the United States.

Over the years, Mother shared only a few details about her marriage arrangements with her daughters. Never once did she say how she felt about this change in her life. When she spoke about how she and Father met, she stressed that marriages were organized by parents—with no questions asked by young Chinese women. She never told us what had become of Father's two children by his first wife, perhaps because she did not know.

In most Chinese families, parents considered it inappropriate to talk about their pasts with their children.

In Boston, Father's life revolved around his small store. I didn't know it at the time, but he had a good head for numbers and business. Father operated his business in the center of our neighborhood and catered mostly to other Chinese families.

In addition to a few standard grocery items, Father sold mainly herbs, tobacco and other odds and ends. At the back of his store, chairs and a bed filled a small room. Regularly, my father gathered here with a group of his Chinese neighbors to share in their favorite activities, which included gambling with cards or dominoes and smoking. Even today, I have heard that the store, which now is a Chinese bakery, has retained a loyal customer base.

According to family lore, Father enjoyed smoking opium on occasions, an activity I do not remember. I know he had several pipes, including a long water pipe with a bamboo stem and another short pipe fashioned from silver. In Boston, and later in China, my father seemed to be absent from the house much of the time. Like many Chinese men, he seemed to prefer the company of his male peers. For Mother, she saw home as her territory.

Father's business generated enough savings to pay for our move to China and provide for our life there afterwards. In Boston, I was so young that I don't remember much about my father in those days. All I remember distinctly is that he always seemed to be looking for ways to make some money to provide for his family. To Father, that included his immediate family and his relatives back in China.

Perhaps owing to his age—he was twenty-three years older than my mother—Father made sure he had a family quickly. My mother soon found herself busy with babies and running her household. In the first eight years of her marriage, Mother had a child nearly every year.

I still recall my Mother as a reserved, but kindhearted woman. Mother never spoke about her feelings. To read her, you had to study her behavior. She lacked formal education, but she made up for that through her ambition and energy. Born in southern China on January 19, 1903, she lived in a time when few considered education important, especially for girls in a peasant village. Still, by her common sense and perseverance, she became a good mother and manager of our home. What I remember most vividly was her confidence and persistence. She could be demanding with her children, but also positive. I admired Mother for her determination. In all she did and all she faced, she held a steady course and admitted defeat only rarely. Complaints in the face of life's trials did not occur with Mother.

When I was born in 1928, we lived in a fourth-floor apartment at 1 Hudson Street. Later, we moved around the corner to 27 Oxford Street. Mother cooked, more out of duty to her family than a love of the kitchen. She woke earlier than the rest of us and spent much of her time at the stove. In a house filled with small children, she took on all of the household tasks and kitchen chores. When my sisters and I were old enough, we helped; but for years she carried a big burden all on her own.

While still in Boston, Mother added to her endless household chores a new responsibility of running her own distinctive business. How she managed to care for all her children, run the household and still find time for this added venture, I will never know. But she did it.

Shrewdly, my mother concluded that her kitchen could fill a profitable double purpose during Prohibition. During the years of Prohibition, from 1920 to 1933, making alcohol at home became fairly common. Authorities pursued home distillers relentlessly for selling illegal alcohol and avoiding taxes, making Mother's venture risky. Alongside the peril came lots of clients. Her customers must have enjoyed her products. And the close-knit community helped keep her operations hidden from the prying eyes of officials. After the repeal of Prohibition laws in 1933, Mother continued her liquor enterprise. Mother never seemed to mind the hazards, and she certainly liked making money.

At the center of Mother's kitchen was her two-burner stove. Turning from family meals to her second career, she produced her own wine and even a bit of whisky. To make her bootleg brew, she relied on rice leftovers from a nearby restaurant and some rice yeast as a fermenting agent. She had a huge metal pot where she mixed her ingredients with water. She covered the container with a lid topped with a series of homemade tubes made of copper. Then she boiled her concoction on the stove, relying on the mass of copper tubes and loops to condense and save her liquid. A separate tube in her condenser system had a spigot where Mother drew off her fortified product. Rice wine came from one distillation cycle. For whisky, Mother might distill a batch two times or more. Her stove-top creations were not high in alcohol content, but their sweet taste appealed to many.

According to family stories, Mother's regular clientele earned her a steady income for her efforts.

Combining energy and business sense, Mother earned enough money from her bootlegging to pay some of our family bills and put aside more savings. Coupled with what my father made from his store, my parents' earnings provided the funds for our trip to China. Mother also converted some of her revenues into purchases of gold jewelry. Her gold stockpile would become a critical resource to our family many years later.

Throughout their lives, my parents kept their emotions carefully in check. It was a rare event when either of them raised their voices to scold or discipline. My father took even greater care to restrain his emotions when in the presence of outsiders. Upon meeting strangers, Father was on his guard, perhaps even suspicious. He took a long time to make friends. He rarely offered any smile or remark that might signal his thoughts.

I have tried to remember the voices of my parents. Father's has become a hazy memory. I recall Mother's expressions, but her voice I have lost as well. To her, remaining composed was important. She was short, built a little wide and solid. She had a high forehead, pronounced cheekbones and straight, black hair. She kept her hair in a swept-back fashion, which emphasized her strong facial features. Many times with her children, her face alone often conveyed her meaning, so she needed few words.

By the mid-1930s, Mother and Father had a plan to find a home back in China, buy land for farming rice and vegetables and live a life of comfortable retirement for Father. Mother, I am sure, expected to manage the household and the land.

As Father talked of his China plans, Mother, by all recollections, also expressed her enthusiasm. She knew China's hardships, but the journey would take her back to a place near her village. I suspect she viewed the trip as a homecoming. Despite her time in America, Mother had no real bond to Boston. Much stronger were the ties Father and Mother had to their native land, likely due in part to their upbringing in the beliefs of Confucianism. To this Chinese way of thinking, ancestors and family are the central concerns in life. The home village was the base for the family, normally for countless generations. Even if they made a long journey, most Chinese expected they eventually would return to their home. By any measure, the individual knew that his or her own life, personal happiness and success came behind primary family considerations.

Most important in terms of reverence and respect were older generations. Grandfathers and grandmothers were dominant, so long as they retained their health and wisdom. Next came parents. Children ranked at the bottom. Youngsters who thought more highly about their status were branded as selfish and thoughtless or worse. In addition to esteem for parents, the views of revered Confucius emphasized ties to family and home village. In China, you grew up with the thought of your family as the source of standing and importance. And, at the end of your life, you expected to be buried in your village, presuming that generations of your descendants would later honor your memory at your grave. All of these considerations must have played in my parents' minds as they planned our move to China.

For my parents, returning to a familiar culture was important, but my mother probably made other calculations. By returning to China, she could tame a great uncertainty facing her. Conscious of her age difference with Father, Mother likely knew she ran a risk of being trapped in the strange land of America with nine children were he to die. Raising nine youngsters was challenge enough. If she found herself alone in Boston with no husband, the burden would be staggering. Better, I suspect she reasoned, to face such a duty in her familiar home of China. There, other family members could help, the language was more familiar and her money might go further. If she were to face stormy seas, a more favorable tide awaited her in China, certainly more so than in Boston. Mother, in her practical way, would have grasped these advantages immediately.

Another economic matter also must have colored my parents' assessment of their position in America. A quick look out the window of our home showed the damage of the Depression up and down our block. By the mid-1930s, lack of jobs and money had damaged all of Boston and our neighborhood. America's financial woes added one more reason in my parents' decision to pack up and return to China.

Not that there was much room for real debate from Mother or any of us about the idea. Father had spoken. Had there been any real objections from my mother or any of his children, my father would have paid little mind. We were a typical Chinese family of the time; Mother and children never questioned the authority of Father. In family discussions, the views of women and the young carried little weight. The voices of children were heard only by specific invitation from Father. Our words were for our parents' amusement or our education, not for serious consideration when making decisions.

To Chinese children, custom held that dutiful respect for parents, particularly the father, was the ultimate virtue. We learned early in life that we must follow direction from our parents without regard for our own feelings. Even if you thought the quality of parental decisions was suspect, you knew to keep such concerns to yourself. Your path was to follow directions. Father, as the oldest son, learned to exert his authority and grew comfortable in the role. At times, his judgments might have seemed unconditional, unmovable and even harsh to his children. But, by custom, we looked up to and relied upon Father. No one, particularly his young daughters, gave any thought to questioning our father's actions. We could add our opinions, but we knew they would not make any difference.

What I knew for certain, even as a little girl, was this: Once Father said we would make this move to China, we would eventually do exactly that—return to his home village.

What was more vivid to me as our journey neared was listening to Father's stories of China and how we would be happier living there. Dinnertime became a time for stories about a land of rice fields, green hills and plentiful water. His scenes told of warm summers, mild winters, lots of neighbors and plenty of celebrations. To me, China remained such a distant land, beyond all comprehension.

Talk of China went on for months, but Boston remained my home. I struggled to see why we might leave it. Boston must have felt a bit like home to Mother, too. She learned the neighborhood, discovering where to shop and which stores carried certain Chinese specialties. She got to know many of the neighbors. What may have been strange to her at first in Boston slowly became familiar. Her transition would not have been easy, for Mother did not read or write either Chinese or English and she spoke no English at all.

Starting with the birth of my sister Edith in 1923, Mother soon found herself with a house filled with children. Florence arrived in 1924, Joyce in the middle of 1926 and I on October 1, 1928. My birth came in the

year of the dragon. Next
came Maymie in early 1930,
Robert in 1931, Dorothy in
early 1933 and Nancy late
that same year.

Another son to Mother
and our family was Cousin
Kenneth. The oldest son of
Father's youngest brother,
Kenneth moved in with us
and became known as older
brother, Wah Goo, to all.
Complicating our family line
further were Father's children
from his first marriage. In my
case, the family tree meant I
was always called daughter
number five, despite being

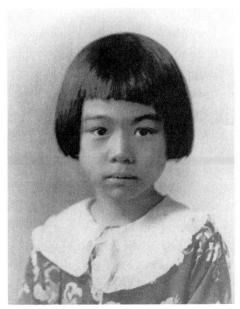

Flora Lee in Boston, Massachusetts, at age six
in 1934.

Mother's fourth daughter. The difference was Father's daughter with his
first wife. Sometimes confusing, the designations became clear to us over
time despite the lost contact with Father's first family in China.

How we were given our Chinese names revealed another family priority: the importance of producing a male heir. According to family lore
and our interpretation of our names, the birth of daughter after daughter brought an increasing sense of urgency to have a son. The first two
girls, Edith and Florence, were given the Chinese names Toy Kane and
Toy Yong, respectively, names for which we had no direct translation to
English. When the third daughter, Joyce, arrived, Mother and Father gave
her the Chinese name Toy Hai, which we were told meant "want to have
a brother" in English. As the fourth daughter, I was named Jong Hai. My
Chinese name roughly translates as "love to have a brother." Then along
came sister Maymie in January 1930. Desperation for a male heir reached
its height with her Chinese name: Oi Hai, meaning "really love to have
a brother." These translations were not precise, but followed my family's
understanding of their southern China dialect. In Maymie's name, the
magic finally seemed to work, as brother Robert was born soon after.

Soon more daughters arrived: Dorothy, named Oi Jane, and Nancy, Oi Lao. Mother gave birth to another daughter, Oi Koon, soon after we returned to China. She lived only a short time. So much was going on as we moved to China that I recall almost nothing about our last little sister.

But about Boston, I have some memories of my childhood.

Because of Boston's small Chinese population, we kept to ourselves. I don't know for certain, but I believe economic conditions probably helped fuel our sense of separation from the rest of the city. Alongside our neighbors, my family sought friendship, common society and refuge in our own part of town among familiar faces. For my parents, I suspect the crowded streets, the open storefronts, the familiar groceries and the vegetables spilling out of stalls helped them feel more comfortable. In Boston's Chinatown, they found a bit of China surrounding them.

At 27 Oxford Street, we lived on the second floor of a brick building, one floor above a business, a store of some kind. Our quarters occupied the rear half of the second floor, facing an alley. We liked it there, as it was usually quiet. Across the street from the front of our building was the Chinese mission where my sisters and I went to Sunday school. For whatever reason, church was an activity only for us kids; our parents never attended services.

Typical for a home in our neighborhood, our apartment had no bathtub or shower. For baths or quick scrub-ups, we used a round wooden tub, something like a half of a whisky barrel. Our tub's rough edges had been smoothed by time and use, but it retained the look of a primitive cask. Kids and grownups alike used our washtub.

My older sisters attended public school, usually from 9 A.M. until 3 P.M. We called it English school. After dinner, my sisters went off to a second round of classes at a nearby Chinese school from 5:30 to 8:30 P.M. The days followed a firm, precise schedule, dictated by schools and parents: six hours English school and three hours Chinese school each day.

In the evenings, my older sisters trooped downstairs and crossed the street to Chinese school. By opening her window, Mother could hear her kids singing or playing. I liked the sounds, but I never attended the Chinese school in Boston. We left for China before I could start.

My sisters tell me I started classes at the English school at age six, but I can't summon any memories of lessons in Boston. My recall is clouded partly by my young age, but more because of my lack of interest in school. I know this: I held onto little knowledge from my classes. Right from the start in first grade, I was a poor student, and my performance slowly declined. Learning in any form came hard for me. Where I thrived was nap time, not study time.

Our parents didn't buy us toys, and I don't recall them encouraging us to play games. But as lively kids, we figured out our own fun. The street outside the apartment served as our main playground. There we amused ourselves in the usual children's games and sports. I recall that Edith, as the oldest, learned to roller skate. Edith's skating showed a streak of rebellion in the family. Father had specific ideas about what was proper for young ladies. Among his lessons: His daughters "would not ride bikes or roller skate." But skate Edith did, with all of her sisters as disobedient partners. Our little revolution consisted of gathering up our single set of skates, sneaking downstairs and running several blocks away to escape Father's notice. Our actions seemed rebellious and thrilling at the time. If Father had discovered our sport, his disapproval and punishment would have been certain.

On rare occasions, Mother took us to a large park close by the house to play on the grass. These were simple excursions: no picnic, no toys, no games, just time together outside in the green setting of the park. For fun, my sisters and I had to rely on each other and our imaginations. I remember these trips as pleasant contrasts to our crowded lives at home.

But our time in Boston was rushing by as the new year of 1936 began.

What began as an adventure into the unknown for me would change all of our lives in so many ways. Yet, as a timid girl, I was more frightened than excited by our departure from Boston for China. My fears increased as departure day approached.

In the midst of their plans to return to China, Father and Mother made one other fateful decision, one that would cause a painful, lasting change in our family. Mother and Father decided to give my youngest sister, Nancy, away to neighbors. Another Lee family, a young couple, lived nearby. They wanted children but had been unable to have any. Mother and Father decided they would help the couple by sending Nancy to live with them as a "seed" for their new family. The theory of one child serving as the starting point for more babies was a concept my parents accepted. One day

Lee family just prior to departure to China. Parents Lee Sing Kim and Chen Sun Ho at center. Children, clockwise from far left, Flora, Florence, Kenneth, Edith, Joyce, Dorothy, Robert, and Maymie.

Mother packed some clothes for Nancy and the two of them departed. Only Mother returned home.

As we packed for our trip, one of us asked: "What about Nancy?"

Mother did not reply. For years, Mother never discussed what had become of little Nancy and why. When we departed for China without her, she became part of another family. Years would pass before anyone in the family had any contact with our sister again.

Decades later, as I reviewed family mementos, I saw pictures of Nancy, her hair permed in a fashion similar to my sister Joyce. In her pictures, with her high cheekbones and tightly curled hair, Nancy resembled Joyce's daughter Virginia. I also saw traces of my Mother's face looking back at me from the photo.

On a visit to Boston in 1993, our family friend Helen Woo took my sisters and me to meet the woman who adopted Nancy. Seated in her wheelchair, the distressed woman cried continually as she related the story of our sister. Nancy married at a young age and soon was the mother of three children. As her adopted mother shared Nancy's past, we understood our lost sister must have been very unhappy. Early in her marriage, she ran away with no warning, leaving her husband and three young children behind. The husband could not care for the kids, so Nancy's youngsters, a daughter and two sons, were raised by Nancy's adoptive mother.

Between sobs, she told us Nancy continued to live in her thoughts but that she never saw our sister again. From time to time, I heard a few more stories of what became of my missing sister, but the facts have drifted away in the fog of the past. No one seemed to know what had become of her. Yet her adoptive mother, holding out hope year after year that Nancy might return, refused to move away. Anticipating that somehow she might be reunited with her adopted daughter, she stayed in the same Boston house until her death.

My parent's fateful choice for Nancy underscored to me just how uncertain life could be. I thought of my family as an unbreakable unit, the one sure fixture in my world. But at the moment of our departure for China, at age seven, I discovered a reality with no guarantees. Even within my family, nothing was assured.

CHAPTER TWO

Lin Fong Lei Village

Our 1936 trip to China began on a train ride across the country to either Seattle or Vancouver, British Columbia. Next, we boarded a passenger ship for a twenty-one-day passage across the ocean to Hong Kong.

I don't remember anything about our time aboard the ship. My older sisters told me we were crowded three or more to a cabin. A mix of rough seas and boredom kept us below decks most of the time—a recipe for seasickness in our first days. As I was already unsettled by the expedition, I can imagine how the expanse and force of the Pacific put me more on edge. I remember I did not look out at the water much, as the distance to the horizon frightened me. I can't recall the name of the ship or what port we arrived at. I am sure we must have docked in Hong Kong, which served as the natural gateway to my family's home province of Guangdong.

For the crossing from Hong Kong to the mainland, we took a much smaller boat than the ship that carried us across the Pacific. The next legs of our journey required several days. Leaving the Hong Kong docks, we traveled across open water along China's south coast a short distance. Then we turned north, venturing up rivers and waterways. Along the way, Father directed gangs of men to transfer our belongings at each stop. At each pier, the boats seemed to shrink in size, as did the waterways. All around us were other watercraft crowded with people, animals and goods. We navigated up many rivers, passing all sorts of boats, including ferries, junks, sampans and rafts. Along the shore, we spotted villages, markets and rice fields. In the distance were low hills. To me, our new home was a confusion of water, rice paddies and people.

For the final leg of the trip, we shifted to the smallest boat yet, this time carrying just my family and our luggage. Two boatmen poled the craft up a narrow stream, using their long sticks to push and steer us. When we landed at a last rickety dock, Father organized a small group of men to load our belongings into carts. Then, he paid for several rickshaws to carry the ten of us: Mother, Father, me, all my sisters and my brothers. As we traveled along a dirt road barely wide enough for one cart, our rickshaws competed for space with people, more carts and a few animals. Some people pushed their own wagons filled with produce, ducks and geese. More carried shoulder poles with bamboo baskets of supplies slung at the ends. Several men drove water buffalo along the road. Our slow progress left me plenty of time to take in all the strange sights.

For most of the last leg of our journey, groups of people in the fields stopped and stared at us and our belongings as we passed. Some pointed and giggled, probably because of our unusual clothing and unfamiliar faces. When we were close to our final destination, a small crowd gathered and followed behind our carts. They made me nervous as they looked us over carefully. Their bold stares seemed to bore right through us. Father knew why they stared.

"They want to see if we are foreign devils. The ones they had been warned to avoid," he said.

Lin Fong Lei, our small village, differed from all I had known before. In place of paved streets, we found dirt roads, tiny alleys and worn pathways. Beyond the paths were neatly terraced rice paddies and irregular fields sweeping out in every direction. Once we left the main port at Hong Kong, I saw no more large cities and few large buildings. We passed small cities, followed by even smaller towns. A small collection of houses, perhaps ten or fifteen altogether, constituted a village. Most homes were two-story and built of brick. Tiny, cramped alleys linked the homes, most of which had the same tumbledown look. And everywhere, I noticed people digging or hoeing in the terraces of the fields.

Row of houses in Lin Fong Lei village, 1936. Lee family house at far left.

In my first days in China, I quickly formed an opinion of this new land. Perhaps it was disruption from the transcontinental rail trip from Boston, the long sea voyage or the shock of arrival in a foreign land—or the combination of all three. Whatever it was, I knew right away I didn't like China. Still a little girl, I did not have my own opinions yet. But my point of view about China was certain. I saw it as dirty, crowded and noisy. For what seemed like the first time in my life, I formed my own view almost instantly.

So many contrasts to my past life confronted me. A drab uniformity marked everyone's clothing. All the people, men and women alike, wore the same two-piece black or dark gray attire. No bright colors, just the same monotonous look. Everybody wore similar pants. For women, their tops had short, Mandarin collars with buttons starting in the center and then off to the right side. Despite the heat and humidity, the women buttoned their collars right up to their chins. The women seemed small but sturdy, a bit like my mother.

Along with dreary colors, the clothing seemed rough and poorly made. Back in Boston, at least we had good clothes, I thought. Where I got this smugness, I don't recall.

I felt a bit of homesickness for Boston. There, I knew the sounds of people talking in English, a language I hadn't yet learned to speak fluently, but one that at least sounded familiar. Boston's noise of cars and commuter trains had not prepared me for this new rustic scene. Now in China, people and animals made most of the noises. I was greeted mainly by the sounds of barking dogs, cackling geese and quacking ducks. The people spoke in what sounded like an unfriendly clatter, a dialect I did not recognize at first.

My most distinct recollections of those first days in China were of earthy smells. As little sister Maymie would remind me for years to come, it smelled nothing like apple blossoms.

My new home in Guangdong Province was near the southern end of mainland China, east of Macau. Our village was in the far southwest corner of the Pearl River delta, below where three main streams, the East River, the North River and the West River, converge. Hundreds of islands made up the landscape of Lin Fong Lei and its surrounding territory. Our new home rested on relatively flat, sandy ground surrounded by brushy terrain. Farmers in the area devoted their lands to rice paddies and ponds for raising fish. Sprinkled among the paddies were some fields of sugar cane, fruits and mulberry trees. The region's only mountains, called the Southern Mountain Range, lay far to the north, too distant to see from our new home.

In our village, rice fields surrounded us, extending in every direction until they ended at barriers of low bushes, bamboo thickets, small forests and low hills. When the rice had sprouted, the fields were an orderly pattern of green. Other times, bare dirt and mud filled the view. Years of cultivation had left the soils tired. The fields had a grayish look, not like the dark colors of hardier fields. This new land was given over to mud in the rainy season and dusty clouds in the dry season. In some fields, dikes held back the water and terraces kept erosion to a minimum.

In stark contrast to our former home was the weather. We had rainy and dry seasons, but fairly consistent temperatures of 75 to 95 degrees most of the year. Our wet season arrived in summer, normally June to August. Typhoons might rush through in summer, bringing wind and heavy rains.

Summertime humidity made the hot temperatures feel even muggier. At this time, I came to like the rain. For me, the showers cleansed, cooled and washed away the dust. Heavy rains, which came from time to time, were miserable, so we often ran inside. A rush of mosquitoes also marked the hot season. Along with welts from their bites, I usually got a heat rash on my forehead. When the bugs swarmed, I welcomed the rain, as it drove away the mosquitoes.

Southern China's dry season came in winter. Even in winter, temperatures rarely dropped below 50, and we spent most of our time outside. Usually a sweater was all I needed for cooler days. Rarely in all my years in

China did I need a coat—good news because I don't think I ever had one to wear. For school, of course, we were indoors, but classes did not last for long. Work and play meant being outdoors. Only cooking and sleeping brought us into our house. We seemed to live outdoors.

Spring and summer transformed village life. From dawn until the red sun went down, villagers worked their plots of land, planting, weeding and harvesting. In most fields, men prodded their water buffalo and plows across the rice paddies. The men yelled and cracked short whips to urge the beasts forward. Around the countryside, young boys and girls bent over to plant their rice fields while younger children played in the water-filled ditches.

Lin Fong Lei had no businesses to speak of. No shops, no stores, no restaurants—only a part-time community market. Our village really just consisted of three or four rows of houses, five to six houses in each row. The town's tight alleys, barely wide enough for two people to pass, made Lin Fong Lei a densely packed square of brick buildings. Where we found daylight was in the surrounding fields. At the outskirts of town stood a community well. Located farther outside the village was a large shrine honoring the dead. Beyond that was land for rice and other crops. Long rows of bamboo trees divided one set of fields from another.

Right off, Father focused on investing in land. Finding a home and as much land as he could afford, I think, was my father's main purpose in Lin Fong Lei. Even before we left Boston, Father made inquiries about land purchases and improvements on a house in the village. Soon, we had the biggest plot of land in our village, a sign to my older sisters that Father and Mother had done well for their time in Boston. Our land holdings, Edith and Florence told the rest of us, would bring us a comfortable life in China and a happy retirement for Father. While workers made improvements to our house, Father moved us to an upper-floor apartment in the nearby village of Gim Woo. Located above a vacant store, our cramped lodging bulged with children and furniture.

Our stay in Gim Woo was short. Within weeks of our arrival, Father's hired work crew finished the house and my family moved in. All the kids marveled at the large rooms, much more spacious than any in our Boston apartment. If my parents worried about the cost or trials of establishing the house and our fields, their children saw no signs of it. Father seemed at ease, taking walks around the village and down to the market area, where he met with a few men from the town. Within a few days of our arrival, he seemed to have acquired a circle of male acquaintances similar to the group he knew in Boston.

When a family moves into a new home, Chinese tradition calls for an open house, or *yeep ok,* to which all villagers are invited. Mother and Father consulted a fortune teller to determine which day would be best for our big party. The choice date must have been in the fall, around October, because I recall the fields were brown and empty following the harvest.

Our new house seemed so big that I thought it could hold the entire village, but Mother and Father put up a big white tent near our front door for the guests. Mother spent a long time preparing platters of food. Father arranged to have a couple of villagers roast a whole pig. When the pig was ready, four members of the cooking team loaded the roast on a platform, lifted it above their heads and carried it into the house. There, they carefully lowered it onto a large table. Looming above the scene was our family shrine, visible on the second floor through our open ceiling. People pressed into each corner of the first floor. Someone, perhaps Father, said a blessing for the house.

The group immediately spilled back outdoors. Knowing that fireworks were next, my sisters and I followed at a safe distance behind the crowd. Father stepped to the front of the throng and lit a string of firecrackers, which dangled on a long bamboo stick above the crowd. The loud noise and bright sparks dazzled me. Better yet was the food Mother had prepared. To serve helpings to the guests, Mother assigned duties to her older daughters. I was too young to be of much assistance, so I just stared at the action. So many hungry people swarmed in line that the row stretched down the street and beyond the neighboring houses. Soon enough the food was gone, even though more unfed guests remained. The stragglers in line seemed to come from the poorer families in the village. When we ran out of food, Father came forward and gave money to people with empty bowls.

Nothing ever seemed to rattle my Father. To me, he was always organized and ready. He knew what to do in any situation.

Right after the party, we settled into the schedules of daily life. In our first year in China, I don't remember having to do much work. Instead, I recall laughter and play with my sisters in the countryside. Butterflies and dragonflies buzzed all around as we played. Lots of other flies, too, but we didn't seem to mind. Mother, too, seemed more lighthearted at first. Outside our front door grew my mother's favorite blossom, called Bok Gnot Lon. Creamy white petals formed a fragrant blossom about the size of my hand. The flowers opened like a lily. As blossoms appeared, Mother often picked one and placed it over her ear.

Soon enough, my easy life ended. During our next summer, my sisters and I learned we had chores. Mother told us it was time for our jobs on the land and around the house. Maymie and I were introduced to two cousins. They were the two figures we had already seen in our fields. In time, we found out that our property in China required lots of exertion. I didn't know it then, of course, but our family stuck with the traditional ways of farming in this part of China. I don't recall any efforts to improve our farming techniques with modern irrigation or fertilizers. Instead, we followed historical practices. To replenish the soil, we mixed human and animal waste with ash from our stove, dried it for a time and then spread the blend on our fields. We farmed just like our neighbors, relying on nature's supply of rain to water the fields. Most seasons we had plenty of water. We irrigated by directing water from surrounding streams from one paddy to another. Our system worked fine when the rains fell. In dry years, however, our irrigation sources dwindled, leaving some crops to shrivel and die. I remember one or two times when we had severe dry years, but when a drought hit, many people suffered in the village. We relied on the weather, basic farming methods, our own hand labor and our water buffalo with a plow to prepare our paddies and fields for crops.

Our home region, too large for me ever to visualize, was a puzzle of rivers, streams and fields, all part of the Pearl River system. What I could see clearly were the low earth walls and terraces that gave a regular pattern to the scene. These plots, some as small as rooms, reached up the hills in terrace upon terrace. Some earthen-wall dikes began right at the edge of our village. Throughout the province, centuries of tilling and planting had left a distinct patchwork of small raised paddies separated by rougher patches of ground. The surrounding brushy hills were home to very few wild animals. Instead, farms with water buffalo, ducks, chickens, pigs and dogs covered the region.

Some years later, I learned that natives of Guangdong Province had reputations for hard work and exotic culinary tastes. A running joke among some Chinese said that Guangdong residents did well in every profession they tried, except as zookeepers. The point of the story, as explained to me, was that the people of our province were so overly fond of unusual foods that they couldn't be trusted not to eat the zoo animals in their care.

Viewed from the fields, Lin Fong Lei appeared as a neat rectangle of houses. But once you ventured into the alleys, our village looked much different. Walls and fences at some houses had collapsed over time as the adobe materials crumbled. Here and there, roofs buckled and sagged. Bricks often tumbled into the street. The village, with its maze of alleyways, had a regular grid for its three or four narrow lanes, but the fallen walls opened new shortcuts through parts of the town. On closer inspection, much of Lin Fong Lei had a decayed look.

In the row of six houses where we lived, ours was built of fired brick while the others were a smooth concrete of similar color and texture. Mottled black in color, our walls also had carved relief work at the roofline and between the windows. Most of the homes in our row had similar carvings that set this group of homes apart from the others.

Just as the building materials in each house were alike, so were the floor plans and furnishings. On the main floor, each house had two kitchens and a dining area. Usually the ground floor also contained a stable for livestock and room for feed. Each kitchen had space for wood storage, usually in a central spot close to the stove. In our home, as in most others, two bedrooms shared the main floor. A central hall with a stairway opened to the second floor, which had four bedrooms, one in each corner of the house. In our house, we also had a storage room and a large chest on the landing at the top of the stairs. Our front door opened directly onto a narrow alley with the house next door just a few feet away.

We enjoyed a distant view of the fields and hills from the second floor windows. One side of our house, with nine windows, looked off from the village toward the fields and thickets of trees, providing a sense of space so unlike Boston. My favorite view was farther west and north, where the countryside rose up to meet the low hills nearby. Farther away, a prominent ridge of green marked the horizon.

Compared to our Boston apartment, our new home had twice as many rooms and nearly three times the space. While we had two roomy kitchens, we used only one. Chinese homes usually have two cooking places, ready for the day when the number one son in the family married. Father and Mother were prepared for the day when Robert would find a wife. Then, our family would have its kitchen, and Robert's new family would have a separate cooking space.

Mother added a special touch in each kitchen: a paper kitchen god hanging above the stoves. Mother's name for the deity in our midst was Zao Shen—the stove god. To Mother, Zao Shen had a very important role: to watch over our household and all of us in it. Mother explained that each year, just before the New Year, the stove god returned to the heavens to report to the emperor of heaven on our activities. She mentioned this kitchen spirit so often that my sisters and I were certain we were being examined thoroughly. Based on our good deeds or naughtiness, the heavens would then reward or punish us. I was never quite sure what to make of our kitchen idols, but I was frightened enough of this mystic power that I usually tried to behave when within sight of Zao Shen. From time to time, far away from the house, I figured I might be able to hide some bad behavior, but I never tested the powers of the stove gods close to home.

Our kitchens occupied opposite corners on the main floor. In between was a large room that served as our storehouse. Two small concrete cisterns held water for cooking, bathing and cleaning. Against a side wall was a line of cages for the chickens, ducks and geese. At the center was a drain for wastewater. This area was part-time home to our pig, which also had the run of the kitchen. Here we cleaned and chopped vegetables and took care of other food preparation duties, such as killing the chickens. A separate part of the open area, which Mother tried to keep orderly, was designated as the area to clean our rice.

A very steep wooden stairway led from the central hallway to the second floor. At the top stood our family shrine, an elaborately carved wooden cabinet sitting atop a bench. Into niches in the cabinet, Mother and Father placed small tablets with written reminders of our ancestors. I can't recall now exactly who was commemorated there, but the list would have included our grandmothers, grandfathers and many generations past. A small ledge on the front of the shrine provided room to place incense sticks and small food offerings. Mother instructed us on how to leave these offerings properly, marked by many deep bows as we backed away. Mother left her respects on a regular schedule each year. Each time, she closed her eyes and bowed silently in respect.

Lin Fong Lei had no sewage system and none of its homes had indoor plumbing. We used a small pot, situated behind a curtain, for urinating. For other bathroom needs, we went to an outhouse a few steps from the house. Both locations, the pot and the outhouse, provided fertilizers for our fields.

Outside our door, the nearly 100 acres of fields surrounding the village required diligent cultivation to support Lin Fong Lei's population of more than 100 people. Most years, with adequate rain and good crops, the fields provided enough food to feed the residents. In times of drought, however, some families faced a grim test to ensure food for all in their households. When lean years hit, as they did at least twice during my time in China, lack of food drove people from our village. They left home in search of food and supplies elsewhere.

Like many villages in China, ours was filled with residents who had the same surname. In the case of Lin Fong Lei, the name was Lee. My guess is we were all related to the early settlers of the village. We considered ourselves distant family. All of us lived in very close proximity, in houses separated by only a few feet. Soon after our arrival, we knew most people by name—at least Mother and Father did. Although we were newcomers, Father had long family ties to the region. Although his daughters had reservations about our new location, my father seemed suited to village life.

Dotting the landscape around the village were graves and tiny family cemeteries. They usually occupied sites on the hillsides above the fields. Some were elaborate, others very simple. Where land was such a valuable resource, setting aside a plot for a grave meant a sacrifice. But honoring your ancestors outweighed the everyday concerns of the farm and food, so most families had gravesites. Larger burial plots were the sign of more prosperity, although I did not know it at the time.

Of my earliest years in China, what I remember most vividly was all the time I spent with my sister Maymie. We shared closeness in age, points of view and roles in family duties. As young girls, we played together, as young sisters do. In Lin Fong Lei, we also worked for many years side by side in the fields. I was very close to all my family, but Maymie and I became almost inseparable.

At first in China, our small village contained my whole world; it was where I played, worked and learned. For eleven years, from age seven until eighteen, my days revolved around my family, our house, our fields and our village. I rarely ventured beyond this space, which was isolated from the rest of the country. Looking back, I can see that much of this new life was hard and filled with physical challenges. Over time, I came to believe this was the way the whole world worked.

As I grew older, a second world came into view in shreds of adult talk, words I barely understood at the time. Now and then, I overheard descriptions of the chaos of invasion, war and economic problems throughout China. These troubles eventually would surround my family, our village and the entire country.

CHAPTER THREE

A New World

W HEN THE TIME CAME FOR US to start working, Mother spread assignments at home and in the fields among her older daughters. Maymie and I pitched in almost every day in our fields. Dressed in sandals, work pants and shirts and topped with straw hats to break the sun, we hoed and chopped weeds, planted rice and vegetables and tended all the crops. Together with Florence, we also took care of the farm animals. Our herd included a water buffalo, a pig, dogs, chickens, geese and ducks.

Most days, we started very early in order to get our hardest tasks out of the way before the heat of the day. Father, I recall, played no role in assigning or judging our work—at least no role that any of us noticed. At home and in the fields, Mother took charge. She managed the big picture, but she directed day-to-day duties with a light hand. Mother might occasionally visit the fields to inspect our work, but she seldom picked up a hoe or harvested rice. After silent observation, she might offer a suggestion or two, nothing more. Most of the time, she left us to figure out what work to do and how to complete it. Where Mother did her gardening was in the family vegetable plot.

Florence, the hardest worker among the sisters, helped Mother with all the kitchen chores and household duties. A treat for Maymie and me in the fields came at midday when we saw Florence trudging across the fields. She came straight from the kitchen, carrying lunch, usually rice with shrimp paste and vegetables, along with a pot of hot tea. Her appearance lightened our moods as we knew it was time for a break. Florence had a tough job. She cooked and cleaned, most of the time around a hot stove made even hotter by the tropical climate. Comparing our responsibilities to the kitchen work, Maymie and I agreed we had a better situation outdoors in the countryside. Still, the field labor was difficult and we often complained among ourselves.

"I don't like these chores. It's hot. Let's sit for awhile," I said to Maymie many times.

"I'm tired too," Maymie replied. "But if Mother sees us, she might put us to work in the house. I'd rather be outside."

Sister Joyce—smart, energetic, with a head of curly dark hair like Mother—also seemed to be something of a favorite to my mother. Outspoken and fluent in English and Chinese, Joyce had what we viewed as the best assignment of all. She accompanied Mother on shopping trips to the surrounding markets. It seemed to be the job that combined fun and excitement. What's more, Mother trusted her with the role of negotiator. At Mother's side, Joyce bargained with vendors for produce and goods. While we secretly resented her good fortune, the rest of us knew we did not possess Joyce's skills with language and math. Mother wisely chose Joyce for the position, but the selection created some hard feelings.

Edith, as the oldest, did the least, or so it seemed to Maymie and me. While we went out to the fields most days, Edith escaped all of the drudgery. Edith had squared off bangs, cut by Mother just like the rest of us. But her longer face and large eyes and mouth gave her a more distinctive look. We agreed she was the pretty one in our family. Edith did not stay long with us in China, only a couple of years. In 1938, Mother matched her for marriage and she moved back to the United States.

Mother saw to it that the youngest members of the clan, Dorothy and Robert, were spared any real duties for most of my time in China. Even our adopted brother Kenneth managed to avoid regular tasks.

In Mother's work design, Maymie and I went off to the fields nearly every day. Early on, she explained our roles would be to tend to the rice and other farm chores. I suspect Mother assigned the various duties based on age, skills and her view of which daughter was best suited to each role. From Mother's perspective, Edith would soon be leaving, along with Robert and Kenneth. Putting them to work would be a waste of training. Based on her practical nature, Mother pushed the rest of us toward tasks necessary to manage household needs. What surprises me still is this: Mother never scolded us, rushed us to complete our work or reminded us why our jobs were important. By some vague notion, perhaps, we realized our labor was a key to the success of our family farming enterprise. Early on, we had a sense that complaints about hard days or unfairness in assignments were out of order. The best approach was to put aside protest and push on.

Father, it seemed to me, enjoyed a carefree life, along the lines of the youngest family members. By the time we settled into the village, Father's life had the pace and pleasures of a retired man. He never worked in the fields. Even a visit by Father to the rice paddies was rare. And he didn't work around the house. At home, he spent most of his time upstairs in his bedroom, especially in the evenings. His room was his sanctuary, off-limits to his children. Mother, too, took care not to disturb him there. His bedroom served as his private dining room, as most every night he took his bowl from Mother and retreated upstairs, leaving the rest of the family to eat without him. Only special occasions would bring Father to the table for a family dinner. Why he enjoyed the solitude I never understood, but his family knew he liked to spend his evenings alone, a practice he had followed in Boston.

Most days, Father walked to the village market or a nearby town to talk with vendors and other male villagers. His task was conversation, not shopping, as Mother and Joyce always purchased the family food and supplies.

Father's daily outings were opportunities to talk, hear the latest news and, on occasion, play cards and mahjongg. Nothing gave Chinese men more pleasure than the chance to get off by themselves to converse. I observed this behavior early on in my father. At the time, I couldn't understand the complexities or protocols of these male discourses, but I always assumed some apprenticeship must be served before membership. With sufficient time and appropriate temperament, a man might finally join the group with full privileges. Because our village was small, my father's crowd was just a handful of men from Lin Fong Lei plus a few more from neighboring villages. By the time I noticed his group, my father had assumed what I took to be a prominent position among his acquaintances. His assembly, I suppose, served as something of an informal men's club for the area. But membership was an honor not all men in the village achieved. And women never sat in on the circle of conversation. It was a tight little sphere that I believe exerted influence in decisions affecting Lin Fong Lei and its residents.

In the fields, Maymie and I saw one day very much like the next. It was hard, mind-numbing effort, especially for two little girls. Most of the time, we were bent over chopping weeds, planting rice and helping to harvest whatever crops had matured. But by working together, challenging and encouraging one another, we could lighten the burden. I always told myself to aim for steady progress down each row of rice and, by day's end, we would complete our section of the field. Over many months, I knew our drudgery paid off because I saw advances on our land.

Our instructors in the ways of farming were not our parents, not even other adults. Instead, our two young cousins, Gnon Him, maybe six years older than me, and Gnon Yee, about my age of eight at the time, served as guides. The two boys taught us how to plant various crops, how to prepare the soil and how to gauge our progress in each endeavor. On any of the farm jobs we tackled, we learned from our cousins. When we looked beyond the day-to-day farming activities, again Mother and Father gave no direction. On what crops should be planted when and where, the cousins took charge. As the first months wore into the following years, Maymie and I learned the cycle of planting, weeding, harvesting and starting all over again. The young cousins explained at each step.

"To grow rice, first we have to get rid of the weeds," said Gnon Him. As the older overseer, he usually took the lead.

"Your job is to pull and to chop. Keep working all the time."

"I see all the rice growing around us. Why worry about weeds?" I asked.

"Don't be foolish," Gnon Yee said. "Get rid of the weeds and you'll make the rice grow strong."

Younger than his brother, he was just my age but happy to give us orders.

"We'll show how to start. First, we plant rice close together in the seed bed." Gnon Him said, pointing to a raised portion of the rice paddy crowded with sprouting rice plants.

"All this work just to make the rice grow?" said Maymie.

Our older cousin nodded.

"We start in bunches like you see. Later we'll come back and spread the plants in the paddies," said Gnon Him. "Watch us and you will learn. We know what we are doing."

In other lectures over many months, our cousins described irrigation, harvests and the cycle of crops during the year. They were our store of knowledge on everything on the farm. Looking back across many seasons in our fields, I am surprised my parents, Father especially, put so much responsibility in the hands of these two young relatives.

Following the example of Gnon Him and Gnon Yee, Maymie and I also learned to tend our animals—the pig, ducks, chickens, geese and our water buffalo. The two boys led the way, and we tagged along behind.

In our water buffalo I faced my biggest challenge. He was the size of a small bull, but with a gentler disposition. His bulk and strength frightened me, so Maymie usually took charge of the beast. As we marched out to the fields, she led our buffalo by rope or sometimes rode on his shoulders. Despite my status as the older sister, I brought up the rear behind Maymie. On days when the buffalo started slowly, we looped a rope around his neck and pulled him toward the fields, both of us yanking on the line. Our task was to steer him to the right rice paddy for that day's work as directed by the cousins. At the end of the day, we guided him home and bedded him down with hay and water. Cooperation didn't always come easy for our buffalo. But he was always fairly docile. Sometimes, when we were not plowing the fields, we simply tethered the buffalo in the field. Then we sat and watched him eat.

Most often, the buffalo had specific chores with the plow, so we helped hitch him to the old wooden tiller. Then, Gnon Him and Gnon Yee took over, driving him back and forth across the paddies to turn the dirt. One cousin pulled the buffalo from the front with a harness while the other drove the buffalo from behind. Any progress required plenty of yelling and pulling by the two, mixed with long pauses by the buffalo. The cousins used the reins but they had another weapon: a rope attached to the buffalo's nose ring. When the big animal refused to move, tugging on his nose ring usually got him going again.

The whole affair was a muddy business. As a first step in the planting process, we flooded the field with a foot or two of water. Next came a day of cultivating, which left a scene like a mud bath with cousins and buffalo alike covered in muck.

Our water buffalo was central to our farm. In one of Father's few farming lessons, he assured us the buffalo's size allowed him to do the work of three or four men. Hitched to the plow, he turned the mud in each paddy quickly. As I tended our buffalo, one thing I learned was this: With vast, silent patience, his steady pace accomplished many difficult, but necessary tasks. Straining on the ropes in the mud and muck of our fields, his sturdy legs slowly dragged the plow forward, cultivating our land row by row, over and over again.

As months passed into years, Maymie and I adopted much the same strategy to accomplish our own chores in the fields. Working side by side, in a steady, common rhythm, we first planted, then harvested. Row after row, day by day, we took our rice from seedlings to a full crop. Then, we set our sights on the next season's replacement crop. Despite the frequent boredom, we repeated the same cycle of work for many years.

As explained by the cousins and dictated by the seasons and rotation of our crops, life fit into a rhythm. February and March each year marked the first rice planting season. Our first step was to plant masses of rice in seed beds, the specially prepared plots of ground where the sprouts would get a faster start on growth. Close by the seed beds were our rice paddies, the terraced fields surrounded by manmade dikes. To prepare the paddies for the crop each year, Gnon Him and Gnon Yee plowed the ground, taking care not to damage the dike walls. Our buffalo was essential for this muddy work.

At plowing time, Maymie and I had the task of harvesting the small fish that lived in the paddy ponds. As the boys and the buffalo dragged the rake-like cultivator across the fields, Maymie and I tracked closed behind and caught the fish stirred up by the tilling. Short with fat bodies, these fish went to Mother's kitchen to supplement our stores of food. A few escaped our small, grasping hands only to die in the paddy, where their rotting bodies became additional fertilizer for our rice crop.

About one month after the first planting, normally in April, came time to transplant the rice. At this stage, the seedlings had usually sprouted to about six or seven inches. That signaled Maymie and me to move the plants from seed bed to paddy. First, we dug and separated the individual plants in the beds, then bundled them into baskets ready for replanting. Rice grew best when you planted it in evenly spaced rows in the paddies, a job that required strong hands and backs. Holding a basket of seedlings in one hand, we bent over our rows and moved slowly, planting each sprout separately with the other hand in a precise spot. Bowed down in the sun or rain, Maymie and I did not last long. My fingers and back gave out often. Most days, our cousins completed most of the planting. As the boys planted, my sister and I turned to sorting the seedlings and handing them over to the cousins, allowing them to move faster up and down each row.

Other times, especially as we grew older, Maymie and I completed the transplanting on our own. We crouched over each strip in the paddy, balancing plants in our hands and pushing them down into the muck of the muddy bottom. Every job in the paddies left us coated in dirt. By day's end, mud covered us from our toes to our knees and from our fingers to our elbows.

When the sun was hot, our brains boiled, despite the woven sun hats we wore to protect us. On rainy days, we enjoyed the cooling moisture. Through it all, Maymie and I moved, with curved backs and aching muscles, for what seemed like hours at a time. Many times Maymie asked me if my back hurt. I said, "Just don't talk about pain because it won't go away." Thinking about it did not help.

Late summer, usually around August or early September, the time came to harvest our rice. To start, our cousins raised a water gate or knocked holes in the earth walls surrounding the paddies. Water surged out, often trapping lots of small fish that flopped around on the muddy bottom. Again, we grabbed them eagerly as we knew they made a tasty addition for the dinner table. We seemed to have a steady supply year after year, either because our cousins planted the fish or because they swam down the irrigation channels from the river above. In a natural cycle, as the rice grew during the season, so did the fish, eating the mosquitoes and other insects that flew around the paddies.

After catching the fish, we put them in baskets and turned back to the rice. Working row by row, we cut rice stalks and stacked them on the paddy wall. Once the cutting was complete, we loaded the stalks in baskets to be carried back to the house. All of us, sisters and cousins, carried long shoulder poles balanced across our backs. At each end of these yokes were woven bamboo baskets filled with our harvest of rice. In our world, the shoulder pole served as the universal transport system. Everything in the field—rice, stalks and even some weeds—went back to our house in this fashion. We carried the fish this way, too, and lugged those to Mother in the kitchen.

On a concrete slab behind our home, we laid the rice stalks to dry. With luck, we had sunny, hot days to help the rice dry quickly. Otherwise, we might have to let it sit for several days. At this stage, Mother stepped in to oversee our labor. She made sure nothing went to waste. Rice grains eventually became food; rice stalks and weeds went to the kitchen for stove fuel.

Here was our process: Mother, Maymie and I shook the rice kernels from the dried stalks. Next, we set the stalks aside and spread out the kernels with homemade brooms for another round of drying in the sun. When Mother deemed the rice kernels ready, we turned to removing the outer hull. For this step, we used a big grinder to separate each kernel from its hard shell. You had to be careful to grind just so. Too much crushing action and you would ruin the tender inner kernels of rice. Too little grinding and you would not break open the tough casing. For our grinder, we used two large, concentric baskets. Very carefully, one of us shook and turned the upper basket clockwise while another moved the bottom basket, slowly breaking down the rice hulls. Executed correctly, the gentle grinding action revealed the inner kernels. Florence tackled the rice milling with us if she had time away from her kitchen work. By Mother's regular presence and interest, we knew we were at the critical point in the process.

Over the years, Maymie and I became skilled at shaking the baskets and hulling the rice. The heavier shells and any remaining unshelled grains would fall one way, while the lighter rice kernels went another direction into their own basket. In an afternoon of hard work, we usually could produce a large basket of rice kernels. A slow, tedious process, for certain, but we got better at it with lots of practice.

Rice polishing came at the end. In our central hall, we set up a mechanism resembling a small version of the playground seesaw. It consisted of a wood plank balanced atop a large stone as the pivot point. At one end of the beam was another smooth, anvil-shaped stone positioned over a shallow hollow in our floor, shaped like a big bowl. We placed our rice kernels in the indentation. Maymie and I stationed ourselves at the other end of the beam. Our job was to push down on the beam with our feet to lift the stone above the rice. Then, using our leg muscles in unison, we eased the beam back down. In a steady motion, we used the rock at the end of the plank to swirl the kernels in the concrete hollow. Slowly over time, our little legs generated enough up-and-down, stirring action with the rice to complete the polishing process. In the past, Mother explained, this stone polishing was accomplished entirely by hand. Happily for us, the practice had been mechanized somewhat by the use of our foot-powered tee-ter-totter polisher. Primitive, yes, but much better than doing all the work by hand.

Still so young for most of our time in China, Maymie and I did not see the direct connection between our labor and the food we ate. We knew, of course, that our work helped bring food to the table. In reality, our fields and farm animals were the source of nearly all the food my family ate. My Mother and Joyce purchased very little at the store for our table. What we as young girls did not recognize was that without the harvest from our land, our family would have a hard time making ends meet. Looking back, I am sure we would have quickly depleted our savings had our farm not produced enough to supply our kitchen. For most of our years in China, the yield from our harvests was enough to keep us happy. I never remembered feeling we had too little to eat or that our diet seemed too monotonous.

At our subtropical latitude with its long growing season, we could have planted a second rice crop. Instead, we usually planted sweet potatoes in the fall, our next growing season. I think our cousins suggested the potato crop so that we would have more variety of produce for the dinner table. Maymie and I liked the transition to a new crop because potatoes were easier to tend. You simply planted, then harvested. No transplanting, but we did have to pull some weeds. With potatoes, start to finish came much easier. We agreed we liked that about potatoes.

In our other fields, we planted all sorts of vegetables, including taro root, daikon and bok choy. Over time, we added jicama, kohlrabi, onions, spinach, mustard greens, pea pods and beans to the list of crops. In our climate, we found we were pretty good at growing most anything if we worked at it.

And we had our livestock. Our water buffalo topped the pecking order as he was essential for the hard work of preparing the fields and paddies.

He was in no danger of ending up as a meal. Our fowl and the single pig we raised each year were for the dinner table—the pig a special delight for the New Year's celebration. Even our dogs were destined for the table. The villagers reserved dog meat for special community events, usually as a stew. When dog was on the menu, Mother did not allow us to complain. But we showed our dislike by playing with our portions and grimacing with each bite.

"No complaints now," Mother said repeatedly. "Just eat what we have and all that is in your bowl."

Another important section of our farm was a small pond near the house where we raised more fish and lily roots. At the time, it seemed like a big lake, but I guess it was about the size of a large room. Every now and then, we drained the pond, much like we did with the rice paddies. Florence, Maymie and I then jumped in and retrieved the fish flopping around in the muck. Before the pond bed dried out, we dug up the lily roots growing in the muddy bottom. These served as another important source of food for the whole family.

Most years in the fall, we worked in the fields on one chore or another. Starting in the potato field, we might move next to a spot where daikon or some other vegetable grew. Guided by the two cousins, we tackled whatever chore came next. I am sure we played plenty of games, but I recall we dedicated most days to tending the crops. What we gathered soon showed up at dinner. If we had any surplus, a rare event, we sold the excess crops to other families in the village, adding a little more money to the household budget.

With help from Joyce, Mother managed the sale of our farm produce. She divided portions for home and market and set prices. As usual, Father was absent, away in the village or upstairs in his room. Our cousins, while in charge of the growing operations, kept out of the business end. In many ways, our lives in the village became a female-oriented society, revolving mainly around my mother and my sisters. The absence of adult males did not strike me as unusual at the time. It simply was the way our family functioned. Mother was our leader and we, as her daughters, recognized our duty to defer to her choices. Father, a distant presence at this stage in our lives, had little influence. Mother was in charge.

Our food was simple fare. At home, we usually ate two meals each day. Morning started with a bowl of *jook,* a porridge made of thoroughly boiled rice. On rare occasions at home, we enjoyed a small snack of boiled or dried sweet potato or taro root at noon. Dinner came in a bowl, almost always rice flavored with *hom-ha,* a salty shrimp paste, and a stir-fried vegetable. Our everyday drink was plain boiled water. Special occasions might bring out a pot of tea to share. When Maymie and I worked in the fields, we enjoyed the luxury of a third feast, the field lunch Florence brought to us at midday. On days we didn't work, we had to make do with two meals.

Extravagances such as meat and dessert showed up rarely, only on very special days, such as holidays. In all my time in China, rice was the mainstay at all meals. Beyond that, we ate whatever vegetables came from our fields in that season. In place of meat, *chong toy,* a preserved form of turnip, added flavor and substance to our meals. Regulars on the menu were taro root, daikon or bok choy. We ate only small bits of these fresh vegetables in order to preserve the excess for later use. To stretch our supplies, we boiled extra bok choy, then dried it for storage as a soup base. If we had too much daikon we chopped it into narrow slivers and salted it in a small clay pot so it, too, would be preserved for later use. Whether it was the rice crop or our vegetables, we wasted nothing that came from our fields. Mother made sure.

On rare occasions, we ate small servings of fish at dinner. Usually, the fish came from our pond or the drying rice paddies. Once in a while and only as an exceptional treat, Mother bought fresh fish at the village market. Maybe three to four inches long with rounded bodies, the fish were small enough that Mother prepared several for a meal. She pan-fried or steamed them. If we had any leftovers, Mother carefully dried or salted them to preserve for yet another feast.

All the foods we ate—fish, meat and vegetables—were very salty. Salt added flavor, of course, but it was critical for another reason. Because we had no refrigeration, Mother used a great deal of salt to preserve our food. Flavor also came from regular sauces like *hom-ha* or *hom gnoi,* a salty fish preparation.

On important family occasions, we gathered inside the house to eat dinner around a rustic square table. Each of the children had his or her own stool with his or her name carved into it. Just as you had your own seat, you also had your regular place at the table, always in the same position.

Mother enforced strict rules on table manners. We ate with chopsticks only, no use of fingers. And you always had to use your chopsticks in the proper way, carefully picking up one small morsel at a time. I remember one night when Maymie devised a new means to scoop food out of her bowl with her chopsticks. Using this approach to take large bites, my sister was able to gulp down her share of dinner quickly. Mother immediately caught sight of this serious breach of table manners. In an instant, she smacked my little sister sharply on the hands with her own chopsticks. This was not the only time Mother served notice that breaking the rules at the dinner table was not allowed, not ever.

Around Mother, you did what needed to be done with no question and no complaint. Her reasoning was to make the most of what little we had—whether food, money or time. If you followed this line, my mother had great patience for her family. Even when Mother had every reason to be upset with us—and we often gave her good grounds—she always stopped short of being as annoyed as she had a right to be. But she never fussed or fretted over us either. Right or wrong, she let us learn for ourselves. We chose whether we learned the hard way or the easy way. When we made mistakes, she did not give us help in recognizing our errors. Nor did Mother offer much recognition when we got things right. Looking back, I think she wanted us to understand that life was unpredictable, maybe even dangerous at times. You had to be gritty, sharp-minded and sensible to make your way through each day. Her message was that you had to stand on your own.

CHAPTER FOUR

Water and Worries

IN SOUTHERN CHINA'S SUBTROPICAL ZONE, the climate was pleasant, but darkness spread quickly in the evening. When we worked late, Maymie and I knew we wanted to be on our way back to the house as the shadows first started to fall across the ground. We hurried home for another reason: We still had plenty of work to do. Once we reached our house, one of us grabbed our little round tub for washing. The other went off to fetch the wash water. Then into the tub went our mud-encrusted feet and arms so we could scrub off. Next came a sponge bath to wash legs, arms, hands and faces. Never did we enjoy a shower or hot bath, but I don't remember missing that luxury because we had never grown accustomed to them in Boston either.

For Maymie and me, mud was our constant companion and washing up was a daily task.

In Lin Fong Lei, the well just outside of the village supplied water for each household. Well duty was a vital chore. Wash water, drinking water, cooking water—it all came from the well. In our family, one of the girls had water-hauling duty every day. Bringing water to the house meant walking to the well with two large buckets suspended from your shoulder pole. Once there, you dropped a small pail down into the well and hauled it back up using the attached rope. It was a long, hard pull from the bottom of the well, even with a small container. You had to be careful to brace yourself at the top of the hole when you hauled up a full load of water. Balanced that way, you could keep the pail level and save enough strength to bring it to the surface. To fill my large buckets, I had to haul up six or seven small pails. By then, my arms were so tired that I found it very difficult to balance my payload for the trip home. With two full buckets at either end of my shoulder pole, I usually had to stop several times to rest and rebalance the cargo. After each break, I summoned more energy to complete my walk home with care. Too much sloshing of your buckets meant spills—bad news because you might have to return to the well if Mother determined that more water was needed. With practice and care, I found most of my water supply made it home with me.

While the water from the well looked pretty clear, we did not drink that stuff—it wasn't safe. Water had to be boiled for some time for use in cooking or drinking. But everyday wash water came right from the well, without the benefit of boiling.

We faced another water-related test. Any standing water in the paddies and fields provided a home to leeches. These bloodsuckers seemed to hear us in the paddies because they attacked as soon as we arrived to work. If you weren't careful, they managed to attach themselves without alerting their victims. Most often, Maymie would spot them on me before I saw or felt their presence. Every hour or so, we took a break to check each other for the pests. Leeches attacked our lower legs first. I always tried to shake them off, and if that didn't work I'd ask Maymie to pick them off. If you didn't find them right away, the leeches sucked your blood until they were as fat as your finger. Often, we didn't find the leeches in time. In those cases, the leeches drank blood to capacity and then dropped off your skin, leaving two small puncture marks. Dealing with the leeches was by far the worst part of my day in the paddies.

Field work and trips to the well weren't our only farm tasks. Every few days, Maymie and I hiked to the mountain to pick up brush, grass and weeds to fuel the stove. What we gathered was Mother's sole energy supply for her kitchen. We called our gathering grounds the "mountain" because it seemed so high to us. Thinking back, this mountain was only a set of small hills. Even though our hike was a round-trip of about two miles, we made the hike cheerfully. This duty, we knew, supplied the fuel to warm the house and cook our meals. Our wood-gathering missions also granted us relief from the fields and a change of scenery. Up the hill we'd walk, carrying just a few strands of twine as our tools. We gathered twigs and sticks until we had two small bundles each. Maymie and I tied these piles together with our twine and attached them to any stout branch we could find. Shouldering our loads, we headed straight down the hill for home. Each bunch alone wasn't much, but working together we collected what we considered to be a big supply of fuel for the kitchen stove. Mother, too, usually seemed pleased with our haul.

Our hikes up the mountain took us past many graves and markers of the Lee ancestors of Lin Fong Lei. By now, we knew reverence for ancestors required that graves be close to the village so families could visit regularly. Our family did not have its own cemetery site, and I remember someone asked Father why not. I was surprised when Father responded that land was "so valuable but we give too much of it to the dead."

We may have felt a bit of a shock from the outdoor labor after city life in Boston, but I really don't remember it. Nor do I recall missing Boston for very long. As I adjusted to the new surroundings, my new life in China did not seem so hard. No one in my family sensed a dramatic break with life in America, that moment where we were jarred out of our lives in Boston. At Father and Mother's direction, we simply moved on. Not only did my sisters never mention any homesickness for Boston, they did not even talk about our past there. Lin Fong Lei simply took over our lives. None of us made comparisons between our time in China with our days back in America. More hard work and less play seemed to be expected of us, so we never gave our duties much thought.

Over time, I came to see my country life as much busier than my city existence, at least what I remembered of Boston. Father had promised that our new lives would be simple. I wasn't so sure. Our new home seemed more primitive, and I did not consider our lives easy. We had lots of work. We wasted little time on play, at least not until evening. If we wanted the farm to succeed and our family to eat well, we had to work. Mother, much more than Father, monitored our efforts and the farm's production.

As kids, we looked forward to our adventures after the workday. As the weather warmed in March and April, we spent many evenings trying to catch a type of large beetle brought out by the weather. Right after dinner, we ran to the fields just outside the village to chase after the bugs as they skittered across the ground. Our exploits seemed grimy and raw compared with our younger days in Boston.

Florence was our most accomplished bug catcher. She charged first into the fields to capture our prey. Florence liked to be the leader. She excelled at being part instructor, part expedition guide.

"Most important is what to catch and what not to touch," she said.

"What is the problem?" asked Maymie.

"Grab just the beetles," she said. "Don't touch the *gow see.*"

Gow see meant "dog droppings" in our dialect. The beetles did look a bit like droppings, especially in the dim light of evening. The warning from Florence got our attention.

Once captured, the bugs went into a large paper bag. Usually, Maymie was entrusted with our collection, but sometimes I got the responsibility. We went from path to path, field to field, bent over looking for our prey on the ground. When we had captured a large mound of beetles, we headed for home. Seated together around the table, we formed a little assembly line for bug cleaning. First we pulled off the wings and hard outer shells. Next we twisted off the heads and removed the innards. Once cleaned, we cooked the bugs, stir-fry style. The best ones were those with the larger bodies, but we cooked them all. Right from the hot oil, we popped the treats into our mouths like snack food. The bugs crunched when you ate them. At the time, I liked them, but I can't imagine eating them now.

More adventure came in the form of frog hunts. Several times each month, we set out as a gang in search of the small animals, for fun and food. Rice paddies provided prime hunting grounds. We eagerly perched at the water gates in the dikes, as these openings attracted our prey. Frogs liked the moving water, so we lifted the gate to start a surge of water to bring them out of hiding. Each time we spied a flash of movement, my sisters and I plunged our fingers into the water and mud, aiming to catch the frogs before they jumped to safety. I didn't mind grabbing them, even though their sliminess made me wince. As usual, Florence was quicker at capture than the rest of us. Any time she saw a lot of movement in the water, she elbowed me out of the way. Because Florence knew I was slow to reach for anything slithering in the water, she took charge.

"I caught you," she said, every time a frog landed in her grasp.

The rest of us were slower.

"I can't hold them," I said.

"Sure you can. Do like I do. Grab their legs."

From the start, we knew Florence, with hands flying, would do most of the work. After grabbing each of her captives, she dropped the prize into a woven bamboo bag. Then she finished by clapping her hands together in celebration.

When our sack was half filled with jumping frogs, our little hunting party headed back to the kitchen. To catch the frogs was difficult, but to clean and cook them was outside my abilities. Maybe it was my aversion to snakes, but I couldn't bring myself to touch the frogs as we poured them onto our table. I didn't wail or leave the room, but neither did I crowd around the table. I let my sisters complete the cleaning and frying. But as soon as the kitchen crew stir-fried the meat, I eagerly ate my share. We dined on the long back legs, or drumsticks, as I called them, because those pieces offered satisfying chunky bites. The rest went to feed the pig.

Only much later did I comprehend the valuable purpose served by our frog and bug collecting expeditions. These exploits helped to feed our family. The frog legs, in particular, added protein to our diet, which otherwise consisted mostly of rice and vegetables from our fields. I remember we also ate a lot of dried sweet potatoes. Most of the time, the frog drumsticks were the only meat we ate for most of the month. We reserved the meat from our farm animals for very special occasions.

To a young girl growing up, our way of life in China could be boiled down to its basic elements. Each of us had a job to do to help the family, and you couldn't be complaining about your responsibilities. Negative thoughts were simply a waste of time.

Apart from my work routine, I often observed that other aspects of days in Lin Fong Lei seemed down-to-earth. All of the families in the village lived the same plain existence we did. I had no concept of upper- or lower-class neighbors. The distinctions did not exist. No cars passed through town and no railroads connected us with distant places. Nearly everything and everybody moved on foot or by wheeled carts. For people or goods going longer distances, you went by water and by foot. Whenever we visited family or shops in neighboring towns, we always walked, no matter the distance. We no longer used the rickshaws that carried us into town. Those were one-time luxuries. Still, life wasn't so bad. If not for my work in the paddies, I might have agreed with Father that life in China was simple and undemanding.

Invisible to me at the time was our status as a landowning family and the distinct economic advantages this offered compared to some of our neighbors. We owned the land we worked. Other villagers with no land holdings hired out for small pay as laborers to other landowners. Or they rented land to grow the food they needed. In my simple view of our village, the division between neighbors, not to mention any resentment it caused, never came to my attention.

Within a year of our return to China, in 1937, my father surveyed our house and land and seemed pleased with the progress of his young family. For a time in the evenings, my parents occasionally sat together at the dinner table—a source of warm memories of time with my family.

Despite all we had accomplished as a family, I sensed worry in each of my parents. What I did not know was that by the summer of 1937, Japan and China were at war. Although the two countries had been fighting intermittently since 1931, the conflict remained in the north of China for several years. In 1937 and 1938, the fighting escalated as Japan's army marched south. I am certain adults in the village discussed these wartime developments and what they meant for our region. I was nearing the age of ten, still too young to guess at what was bothering my parents and other villagers, although I sensed some problem was at hand.

At an age when they might have been content and ready to enjoy what they had built in China, my parents instead began to face troubled times. Our village was remote, a walk of several hours and then a daylong boat passage away from Guangzhou. Even so, my parents and our neighbors knew enough to be concerned.

In our second summer in China, battles between Chinese and Japanese soldiers no longer seemed so distant. The armies were coming closer to our doorstep. Mother and Father tried to hide their apprehension from their children, but we picked up tidbits of the stories. Some nights when they were together, Mother and Father were much quieter than usual. When this happened, none of us said a word. After a pause, Father might break the silence by saying to Mother that we would find a way to get through this newest difficulty.

Many evenings after the children were sent to bed, I tried to listen in as my mother and father continued their talks in quieter tones. I never understood all of what they discussed. Looking back, I am sure they worried about what we should do as a family in a country facing war and the political and economic upheavals that were sure to follow. Very shortly, we would discover how Japan's actions set in motion major changes for our province. In the long run, the fighting would start a decline, followed by the beginning of a new China, all changes that none of us could imagine.

CHAPTER FIVE

五

Can't Everyone Be Smart

OR A COUPLE OF YEARS, my tasks at home and in the fields did not
fill all my daytime hours in China, so I attended school briefly. My
older sisters and I started lessons in the village. All went to classes except
Dorothy, who was too young to start school with the rest of us. For Mother,
school did not seem to matter much. She never attended any classes and
I think she believed you were better off being practical than book smart.

Although I went to first and second grades in Boston, I remember very
little about my school days there. I'm sure I studied reading and writing in
English and basic math in elementary school. I really don't remember. None
of those skills made the voyage with me to China. Of that I am certain.

My learning challenges continued in China. In my two years in the village school, I don't recollect reading a single book. My interest in lessons
faded week by week. By almost every measure, I was a poor student. Math
gave me my biggest challenge. Even the simplest rules for adding and sub-
tracting seemed too complex. Multiplication and division were so hard as
to remain nearly incomprehensible. Years later, I still find that I am not
good with numbers.

School was my time to learn and develop some awareness of the rest
of the world, yet I missed the opportunities. In the Chinese custom,

I remained focused on my sisters, my family and, to a lesser degree, on my own life. School left me feeling dull, lacking in curiosity about how the world worked, how my classmates lived or where the future would lead me. My thoughts never wandered beyond my own family. Perhaps it was my wariness, fear, lack of confidence or Chinese reserve. Whatever it was that held me back, I missed many chances to advance my education.

My one bright spot was calligraphy, where I enjoyed some limited success. I learned Chinese characters, and I liked that part of my schooling. Sensing my struggles in other topics, the teachers were happy to concentrate on my Chinese writing. They were strict, drilling me on how to sit and stand up straight—no slouching allowed—and how to hold my pen just so. For once, I didn't mind when the teacher stood and looked over my shoulder at my work. To improve my technique, they gave me characters to trace and copy. I found writing the precise characters difficult, but I grew to enjoy this part of school. On this assignment, my approach mimicked what I used working in the fields: just keep moving on to row after row. After a time, Mother recognized my success by giving me my own ink and brush set.

School did have one attraction. By comparison to work, it felt like vacation.

School days in China went by as if I were in a cloud. I never wanted to stand out in class. I tried not to attract attention from teachers or classmates. Only rarely would I talk with classmates or seek help with my lessons. I was happiest when the school day ended without the instructor sending any questions in my direction. It was simple: I realized I did not like school and I had no desire to be taught.

"Why can't I figure these questions out?" I asked myself at the end of some lessons.

To justify my lack of educational direction or progress, I told myself, "Can't everyone be smart," which was my way of explaining that not everyone can do well in school.

Soon, my lessons and learning ended, lost to me for years as it turned out. After only two years of class in China, my career as a student halted without notice. In contrast to most public school systems, China's education system in our day offered no free schooling. Parents paid tuition to the school for the education of their children. Add to that the cost of a few books and supplies, and school became an expensive proposition. With six or seven children of school age, my family could not afford to send us. One by one, usually before the age of ten, we dropped out to save money and to concentrate on our duties at home.

The Chinese practice emphasized education for boys, much more so than for girls. Sending a boy to school yielded a better return on investment in most Chinese households, because the oldest male usually retained the family home and lands. For our family, with only two sons and limited money, education was not a priority, especially for daughters.

So it was that Mother took me aside after my second year of lessons to tell me my school days were over. I was delighted, glad to be free from the confinement of classrooms and the supervision of teachers. Already, I knew the hardships of the mud and toil in our fields, but I preferred being outside working with my sister to the time being cooped up in the schoolroom.

Leaving school so early, of course, I never received a degree, not even a grade school certificate. Many years later, I struggled to read and write just a little English, but I retained a bit of my Chinese language skills, put to use most often around my family Always, in either language, I struggled to organize my thoughts, whether composing a letter or following complex conversations. And yet, I found if I set my mind to the task and concentrated long enough, I could make sense of most anything. Only much later did I realize just how little schooling I had and how much my lack of education had held me back.

Lucky for me, in place of formal education, I found other ways to develop. I learned plenty by working our land. All my sisters were generous in playing with me. We explored the hills and roads surrounding the village. I am sure we scuffled and quarreled at times, but what I recall most is how, with gentle temperaments and even emotions, we got along. That is not to say every step in growing up was easy for me.

I was clearly the most timid member of my family group. My sisters picked on me, calling me "scaredy cat" or "cry baby"—*hoke bow* in our Chinese dialect. My sisters took great pleasure using my phobia of snakes to scare the dickens out of me. Whenever they could, usually on our walks outside the village, one of the group would run ahead to put a rope across my path. When I arrived on the scene, they hollered, "Snake!" and pointed to the slender menace on the ground. Because the road was really just a narrow trail between rice paddies and dikes, I had no way around the "snake" in my path. Paralyzed by fear, I stood still and cried until one of my sisters tossed it aside.

My mother must have thought I needed to learn toughness because she made no effort to scold my sisters or otherwise make them stop. I didn't respond well to this teasing and became more frightened as time went on, but I never complained to Mother. My fright was not without reason. We often saw small water snakes in the rivers, rice paddies and ponds. Dangerous, venomous Chinese vipers also lived in our region. Although we were warned to watch out for the deadly snakes in the surrounding bamboo groves, I don't recall any of my sisters ever seeing a real one.

Years later, I discovered that the teasing from my sisters formed a basic part of Chinese culture, a way to educate youngsters. Looking back, I am sure Mother encouraged it for her most timid daughter. In the process of being taunted, a child discovers how to control emotions and show strength. Here was my lesson on how to avoid torment: Limit your reactions and the mocking eventually ends. Mother set out to teach her children how to guard against displays of emotion or personal sensitivity and why feigning indifference was important. Mother, I suspect, watched my nervous reactions and felt more teasing of Flora was needed. She saw plenty of evidence that I had little control over my nerves and emotions. Looking ahead to what life would throw at me, she concluded I would have to grow more independent to cope.

Most evenings, my sisters and I filled our dinner bowls at the kitchen stove and ate together as a group on the porch. It was a time for just us kids to eat and play once we finished our meal. A favorite memory is singing simple country songs together with my sisters on warm nights. We had trouble carrying a tune, but the songs were fun. Mother did not join in our songs, but she often sat and listened, usually crocheting hats, which she sold later in the village market.

On the few nights when it was cold, we moved inside and gathered around the kitchen stove for warmth. Our smaller farm animals, responding to the chill, joined us there, too. Our pig, especially, liked his place just to the right of the stove where we kept the twigs and other fuel for cooking. He burrowed right into the pile of sticks to make a bed.

On the coldest nights, my mother might slip a few more twigs into the stove to keep it burning into the evening, a real luxury to us. Then, we all sat close together in the warm glow of the kitchen. Extending our evenings in front of the stove was not only enjoyable for the extra heat but also meant that Mother would send Maymie and me to the mountains the next day to gather more twigs—a nice diversion from our day in the fields.

No matter the time of year or the weather, darkness ended our outdoor play and drove us indoors. After dark, we had been warned, the many ghosts who lived in the graves around the village became active. We knew about the graves surrounding Lin Fong Lei, so the talk about all the roaming spirits scared us. Children heard stories of ghosts with fiery mouths and big teeth, ready to devour any youngsters they might meet at night. For a timid girl, those tales were sufficient warning to keep me close to home nearly every night.

CHAPTER SIX

War: A Country Broken

W E HAD NOT BEEN IN THE VILLAGE long when the first stories about the war with Japan began to circulate among our neighbors. But the fighting seemed so far away to the north. In Lin Fong Lei, we would be safe, we thought.

The village had no regular newspaper, radio or other means to learn what was going on outside our region. Father read any Chinese publications he could get his hands on, but few were available. Most of his news came from his acquaintances and the few travelers who passed by. Both of my parents gleaned information and gossip from neighbors and residents of nearby villages. These reports included talk about the Japanese invaders marching down from northern China toward the south.

Japan's confrontation with China began early in the 1930s as an undeclared war in Manchuria in the north. Open war broke out between the two nations in July 1937 at the Marco Polo Bridge outside Beijing. Using this incident as an excuse, the Japanese Army launched a full-scale invasion of China. The two armies fought back and forth through the summer of 1937 as the Japanese advance continued. Shanghai fell to the Japanese forces in November, followed by the brutal capture of Nanking, then the Chinese Nationalist Party capital, on December 13, 1937. We did not realize it, but the fighting was coming our way.

On October 12, 1938, Japanese troops landed on the east coast of Guangdong Province. To resist an attack, Chinese soldiers had set up fortifications along the main waterways leading to Guangzhou. The Japanese reacted by pushing ahead overland. Conditioned by rumors and false alarms, many people in our region at first could not believe the Japanese invaders had advanced south so quickly. Once the reality of the reports sank in, people clung to the hope that the Chinese Army would turn back the attack. Any optimism was hollow. Within days, the Japanese troops advanced to the eastern outskirts of Guangzhou itself. On Friday, October 21, the invading army entered the city. Soon the city was ablaze, with many of the fires set by the Chinese Army to prevent military supplies from falling into the hands of the invaders.

News of Japan's defeat of the Chinese defenders in Guangzhou and the occupation of the city stunned our village. In the wake of the raids, the provincial transportation system collapsed for a time. Railroads and roads were damaged. Guangzhou and major cities were cut off from one another.

The chaos spread as people from the city fled into the surrounding province. Lin Fong Lei, due to its small size and relative isolation, did not see any refugees, but we heard about their flight to nearby towns. Planes began to fly over the village regularly. As they first appeared high overhead, adults in the village paused to point at the spectacle.

Word of the Japanese cruelties horrified all who heard. The invaders followed the policy of the "three alls," which we were told urged Japan's soldiers to "burn all, loot all, kill all." Parents warned their children of terrible Japanese rituals. Rumors spread that the Japanese prepared for battle by practicing bayonet charges on Chinese people, slicing off the heads of captives and pulling up trees and planting children in the holes. A few stories from Shanghai and Nanking reached our region, and the accounts shocked all who heard them.

As fighting spread beyond Guangzhou, fear increased. Stories of Japanese troops attacking surrounding villages led to increased vigilance in Lin Fong Lei. More and more planes flew over, almost always at a high altitude. We were never sure if the planes were Japanese.

Although the events caused enormous worry to my parents, I still didn't grasp the seriousness of our circumstances. My days passed as they always had. Maymie and I worked in the fields as usual. Our biggest distraction most days remained a welcome visit from Florence with our midday lunch.

Not long after the first airplanes appeared in the sky, other more ominous reports about the war soon came to Mother's attention. Gossiping with the neighbors and others who traveled to nearby cities, she heard details about threats and violence caused by Japanese troops nearby in the Pearl River delta. Mother never shared with us all of what she had heard. But she made it clear we had to be careful every day. Watch for any sign of troops or airplanes in our area, she warned. The Japanese soldiers would harm us or kidnap us.

About the airplanes, Mother's instructions were specific: "Japanese airplanes can drop out of the sky and shoot at you in the fields," she said. "Always be ready to run and hide in the brush."

For me and my sisters, all aspects of war were frightening, but the thought of airplanes worried me in particular. I turned Mother's words over and over in my mind. Most upsetting was how quickly the planes would come upon us. How she knew this I could not guess, but I listened. She told Maymie and me to watch the sky at all times. "Run fast. You have to hide," she said. Mother's words on this new threat terrified me, but I knew we had to stick to our chores.

Swirling around the country and my family at this time were many troubling events: the invading Japanese, a long civil war that still simmered between the Chinese Communist Party and the Nationalist Party, the hard economic times. As a youngster, I had no concept of how these problems had begun to weigh on my parents and our family finances. Our farm still provided much of what we needed for food, but crop production fell so we started to purchase more items to feed the family. And prices rose dramatically, pushed steadily upward by the fighting and the shortages of food and other goods.

What I did sense was that my parents talked more openly about what lay ahead for our family. We had been in China for a year now, and Mother and Father could see that their children were hardy and adjusting well. But we had a crumbling government and a war at our doorstep. Father seemed to be more concerned, seeking out other men at the market to talk and visiting other nearby villages for news. In his practical way, he must have known the time had come to assess plans for survival or escape. Could we escape into the mountains if necessary or would we have to flee the area entirely? Would we go back to America? Was that measure even possible?

Mother, I am sure, worried quite a lot about her children at this time. But she and Father did their best to shield us from the worst of the war stories. Even so, my memory is of continual anxiety throughout the days following the Japanese invasion of Guangzhou. Meat, fish and vegetables disappeared from marketplaces. Precious salt used for food preservation became more scarce, a real hardship as we had no refrigeration.

At the close of 1938, spurred on by the Japanese advances in our region, Father began to talk openly with Mother about plans to return to America. Despite his determination to fashion a comfortable life for his family in China, Father sensed our peril and had been studying how best to proceed. Later, I came to see this moment as both a crossroads and a dilemma for my family, weighing the stability of America against the volatility of China. I heard enough talk about the troubles facing Lin Fong Lei that I found myself thinking we had a real chance to see America again.

On several occasions, Father and Mother called us together as a family to discuss the war and what it might mean for us. Whether my father had made up his mind when he said we might head for Hong Kong and then America, I could not tell. But I knew that he would not bring up the topic for discussion on a whim. If the time for a family talk about the subject had arrived, then I suspected Father had already decided what to do.

A part of me was pleased the war had pushed my parents to consider a return to the United States. I had always been too young to express my wishes at family meetings. But I was getting older, and this war presented me with an opportunity to be heard—and to speak up about my desire to go back to America.

One night, when talk of leaving China again came up in a family discussion, I showed up prepared. In the days before our gathering, I guessed that I might have a chance to speak, so I planned my speech. I collected my thoughts and courage. When Father brought up the idea of departing for America and said he was thinking of a plan, I stood up without waiting my turn to address my family. My boldness prompted a stern look from my father. He scowled directly at me, but made no move to cut off my words. Surprised that no else made a move, I looked around the table, took one deep breath and proceeded. My heart pounded loudly from fear of my father and nerves at addressing my family, but I spoke my mind.

"If we go back to America, that would make me very, very happy," I said, holding my hand over my heart as if to emphasize my strong feelings. "I don't like it here anymore."

Father still said nothing and made no move to silence me. I spoke again.

"I think it's time to go back to America. I am too frightened here. Trouble is close. I am afraid of the Japanese."

Even my older sisters Joyce and Florence seemed impressed that their modest little sister had found the nerve to speak out. They knew courage was required to stand up in front of Father. Looking back on my little speech, I know my father paid little notice to the views of one of his younger daughters, but my spirit in speaking out might have impressed him a bit.

"What do you think we will find back in the U.S.?" Father asked.

I didn't have an answer for that question, so I sat quickly. Why didn't I realize Father might quiz me? Still, I felt proud of what I had accomplished on my feet. What I remember most is that I selected the right time to speak up. Here was the right moment to influence my family, and I had voiced my views. Even as a young girl, I knew decisions about our future were being made. I had to stand up or my opportunity would be gone. It was quite a moment for a little girl, especially this mild and compliant one.

That evening, Father did not give his verdict on our future. I was sure he had selected our course; he was simply waiting for the right time to tell us his choice.

"The most important thing in life is to be prepared for whatever may come," he said, as he closed our family meeting.

t

Edith's Live Fowl Day

FATHER, I BELIEVE, HAD HIS PLAN for how our family would survive the threats of war, while Mother had hers. Whether they even agreed on what to do was something I never knew. But as Japanese first began moving south toward Guangdong Province, Mother initiated the first step in her own plan of protection for our family. As far as I could tell, her precise strategy and tactics were never explained to any of her daughters, perhaps not even to Father. For Mother, action mostly came without words. Sometime in 1938, she began a campaign to protect her family by moving them back to America. As I was to learn, when Mother concentrated her mind on a fixed goal, she would not be discouraged.

Sometime during in July or August, the rainy season of 1938, weeks before the Japanese captured Guangzhou, Mother called on a matchmaker, an arranger of marriages, in another village. Her first aim: Arrange for fifteen-year-old Edith, the oldest daughter, to marry. Soon enough, the matchmaker identified a prospective husband for our sister. Mother kept their conversations quiet as she considered the qualities of a man we later came to know as Uncle Joe. He lived in Mississippi, and he was searching for a wife in his homeland of China. He had written to his family living in a village close to our own for help. Just as Joe's mother sought out a matchmaker, so did my mother. They had turned to the same go-between. Joe was not able to return to China, so he asked his mother to take care of the marriage details for him. The matchmaker, after an exchange of photographs, had no difficulty linking two people on opposite sides of the world. Matrimonial interests and intentions were quickly assessed and family approvals obtained. Within a few days, the matchmaker had the couple paired up and our first family wedding had a date on the calendar.

Soon, our house buzzed with all sorts of wedding preparations. My family collected dowry items—mostly clothes and some furniture—to serve as Edith's contribution to her new family. In all, the final engagement and wedding planning took place in a span of a little more than two weeks.

These days were exciting, but I remember thinking that Edith was so young to be setting off on her own. And things happened so quickly that there hadn't really been time for the five younger sisters to ask questions. We weren't sure what a wedding meant. And we knew nothing about how this event would change Edith's life. Amid the uncertainty and the turmoil of the war, all the kids were glad to have a happy diversion in our household.

On the eve of her wedding, Edith and all the sisters slept in a main floor bedroom together, all in one big bed. I recall this as something of a tradition for the night before a wedding. For us, it turned into a very crowded slumber party, Chinese style. Some of our sisterly conversation was serious.

"Will we ever see you again?" someone asked Edith.

"Oh, yes. I'm positive," said Edith.

"When?" came the next question.

Edith had no answer. Neither did anyone else.

The next morning, when members of Joe's family and the matchmaker arrived to take Edith to Joe's village for the event, all the Lee sisters sprang into action. We surrounded the bride and put up an imitation fight to keep Edith from being taken from the family home. The matchmaker tried to break through our protective ranks. In line with Chinese traditions, we pushed back at the matchmaker and Joe's family, pulling Edith away from the clutches of any outsiders. We declared she couldn't be taken from our home. Next in this game, we stuck pinecones in the matchmaker's hair. Coated in a sticky substance, the cones made a small mess for the match-maker in keeping with our ruse to foil the wedding. All the push and pull, an expected part of the day's festivities, amounted to playful drama.

After some more teasing, we finally relented. Finally, the matchmaker hoisted Edith onto her back and took her to a waiting carriage for the trip to Joe's village.

A band of Joe's family members loaded Edith's dowry onto the carriage. The procession, with the overloaded wagon in the lead, departed for Joe's village. By tradition, only the bride makes the trip to the bridegroom's home, so our family stayed behind as the procession pulled away from our door. Two men from our village accompanied the wedding party to help watch over the bride and her gifts. I felt an ache of sadness as I looked on. With all she had packed, Edith, it appeared to me, really had no plans to return to our home again.

As the wedding party set off, the sun shone brightly. Before long, rain began to pour. Mother appeared a bit shaken by the bad weather. In China, a wedding-day downpour means the bride will be stingy. A four-hour trip to Joe's village in the driving rain drenched the carriage, riders and much of the furniture and clothing. As Edith recounted her story later, by the time the wedding party arrived, they looked a soggy mess. Clothes and hair were soaked. Mud coated the furniture, including a fine dining table. The group attempted to straighten up in time for the festivities. Inside her carriage, the bride dodged the worst of the rain. Edith kept her bright-red wedding tunic, red veil and black skirt tucked away from the heavy showers.

At Joe's family home, what a surprise awaited the bride. Because her husband-to-be remained in Mississippi, his family had to find a substitute for the groom. As Edith lingered in the carriage and peered shyly out the window, Joe's family brought out a rooster. All that day, for the wedding and through the afternoon's banquet, the sturdy fowl served as the stand-in for the absent Joe. Edith had seen plenty of roosters in her time, but she said this one particularly seemed to enjoy his prominence that day. He strutted ahead of the rest of the wedding party, puffing up his white feathers and prominent head to put on a show.

Edith knew Joe would be absent that day, but she had no idea a rooster would be his stand-in. By her wedding date, Edith had not heard anything directly from Joe, not even so much as a letter. All communications had been between the two mothers, with the matchmaker as the go-between. I don't think Edith had even seen a picture of Joe until a few days before her wedding.

In reality, having a fowl represent an absent bridegroom was not an

Sister Edith Lee in wedding portrait at age fifteen.

unusual choice. In our part of China, the ceremony even had a name, which I no longer recall, but it translated from our dialect as "a live fowl marriage." Most Chinese families believed that every man and woman must be married at the proper age and on the appropriate day. For families with men overseas who were not able to return to China on the specified date, a solution had to be found to ensure the marriage would occur on schedule. Substituting some sort of fowl, usually a healthy rooster, for the absent groom came to be the accepted practice. The rites and feasts took place at the moment deemed suitable, just as if the groom were present. I learned later that Edith's own circumstance that day also had a name. In our region, my sister would be called a "live fowl dame."

My family heard the details of the rooster's appearance and the rest of the day's activities some time later. By convention, Edith could not visit her family for at least three days after her wedding. When Edith returned home, she stayed just a short while, but she shared with her excited sisters all the stories of her wedding. Then she returned to Joe's village to prepare for her trip to America.

In December 1938, Edith reached Hong Kong, despite the Japanese Army's presence in the province. There, she caught a boat for Seattle, a twenty-one-day ocean voyage that eventually brought her face to face with the man she had married. Joe finally replaced the rooster.

In China, most people viewed marriage as a significant family and economic rite, not as a romantic and emotional ceremony. Prearrangement of marriage by other family members was a normal course. Yet to wed at fifteen, as Edith had, was unusual; the typical age for marriage was eighteen to twenty. In normal times, my mother likely would have waited a few more years to arrange for Edith's marriage. But she recognized the danger of the war circling around her family and decided there was no time to waste. She had formulated the beginnings of her escape plan for the family.

In keeping with her relocation strategy, Mother sent brothers Robert, eight at the time, and Kenneth, then seventeen, along with Edith. Edith and Joe took over the job of raising Robert for many years. He lived with them until he graduated from high school in Mississippi. Kenneth, in the meantime, went to live with other relatives in Indiana. There he grew up, eventually found a job and established his own family.

In an instant, my family shrank from ten to seven.

CHAPTER EIGHT

Silence and Storm

MOTHER FEARED THE TURMOIL of war. She also worried about Father, who had begun losing weight, walking at a slower pace and talking in a softer voice. Even as young girls, we noticed he did not look healthy. For my father, fears about the war and the ruinous economic conditions began to take their toll as 1938 drew to a close.

My father kept his usual routine of meeting with his group of friends and acquaintances, but he had a difficult time on his walk around the village. After awhile, he spent more time at home in his room. Mother never shared details of Father's poor health with any of us. Mother may have guessed at the nature of Father's sickness, but my family never visited a doctor, so no diagnosis was available. Mother and the rest of us thought Father had simply slowed down because of his worries about the future.

Before spring arrived, Father became too sick to get out at all. He no longer walked to the village market for his gathering with friends. My sisters and I knew the situation was serious when Father could not climb the stairs to his favorite place, his room. Mother arranged to have a bed set up in a corner on the first floor where he could face the front of the house. For days on end, Father did not leave his bed. He talked to his children at his bedside, but the words came slowly. He pulled the blanket up around his face until you could barely see his eyes. Most days when I watched him in bed, he was asleep.

Then one day, as Maymie and I came home from the fields, we saw all our doors and windows closed and shuttered tight. An instant feeling of fear hit me. As soon as I saw the house sealed up, I knew Father was dead. Walking inside with my head down, I joined my Mother and sisters. Once Mother had all of us assembled inside, she directed us to the side of Father's bed. Facing his body, we all bowed deeply a number of times. We were ushered from the room. Later, when we were allowed to visit Father again, his bed had been turned so that his body faced the back of the house.

He died on April 15, 1939, one month short of his sixty-first birthday. Years later, I wondered if he had just decided to stop worrying and let the end come.

Father's body remained in the house for nearly a week until his funeral. He rested on his bed, still on the main floor of the house. By Chinese custom, Father's body occupied what Mother described as the supreme position in the house during this time of mourning. Out of reverence, we were not allowed to be above where he lay at any time. The restriction meant none of us could go upstairs at all during this time of respect. With our upstairs bedrooms off-limits, we all slept together on the first floor in his honor.

Despite the presence of his body and all the funeral preparations going on in our house, I didn't really believe my father was gone. I went about my daily chores in a state of numbness. Haunted by the phantom of my father in our house, I was troubled all the more because I could not call on him for help or to explain what was happening. By now, I had learned the important lesson that personal feelings and emotions must be controlled, at least on the outside. So I kept quiet. Mother, I knew, would be upset by any outbursts from her children. With some difficulty, I kept my dread in check.

Someone from a nearby village arrived to prepare the body for burial. We ordered a special wooden coffin. In the days leading up to the funeral, Mother worked late into the night sewing mourning clothes out of special cloth for her five remaining daughters.

On a day that seemed much colder than normal, we dressed head to toe in white, the Chinese color for mourning and death. Before going out the front door of our house, we formed a procession of all six remaining family members. We walked in single file from the house to the gravesite, wearing white pointed hats, another sign of mourning. After a long walk across fields and hills, we stopped at a site above the village. Before us was the open grave for Father.

At the burial site, we burned paper money for Father, so he would have money to use in the afterlife. We also left food, a rice bowl and whisky to help him on his final journey. Before departing, we burned punks of incense around all sides of his open grave and stood in silence. As men covered the coffin with dirt, Mother turned away quietly and began to walk home. I don't remember that we cried. I know Mother would have been upset if we had. All the way back to our house, I don't believe she said a word to anyone.

In her final act before leaving the gravesite, my mother had placed a small amount of gold inside my father's coffin. She'd intended it as assistance to ease Father's way into the afterlife. I suspect it was gold, or at least something of great value, because we were told someone dug up Father's grave and opened his casket soon after the funeral. Whoever did the grave robbing must have thought we put a lot of gold in my father's grave. It was a desperate act in a small village where you knew everyone by name. For someone in our own village to commit such a deeply disrespectful deed should have served as a warning to Mother and my family. In many ways, life had been hard in Lin Fong Lei for Father, even at the very end.

Back in the village following Father's service, a few other family members and neighbors gathered outside our house. We somehow held up through the nightmare and coldness of the day. Those few details are all I remember of Father's passing. I was so young, just ten. Reacting to our sadness over Father and our concerns at Mother being alone, my sisters and I filled the house with sadness and tears for days. For us, it was an unusual show of emotion. But we tried not to let Mother see. Everyone pined away but Mother. In the weeks after Father's death, she seemed determined that no one would see her break down. After all, she had a big family to support, all on her own. She wanted her family to know she would not collapse under the responsibilities and sorrow she now carried.

What I recall about my mother, at this time and during the many events to follow, was that she rarely drew back under difficult circumstances. Her response to pain or fright was to fight. In the days following

Father's funeral, she kept busier than usual, looking after each of her children, trying to make everybody in the house feel safe and happy.

In spite of her steadiness, my sisters and I noticed changes in Mother after Father's death. Her reserved character turned even more withdrawn from her family. In normal times, she never spoke more than necessary, but for some time after the funeral she said even less.

One day, soon after Father's burial, Mother gathered us together. With Robert, Kenneth and now Father gone, we were a house full of women without a male leader, an unusual circumstance in China. As I recall, this was the only time Mother spoke about how her daughters should respond. "You are strong. You are young. You have good spirits. You must respect and remember your father, but he is gone," she said.

Except on special occasions, she rarely mentioned Father again.

Some months after Father's funeral, Mother seemed to grow stronger, as if a bit of her liveliness returned more every day. I was troubled that, like most people, I took Father, Mother and my family for granted. In part, I was reluctant to reach out. Beyond my hesitation, I really did not know how to talk with my family.

What few distinct memories I have of Mother and Father I value deeply. But I regret there is so much I never knew about my parents. And so much that I have forgotten. Much later, I realized that my happiness came not from our house, our farm or the times we had money, but simply from time with my parents and other family members. And I realized that the sorrows of life helped me enjoy the high points even more.

CHAPTER NINE

Run and Hide

IN THE SUMMER FOLLOWING my father's death, Maymie and I had our first brush with the war. It was a warm, humid day in 1939, nearly a year after the Japanese invasion of Guangzhou.

For months, we often saw planes zoom high above us, but none flew low over the village. And during this time, we had never spotted soldiers anywhere near Lin Fong Lei. Other than the occasional streaks in the sky, our days in the fields passed as they always had.

One particular morning, Maymie and I were working in the paddies as usual. Coming from off in the distance, I heard a distinct hum. As I scanned the horizon, the noise grew louder. At first, I was not sure what it was. Then it became a roar. Following Mother's warnings about Japanese airplanes, I searched the sky. The source of the noise was no longer a dark speck. It was an airplane headed directly at us.

I reacted immediately. As instructed by Mother, I dropped my hoe and grabbed Maymie by the arm.

"Come with me quick. Run for the trees," I said.

"Why, what's wrong?" said Maymie, who was not paying attention.

"Airplanes are coming. The Japanese devils, Maymie. Mother warned us. Run now," I said as I grabbed her arm. I wasn't usually this forceful, even with my little sister.

"Why?" asked Maymie. "I'm too tired to run."

"No, we have to run now for the bushes. They can't see us there."

When Maymie finally looked at the sky, her eyes flew open wide. We dashed toward the brush. Dropping their tools, our cousins ran up to take cover with us. We ducked into the trees just before a lone Japanese plane swept low over our home and the fields. I expected to hear explosions coming from the plane as it passed above our heads. We had been warned of the racket of hundreds of New Year's firecrackers when the planes shot at people. But I heard nothing like that, only the loud growl of the engine. The plane swept close enough that I saw the pilot and the red rising sun insignia on the side. In a moment, it was gone.

The four of us stayed in the trees for a long time, waiting to see if the plane would return. No one stirred in the village. After a long period of silence, we did not know what to do. The best choice seemed to be to go back to work, so we did.

After that first airplane flew low over our corner of China, we saw planes in the sky more and more frequently. Usually, just one or two flew by in a regular pattern at high altitude. Occasionally, the planes screamed by just above the village. The thundering sounds drove us out of the fields and into the underbrush. Never did they actually shoot at us. But we heard they had fired at people in villages nearby, so Mother made sure we kept our eyes and ears on alert. Our work in the fields never stopped. But any time a low-flying airplane approached, Maymie and I quickly dashed for cover.

I never could make sense of what these airplanes were doing. They came without warning, on no regular schedule, with no regular pattern of flight. Finally, I decided the planes flew above us as if we were unworthy of their attention or notice. For me, they seemed headed for a far-off rendezvous. What did they care of Maymie and me below, in our fields?

Japan, I was told, lay far beyond the ridge to the east where the sun rose. There, the Japanese generals were making their plans, reviewing land to be taken and lives to be lost. In our isolated little village of Lin Fong Lei, what plans could we make? What could we do but run for cover when the planes came?

Adults in our village realized the fix we faced. Years of war had challenged China's leaders and weakened the economy. Generalissimo Chiang
Kai-shek, leader of the Nationalist Party, remained in command, but his
government moved frequently as the Japanese soldiers advanced.

Despite the fear and uncertainty in our village, we saw none of the
destruction firsthand. At times, my sisters and I listened to the rumors
of war with a sense of excitement almost, a bit of excitement for our dull
lives. Adults, of course, knew better and did their best under maddening
circumstances. Years passed and no soldiers ever appeared in Lin Fong Lei.
Airplanes swooped down but flew on without a shot.

While I don't remember being painfully hungry, I do know that our
food supplies began to dwindle steadily after my father's death and the
Japanese invasion. My family had enough to eat, but hunger lurked as
a killer in our village. Maymie had made friends with a little girl who
lived with her family in a house a couple of alleys behind ours. During
one dismal season, when crops failed in many fields around Lin Fong
Lei, Maymie's friend disappeared. When Maymie went to check on her, a
neighbor explained that the girl and her brother had died days earlier from
starvation. If this news made a real impression on us, I don't recall it. We
should have been alarmed that Maymie's playmate had died from lack of
food, but the thought that we might not have enough food at our house
never occurred to us.

Mother did her best to keep us fed and healthy. But after several years
alone, weighed down by Father's death and wartime distress, Mother
seemed to lose some of her force and enthusiasm. Her daughters didn't
understand the causes, but we all noticed that Mother seemed tired most
of the time. She made no complaints and kept up with all of her household
chores. But a sluggishness came over her and her mood darkened, more
than at any time I can remember. Faced with the burdens of her family
and without the support of Father, her pain must have been heavy during
those days.

Life would be easier for Mother, we thought, if we could do more to
help her. About this time, Florence, our leader in the kitchen, said we had
to make sure Mother was eating better. We agreed, so Florence began to
give Mother the first and largest portion of rice and vegetables from the pot
each night. Then we added more water to the pot, stirred the contents and

served our own meals. We were pleased with our resourcefulness, and we watched for Mother to get better.

As a family, and as a village, we were safe but reeling on the edge of peril. We were pulling together as a family, and the villagers of Lin Fong Lei were starting to look beyond the seeming quiet to prepare for what the Japanese might bring. The villagers realized that most of the escape routes were gone. The Japanese controlled the largest city in our province, had stationed troops throughout the region and had expanded their hold on a broad swath of the neighboring countryside. Trying to run away would be very difficult. Most in Lin Fong Lei simply waited for whatever might come.

CHAPTER TEN

Auspicious Times

A S THE CONFLICT WITH JAPAN took hold all around us, my sisters and I continued our normal duties with little change. Lin Fong Lei's isolation along poor roads helped keep foreign troops away. Life in the village remained mostly quiet, moving at its normal pace amid the tension. We still made time for fun.

Favorite memories centered on the celebrations of Chinese New Year. We eagerly anticipated this celebration, the largest for the country, our village and my family. Normally a fifteen-day observance and festival, the New Year gave people time to rest, play and visit with friends. Even our small village organized its own festival. Everyone joined in the gambling, eating, drinking and parades. All rejoiced because the harvest was over and toil was at an end for a time. For villagers accustomed to hard work day after day, this time of year provided our only holiday.

Mother began her preparations weeks beforehand. First came a thorough house cleaning, more complete than any other during the year. Mother directed us to take everything out of the house. We stripped rooms of all we could move, arranging stacks of furniture outside. Back inside, we scrubbed all the rooms, with special attention to the kitchen. Then, we moved the whole lot back inside. Her goal, Mother said, was to sweep away any family misfortunes and prepare for good fortune in the future.

"Time to wash away the dirt, wash away the dust," Mother said.

She repeated her message at each annual cleanup. Her children knew the most thorough purifying frenzy of the year was coming each time she mentioned the approach of the New Year.

"Make way for family good luck and auspicious times" was her constant refrain as we worked.

Once we finished our house chores, Mother turned to the New Year cooking. All of us crowded around the kitchen stove and, starting early in the morning, we cooked all day long under Mother's watchful gaze. Florence, number two in the kitchen after our mother, took her command role seriously as she ordered us about. Maymie and I planned on extra trips to the hills for more fuel. Even Joyce and Dorothy helped out with the cooking chores at this time of year.

For me, the highlight of the holiday cooking was the preparation of what we called *tays*, special dumplings essential to our New Year's feast. Made of rice-flour wrappers filled with vegetables and meat, *tays* topped my list of food favorites. We rolled out the rice-flour dough then stuffed each dumpling with vegetables and a little meat if we had it. Mother helped us fry the *tays* in a big pot of hot oil, dropping the morsels in one at a time. We took great care to avoid burns from the boiling oil, but we had some close calls as each of us crowded in to get our treats. I was ready to eat as soon as they cooled just a little, but Mother made sure none of us touched even one. She had definite plans for all our dumplings.

She set aside the first small batch of *tays* for a very special purpose; they would be used as offerings to the memories of our deceased relatives. Along with the *tays*, we added tangerines and oranges purchased solely to honor our family members. Mother also had incense sticks and whisky for her ceremony.

In our center hall, just below the family shrine standing at the top of the staircase, sat a table. Here, Mother solemnly made offerings to our ancestors. We knew from long experience to be quiet and pay attention during her ritual at the shrine. Facing the carved memorial, she performed her long and deep bows, first as she placed the whisky at the shrine, and again when she lit the incense. In silence, Mother completed another round of formal bows, came down the steps and led us into the kitchen. There, we had two more family memorial shrines at opposite ends of the room. At each, Mother again left tangerines and oranges to honor our relatives. Here, Mother carefully selected the fruits with leaves and stems as her offering. She told us that fruit with green stalks attached showed the highest level of respect. She chose only the best for her presentation to the dead.

Mother had a final round of worship to complete. Alone, she returned to each shrine with incense sticks, called punks. She lit a bundle at each stop. For the next two weeks, she also burned punks each morning next to the front door.

Once Mother completed her rites, we cooked the remainder of the dumplings. When the next batches of *tays* had cooled, we placed them in a large basket. We had to use all our willpower not to sample them. For me, the wait turned painful.

Mother assembled her daughters and the basket of *tays* for visits to the neighbors. My sisters and I watched as Mother stopped at each house, chatted with friends and offered the delicious holiday treats. By the time mother had completed her stops, the neighbors had taken most of the *tays* we had worked so hard to prepare. Each year, we waited with growing agitation at each door, afraid that none of the *tays* would be left for us. We should have known better. No matter how many of the *tays* the neighbors took for themselves, they always left a layer at the bottom of the basket for us. Chinese manners dictate that you never take more than one item offered at a time, and you never remove the last item on a plate, bowl or platter. If you lapse and leave an empty plate, you are expected to add a *fong bow*, a red envelope filled with good luck money.

And Mother always made sure we prepared enough *tays* to go around. When we reached home, she allowed us to pick the treats from our basket. We knew if we had behaved, Mother would allow us to eat more than one. After a bit, Mother separated her dumpling basket from her contingent of children one final time. Visiting, she reminded us, was not over. Almost on cue, the neighbors were at our door waiting to come in. Holding their teacups, they gathered in the main hall, adults seated and children on the floor. Mother served tea with *tays,* and the holiday celebrating began once more.

As Lin Fong Lei took its New Year break from work, the village appeared to settle down. Even Mother seemed more peaceful for a time, ready to talk with the neighbors and put her normal cares aside. And, to me, the talk went on for hours at a stretch. How could Mother, normally so quiet, talk so much at these gatherings? It was a riddle I never solved.

My sisters and I eagerly anticipated these blissful times. I felt we could do no wrong during these festivities. We got out of work, and people gave us money. What a perfect combination of events. As we walked through the village, we greeted people we knew and gave them a New Year salutation. And in return, they usually handed us some money. Maymie and I saw this as pulling a fast one, where we sought out familiar faces, expecting our efforts to yield easy money. Many of the village children accosted any adult who walked by. Maymie and I greeted just the people we knew well.

Usually the money came in red envelopes and in even numbers. Even numbers meant good luck. Only at funerals would you see money handed out in odd numbers. For us, New Year greetings were great fun and resulted in something unusual and special, our own money to spend. Splurge we did, on cookies and candy, although we never bought much. In Lin Fong Lei, people had little money to give and the village offered few places to spend it.

The promise of cash was nice, but I remained much too shy to approach most people. And Mother scolded us if we got too greedy in the game of handing out greetings, one of the few times I recall discipline from her.

The New Year fun jammed Lin Fong Lei's tiny paths. Dressed as dragons and lions, people marched in a procession, winding through the few alleys and streets until late into the night. Everyone seemed to be dressed in red, the color of joy for Chinese. Red mixed with splashes of gold also signified truth and virtue in China. Lin Fong Lei had its own dragon costume. Worn by several people, the makeshift dragon created a scare as it reared its head and charged at people all along the route. I was both frightened and excited. In the background, I remember firecrackers exploding, drums and cymbals crashing. Even our little town generated lots of noise and excitement. Late into most evenings, firecrackers, rockets and sparklers lit up the sky. More fireworks were tossed at the feet of people in the parade. Mother, accustomed to fireworks from the old days that were made from gunpowder packed firmly into bamboo stems, worried all night. To Mother, every small explosion brought danger. Even later, as firecrackers took the form of tightly packed paper tubes, Mother saw them as a menace to her children. This part of the show put her on edge.

During village festivities, Mother kept mostly to herself on our front porch. She knew that the procession, which moved up and down each alley of Lin Fong Lei, would eventually turn up at her doorstep. I also think she saw the celebration as a way for her children to develop some added independence. For this one occasion, she appeared happy to let us venture out into the night with the crowd. She sat comfortably at our front door as we went off on separate forays throughout the village. She knew we would not wander very far.

Gambling, too, filled most days of the New Year period. Taking our cue from the other villagers, my sisters and I bet with one another. But instead of cards and other games of chance, we adapted and invented our own diversions. We had a coin contest in which we placed loose change on edge against a wall. The object was to step about five feet away, take careful aim and toss remaining coins at the wall. When you knocked over the balanced coins, they were yours to keep. Using pieces of broken dishes, my sisters and I competed in another contest, our own version of checkers. Yet another sport was a version of dominoes, with our small amounts of greeting money as our stakes.

Maymie and I jumped right into the town party, partners as usual. We gambled among ourselves and talked to lots of people. We watched the adults, some quicker at the games and others slowed by drinking. Everyone seemed particularly carefree for this two-week period, with little to do but gamble and call on neighbors and relatives. Best of all for us, there was no work because the harvest was complete and we had several weeks before planting time.

For New Year's Eve, my family enjoyed our most exceptional meal of the year. My sisters and I crowded around our table, usually joined by my mother's stepdaughter-in-law and her two children. At other times, the scarcity of meat limited Mother's menu. But, for this occasion, we had several types of meat in what looked to be enormous abundance. Chicken, pork, duck and goose—all these delicacies were set upon the table. For the pork, we butchered the pig we had been raising all year long. The chicken and goose, too, came from our stock of farm animals. Only beef, a special addition if we had money, came from the market. Mother purchased very small amounts if she felt our budget would allow us to indulge.

Once Mother finished cooking the chicken, but before we could be seated, she had another important task to perform. Mother placed the bird on a platter and took it to the table, where she looked solemnly up at the shrine above. Then, Mother bowed deeply before the chicken platter and nodded to each of her children to repeat the bows. As always, Mother remained silent during this small ceremony. Only when each of us had honored our ancestors could the chicken be returned to the kitchen, where Mother chopped it into small pieces and served the dinner.

Even before Father's death, Mother played the central role in these family memorial services. I don't recall my father doing much more than following along in the procession with his children. He never stepped forward or said anything; he simply bowed along with the rest of us. The first year after Father's death, Mother broke her traditional silence and spoke in memory of Father. Every year thereafter, she made sure we honored Father as part of our ritual.

After we finished our New Year's Eve meal, Mother performed one final rite. Into several small cups she poured a bit of whisky. Then, one by one, she placed the alcohol offering at each of the family shrines around the house. She remained very still as she bowed at each stop throughout the house.

Recalling my mother's silent reverence, I realize how little I knew about her view of life and death. Looking back, I believe she felt stranded after Father's death, left without a partner to help her, trapped in her own silence and surrounded by children who could not offer much counsel. Mother would remain isolated for many years. Widowed at a relatively young age of thirty-six, she had only her young children, who offered companionship but limited conversations. Hers had to be a lonely existence.

I often wonder what my mother looked like when she was young. We have pictures of her, of course, when she was older, after she and Father were married. In those photos she is very proper, very stiff, no smile—as was appropriate for Chinese portraits of the time. I cannot recall her voice any longer. For me now, it is as silent as those silent New Year offerings.

The next day, New Year's Day, we gathered again to eat leftovers and vegetable dishes. Still later, on another part of the holiday, called Open Day in our family, we assembled for yet another meal with lots of food. The entire New Year holiday spread over a couple of weeks and across many happy meals. I'd never thought much about food before, but I realized this holiday was made for eating.

New Year dishes included another special treat, arrowroot. To us, it was known as *thloo coo*. A starchy vegetable grown in our fields, it resembled a water chestnut, but a bit larger. Each arrowroot had a small stem protruding from one end. Mother liked them, either boiled or braised. At each step in the cooking process, Mother made a point of telling all her daughters to be very careful to keep the stem intact.

Mother said to us: "The stem is very much like the special part of a little boy."

We heard this description each year, but one of us always asked: "What do you mean, Mother?"

"It is something only boys like your brothers have. Not anything like you have. As you clean the *thloo coo*, be careful. Keep the stem together with the rest of the *thloo coo*," she said. "That way, when you have a husband, you will have a good chance of having a baby boy."

Mother provided no further details about anatomy and biology, neither then nor at any other time in my life. Our arrowroot talks were as close as she ever came to discussing male and female interactions or human biology with her daughters. Mother worried about arranging the right husband for her daughters, but she did not waste time telling us anything about marriage and what would follow.

Each time I listened to Mother's advice on arrowroot stems, the story made no sense to me. I just wanted to eat them. Cooked just right, the roots had a consistency between a potato and a water chestnut, with a unique nutty sweetness.

After New Year's, the next best celebration happened in late summer: the Moon Festival. Mother told us we celebrated because the harvest moon rose then. To me, the moon did look bigger and brighter than any other time of year. Some nights, a hazy layer of clouds obscured the moon and the stars. Even so, I would sit on our porch and stare hard into the night until I spotted the moon. It almost always worked. Eventually, the promise of food stopped my evening observations and I turned to eating.

From the kitchen came tasty treats, fried dumplings and *woo doy*, our name for boiled taro root. At the store, Mother purchased the moon cakes, a specialty reserved in the village for harvest time. About five inches in diameter and very thick, these desserts were not an easy mouthful. Made with thin pastry layers, the cakes came with a sweet cream filling made of soybean paste or ground lotus pods mixed with pork fat. Mother cut the cakes into small, bite-size wedges. On most Moon Festival evenings, she sat on our front porch, eating a few slices as she slowly sipped her tea. Her daughters joined her at the front of the house, watching the villagers stroll by and gazing at our fields.

For me, Moon Festival never became a favorite, mainly because I didn't have a taste for the cakes. Their heavy sweetness overpowered my tongue. Oddly enough, for someone who liked food so much, I responded to the moon more than the festival. My eyes filled with awe as I stared at the sky, but I left my portion of the cakes untouched. On these nights, Mother didn't know what to make of me. As someone who loved food so much, how could I pass up my moon cakes?

CHAPTER ELEVEN

Hard Choices

B Y MOTHER'S RULES, laundry day came once a week. Maymie and I came home most days caked in mud, so we washed a little each evening and then gave our clothes—we only had two sets each—a thorough washing on laundry day. Our tools were simple: a bucket and a wooden washboard right outside the door. On rare occasions, we used the farm pond for washing and rinsing. During summer, clothes dried quickly outside. But in the wetter seasons, we moved our fresh wash inside to dry on a temporary clothesline fashioned from bamboo sticks supported on two posts. Mother never liked the look of clothes draped around the house. At the first sign of dryness, she had us fold our clothes and take down the clothesline.

In all my years in the village, our wardrobe consisted of two-piece Chinese-style outfits of pants and shirts. We made them ourselves with guidance from Mother, stitching them by hand because we had no sewing machine. With no patterns to guide us, we somehow figured out the process with just a few directions and corrections from Mother. Once we went to work on our sewing, she rarely intervened.

Even more basic were our shoes. Mother purchased our first pair. After that, we were in charge of shoe adjustments, repair and replacement. The soles consisted of plain wood platforms, resembling clogs. To the base, we nailed a thick leather strap to grip your foot. If the strap did not fit just right, we simply pulled it loose and renailed the leather for a more secure fit. Whether dealing with clothing, food or life in general, we aimed to keep everything uncomplicated.

Even the way we slept was kept as simple as possible. Our beds, built upon a series of wooden boards atop a pair of short supports much like sawhorses, had no mattresses. It wasn't luxurious. Sleeping on the boards—which had a bit of give—afforded only slightly more comfort than sleeping on the floor.

Our real troubles were the bed bugs. Just a few did not present much of a problem, but they multiplied fast. Their bites itched so much that you could not sleep. They laid eggs in the seams of the covers or along the cracks of the bed platform. Mother inspected the beds regularly, checking for any sign of blood or bugs. She often looked us over, too, watching for signs of bites on our arms and legs. If she spotted too many welts, she spurred us into concerted action. Getting rid of bed bugs seemed impossible, but Mother had her plan. At her command, we smashed the tiny insects with our fingers. Each time we struck, we left a smear of blood marking the spot. I got to be pretty good at this extermination business.

Unfortunately, the dead bugs gave off a terrible smell. So, simply killing them did not provide an effective long-term solution. Mother then directed us to take our beds apart, separate the boards from the bedcovers and carry all the parts outside. In the courtyard, we shook out the bedding as thoroughly as we could. Next, we pounded on the bed frames, driving out the bugs and killing the escapees. This bed cleaning and frame pounding—always tough work—never produced complete success, so we repeated our extermination work every week or so. When we finished the job, we lugged the covers and frames back upstairs to reassemble our beds. This same routine took place throughout the neighborhood. Otherwise, the plague of bed bugs would have been unbearable.

Another sort of pest was nearly as bad: head lice. As school girls, we often came home from class with these pests in our scalp. One day, I remember Maymie alerting me to the problem as we walked home.

"Oh, what's in your hair?" she said.

"What is it exactly?" I responded smartly, thinking she was pulling another sisterly joke.

"It looks like dust in your hair," she said as she tried to brush it off. "Well, we better go to Mother. She'll know what to do," she said.

I nodded knowingly, thinking I would just play along with her prank. "Yes, let's go home and see what Mother has to say."

A surprise awaited. When Mother saw the strings of tiny eggs in my hair, she immediately sprang into action. To get rid of the bugs, Mother used her special remedy. Mixing whisky with tobacco, she fashioned a foul-smelling paste and applied it, layer upon layer, on my head. Next, she wrapped a towel tightly around my scalp to seal up the mess. While I sat still for the treatment, she made me shed my clothes. Meanwhile, she heated a big pot of water on the stove and boiled my outfit for a long time. When my head towel came off, we retrieved my clothes from the kitchen kettle and dried them. Usually, one such treatment would be the end of the head lice, but sometimes the pests were transmitted from one sister to the next, requiring repeat sessions with the awful paste. Mother's mixture smelled terrible, but sitting still while the others played outside was more than I could bear.

To this day, I suspect these head lice treatments are the reason I never developed a taste for whisky or tobacco.

Despite these regular challenges of housekeeping and cleanliness, I remember all of us—my sisters and I—as being remarkably clean. And even with the seasons of dust and mud, our house always looked nearly spotless. Perhaps this was not so surprising. To Mother, neat and clean ranked near the top of her list of values. Despite the constant dust and dirt of rural China, she believed nothing but a clean house was acceptable. Washing and scrubbing, particularly in the kitchen, were central events in her regular daily routine. Fortunately for the rest of the daughters, Florence functioned as Mother's main kitchen assistant. The two were on the job every day, ensuring a busy but tidy kitchen. When it came to maintaining the rest of the house, all of the daughters made up the work crew.

Mother had her own meticulous idea of what constituted spotless. All of her daughters were introduced early to her theory of neatness, and the lessons remained ingrained throughout our years, long after we departed from China.

Mother did her best to keep us all healthy, but Maymie and I encountered a hidden affliction in the rice paddies: malaria. It brought on fatigue, shaking, fever and sweating. Our difficulties would last for days and we didn't understand the cause.

When our malaria first hit, we experienced chills, then violent shaking. Next, a high fever came over us. At this stage, Maymie and I usually broke into heavy sweats. We had numerous attacks of the illness, first as young girls and later into our teens. The misery continued to strike us for years to come.

I can remember days of shivering in the rice paddies despite the heat. I crouched down cross-legged, wrapped my arms around my legs and trembled for long stretches of time. Frequently, we felt too weak to work or even to walk. The two of us took turns getting sick.

Our troubles came from mosquitoes. None of us, Mother included, knew the biting insects caused our illness. At the time in Lin Fong Lei, malaria had no known treatment. Other parts of the world used quinine, but we had none in the village and wouldn't have known to use it anyway.

My mother believed that some parts of our diet made the malaria symptoms worse. When we were ill, she made sure we did not eat tangerines and star fruit. Something in their composition seemed to make our suffering worse. To help us feel better, Mother fed us plenty of garlic, which she believed relieved our miseries. She prepared pots of steamed garlic and salt, usually ladled generously over our rice. Whether any part of this diet really helped us get better, I don't know, but Maymie and I seemed to improve under Mother's watch.

I don't recall getting much of a break from work even when we were sick with malaria. We wanted to rest, but we knew we had work to do. When one sister fell ill, the other played the role of persuader. In the end, both of us marched off to work most mornings, resigned to toil away. As we grew older, we reasoned that our responsibilities were important and nothing should get in the way.

Our sisters had their bouts of malaria, as well, but they escaped the worst reactions, perhaps because they did not work in the fields and so avoided the concentrations of mosquitoes.

I cannot say how much of my memory is colored by resentment, but I recall thinking at these times that our sister Joyce, in particular, had an easy life. Mother was closest to Joyce, although she also doted on youngest daughter Dorothy. Mother had a theory for dividing labors among family members that I grew to resent. In the apportionment of duties around the house and in the fields, Joyce and Dorothy seemed especially blessed. Joyce had a plum job, accompanying Mother on shopping and trading trips into nearby towns. Joyce, with a sharp mind for numbers, became a good negotiator, making her well suited to the tasks.

"We work out here in the sun, rain and dirt. Joyce gets to shop," said Maymie, in one of our talks about what we saw as an unfair division of labor.

"Hard for us, sweet for her," I said.

All of the sisters regarded Joyce as the intelligent member of the clan. She spoke Chinese and English well and she knew her math. She could be very blunt, with a sharp tongue. All of us felt the sting of Joyce's taunts from time to time. Even Edith, when she still lived with us, was a target. And Edith, like the rest of us, allowed Joyce to speak bluntly.

"I'm the prettiest," Joyce frequently reminded us. "And I'm the smart one."

Joyce, I thought, singled me out when I was younger. I tried to avoid her gaze and attention as much as I could. For a long time, some memories of my sister Joyce made me uncomfortable, as she seemed unkind toward me.

One summer day, I made the mistake of pointing to the hair I noticed growing on my arms.

"You. You are just like a monkey," she said, using the Chinese term *mow low noy.* Later, I cried, but I made sure to hide my tears while Joyce was watching.

Through the years, she aimed much of her heckling at Maymie and me.

"I'm the smartest and Mother knows it," said Joyce.

"I'm going to town to shop with Mother. You two stay here and work in the fields. That is your kind of work. I don't have to do those jobs."

It was a little speech we heard often from older sister Joyce. Always quiet and restrained in the face of her behavior, Maymie and I should have rebelled, but we didn't. Joyce was older, smarter and more assertive. I don't remember either Maymie or me mounting more than small resistance to her conduct. Joyce outranked us, and we had always been taught to have respect for our elders. So we did. It was our Chinese way. Still, her comments stung.

One day, I asked my mother about why we worked on the land while Joyce got to shop.

"This is something you will have to accept," Mother said.

"But I don't like it in the rice paddies," I said. "Maymie and I want to go to the shops, too."

"I know, but the decision has been made. I have my reasons, so no more questions."

Mother, I think, figured Maymie and I would be just fine, especially because we relied on one another. While Mother and Joyce enjoyed the excitement of a trip to town, we stayed home to hoe, weed and plant. Maymie and I understood the necessity of our work by this time, but we longed to have small roles in those shopping journeys. How much happier we would be if we could just visit the big city.

First in Boston and later—and more so—in China, turbulent and uncertain times forced Mother to be a capable, quick-witted manager of her home and finances. My mother's supply of gold, much of it derived from her bootlegging project in the United States, sustained our family for many years. Her valuable stash of gold became more crucial after Father's death. Because our farm did not always supply enough to feed us, Mother carefully traded her gold for food and other provisions at shops in the area. She kept her gold in a small box, carefully hidden in the house, which she watched over very vigilantly. Not even her children knew of its precise hiding place.

Years before in Boston, in preparation for the voyage to China, Mother converted much of the family money to gold, mostly in the form of necklaces, bracelets and rings. This accumulation of jewelry, she correctly guessed, would be needed to shore up her family's budget. Gold had great value in America, but the precious metal held even more value for us in China. Early in my life, I remember seeing a lot of gold jewelry in Mother's care. In essence, this reserve served as our family savings account. Without Mother's gold, I can't imagine how we would have survived in later years, especially when our farm output dwindled.

Mother's jewelry also became a source of gifts for her daughters. I remember Mother's beautiful jade bracelet. It disappeared one day; she had taken it to a local shop. Several days later, she returned from the shop with jade rings for each of us.

I am embarrassed to admit that some of Mother's decisions about her stock of gold jewelry hurt me. All my sisters seemed to be the recipients of gifts of fine jewelry from my mother, but I felt slighted. I noticed that each of my sisters received a bright gold necklace from Mother while I got a small jade ring. I came to believe my mother handled my gift of gold this way because she believed I soon would have a husband to provide the jewelry I wanted. Her decision reflected Mother's commonsense approach in family matters. Still, I thought at the time, life was not fair.

Mother hid another stockpile of money. In a woven straw bag, she kept a small supply of Chinese coins. On special occasions, we had access to this loose change, usually as a small allowance to buy cookies and candy. Saturday, the normal weekly shopping day, was our only opportunity to find these treats. When the market opened, we raced off in excitement with a little money in our pockets. I always had a hard time making my selection. Too many choices and too little money.

Lin Fong Lei offered very few places to look at and buy anything. A true shopping trip took us to nearby small towns. Our most frequent destination was Gim Woo, another small village just a bit larger than our own. Gim Woo, about an hour's walk, had true shops and market stalls. On rare occasions, Mother invited Maymie and me to come along. Once there, we carefully searched for just the right delights and spent our meager allotment of money. If her budget allowed, Mother might splurge and buy crackers in a tin. After a day shopping for treats with Mother, I could hardly believe my good fortune.

CHAPTER TWELVE

East to Montana

NEARLY A DECADE WOULD PASS between Edith's 1938 wedding and my engagement in 1947. During this time, my understanding of marriage and relations between men and women did not advance at all. I tended our fields, did laundry and fed our animals; my horizons did not expand much further. My family focused on surviving World War II. Mother imparted her household knowledge, but spoke very little about human relations and not at all about human biology. Nothing of what I call "the bird and the bee" ever reached my ears.

Not only was I woefully lacking in experience, I did not even know enough to speculate much about love and marriage. Even if boldness had prompted me to speak with Mother on those topics, I doubt very much that she would have offered any insights. By Chinese custom, family members were taught to be unemotional, composed and passive. Throughout her life, Mother lived that model for her daughters. In Mother's China, you did not talk with your children about marriage or most private subjects.

Our uncertain life in China also hindered many everyday discussions. For me and my family, more immediate problems were at hand. Soon after our arrival in China, the conflict with Japanese invaders caused the first disruptions in our lives. By the 1940s, the war with Japan grew into World

War II. China's countryside was in turmoil, and the declining economy commanded our attention. Fear and doubts about the future seemed to increase daily for people in our village.

From the late 1930s into the early 1940s, our village had been spared from the actual fighting. But the resulting financial chaos began to hit closer to home. And China had another confrontation in its midst. The effects of the conflict between the Chinese Communist Party and the Nationalist Party, which began brewing in the late 1920s and lasted for more than twenty years, were becoming more evident throughout the country.

Sometime before the end of World War II, a friend of Maymie's disappeared. She and her family had been killed when a band of men attacked their home. To fend off the marauders, identified as either Chinese rebels or Japanese troops, the family locked themselves inside their house. The assailants set fire to the house, and all the occupants perished in the blaze. It was a shocking loss of life so close to home, but we had grown somewhat immune to events like this, as war and instability had become a part of everyday life.

During World War II, our crop harvests declined. To put food on the table, we learned to be more resourceful. As our rice supply shrank, we shifted to potatoes more often. In search of new alternatives for the dinner table, Maymie and I roamed the hills outside the village. Among the bamboo groves, we dug up various roots. These we loaded into our woven baskets to carry home. At the stove, Mother and Florence washed and boiled them to add to our dinners. I also remember cutting the long bamboo stalks at the edges of our fields for the seeds. Carefully separating the seed kernels from the shoots, Maymie and I filled a small bag, which we took home to Mother. She showed us how to grind the seeds into a paste, which we could then use as a topping on pastries and other food. I never really liked the bamboo flavor, but it did add a new taste to our diet.

My reaction to the hazards—the conflicts and financial hard times— was to separate myself from the problems. By this time, escaping from our predicament, as we had discussed when Father was alive, somehow never came to mind again. Memories of Boston had faded. China was all I really knew. If we gave any further thought to going back to Boston, I have no memory of it. The departures of Edith, Robert and Kenneth ten years earlier, along with the possibilities of escape they held, were distant ideas. I came to accept my life in China. But I did so by blocking out our struggles. Disorder in the countryside filled our days. I saw no point in fighting it. What helped was the slow, steady pace of village life, which still seemed comforting to me.

Thinking back to this time, I am surprised that I felt relatively happy and safe most of the time. Our family still enjoyed time together in the evenings, usually spent playing dominoes and other games at our front door. Mother still sat and gossiped with the neighbors about local news and people in the village. Faced with the country's chaotic economy, Mother maintained a steady course by her own means. Her composure kept us in high spirits.

Although World War II ended in 1945, the ongoing fight between the Nationalists and the Communists flared anew within China. At first, the warfare between the two parties occurred far to the north and east. Even so, our village continued to suffer the economic impacts. Looking back, I believe Mother recognized that the end of World War II would not bring peace to our country. She was left with five of her daughters —Florence, Joyce, Maymie, Dorothy and me—still to shelter. She could sense there wasn't much time left to flee. Sometime in the mid-1940s, Mother again decided to act.

Even if I was not puzzling over the future, Mother knew what to do. In her silent, unflustered way, she set about orchestrating the marriages of her daughters as a means of escape back to America. I am sure she saw this course as the best way to preserve her family, something she must have sensed would be increasingly difficult in the changing China. Faced with the growing Communist advances and with little time to act, Mother proved to be wise in protecting her daughters from the harm coming to our village. Once again, Mother dipped into her savings to hire a matchmaker.

Without my knowledge—and likely without the knowledge of my sisters—Mother selected eligible bachelors in the United States for Florence and Joyce. If they had any advance notice, they never let on to Maymie and me. Florence's husband-to-be was Henry Woo, a restaurant owner; Joyce's was Bill Chinn, another restaurant owner.

For all the sisters, mail-order marriages became the standard course. We had witnessed this choice for Edith, so we came to expect the same for ourselves. Not one of Mother's daughters would have thought to resist her wishes. I knew that my own wants, and those of my sisters—to the extent we even thought about our own desires—were not important. Family considerations came first. Families arranged marriages, settled disputes and made major decisions. Always act in the family's interest. Father taught us this fact early on in our lives, and Mother made sure we did not stray. To this ancient force of family devotion, war added a strong, new imperative. Renewed conflicts between the Communists and the Nationalists had sealed our fates.

Sometime in 1946, after concluding her matchmaking assignments for Florence and Joyce, Mother turned to me. Without a word, Mother sought out her trusted matchmaker to orchestrate my pairing. At the same time, a resident of Helena, Montana, began his own marriage inquiries. He had been born in a village close to Lin Fong Lei but had left for America in 1922. His first wife had died at a young age in 1946, and he wanted to find a Chinese wife to join him in Montana.

One afternoon late that year, around my eighteenth birthday, Mother took me aside to tell me the news: I was engaged to be married. Her announcement came in the most matter-of-fact tone as we stood in the kitchen. Mother offered no advice, no discussion and certainly no opportunity to express feelings. True to her nature, Mother gave nothing away about what marriage meant to her as she explained the course I was now on.

"You have time to think about this step. But do not question it," she said. "This is your direction in life."

I started to speak, but Mother waved me off.

"This will be good for you in many ways. You have a strong personality, stronger than you think," Mother added. "You will be fine, better off, really. His name is Charles Wong. We have sent him your picture."

I said nothing.

"He lives in Montana, in the west of America."

Uncharacteristically, Mother reached out and patted my hand. With that, I was on my way to marriage. All I knew of my future husband was his name, that he lived in the United States and that he had family nearby in our province. There were no chances to meet beforehand, no conversations, no letters. As the ceremony drew closer, Mother finally showed me a small photograph of Charles Wong. I don't recall my reaction, other than I liked the handsome face looking back at me.

Later, Mother shared two other facts: My future husband was forty, twenty-two years older than I, and he had been married before. What a match. I had no experience with boys, and he was a man who had already been married once. And no one warned me that, because his first wife had died young with no children, he was anxious to start a family.

True to her nature, Mother said little as my wedding drew closer, declaring simply that all arrangements were complete and the matchmaker was in charge of final details. Too timid to ask questions, I complied with my mother's will. So far as Mother was concerned, that was the end of any discussion.

Yet, my direction into the future did interest me. As the days passed, I began to wonder: What would this man Charles Wong be like? What were his interests? What might we have in common? Where was Montana? If I had had a map, I might have traced my finger along the route east to Montana. But we had no maps. Yes, I had been born in the United States, but I knew nothing of its geography. I could barely remember any details of Boston. After years in Lin Fong Lei, I had little idea about anything beyond our hills.

What I remember is that, on these questions of my future, the doubts left my thoughts as quickly as they entered. As with so many aspects of my life in China, there was no point in asking a lot of questions; Mother had charted my life's course, in details well beyond my control.

Sounding like Mother, I reassured myself, "No matter what comes, you will adjust."

That my husband-to-be came from a Chinese village not far from my own seemed a good omen. Our life together will be better, I thought, with our shared history and sense of family. These would be bonds to build on.

Right after Mother announced my engagement to Charles Wong, I remember our lives changed for the better. Almost immediately, my future husband began to mail money to my family. How much money I never knew because I did not see the sums as they reached us. Whenever a check or cash arrived in a letter from Montana, Mother took charge of the funds right away. Regular money allowed my mother to buy more food, which spelled relief for Maymie and me in the fields. We took some time off, which was wonderful.

Charles's generosity left room in the family budget for exciting new ventures. Best of all were the shopping trips that replaced our days at work.

Late in 1946, I finally traveled to Guangzhou. Now almost back to normal after the departure of Japanese troops at the end of World War II, the large city featured countless clothing shops, fruit and vegetable stands and candy stores. I had never seen such a concentration of activity. These were places I had only heard about in stories related by Mother and Joyce. Now came my turn.

The "picture bride" photo of seventeen-year-old Flora Lee that was sent to Charles Wong.

Our journeys to the city were long, twelve hours or more on foot, boat and, finally, by bus. But I loved each moment. These were festive times for me, my mother and my sisters. The city stretched out before us with shops and people. Aided by Charles's money, we visited plenty of shops, buying fabric for new skirts and dresses as well as other treats. I got my first perm, bought my first new dress and brushed on my first lipstick. The city and its diversions presented unfamiliar pleasures to young girls from the countryside.

My upcoming marriage was never far from my thoughts. Ideas about a new life in Montana with Charles fascinated me, but I never could get a clear picture in my mind of what my new existence would be.

Yet, even as I prepared for coming adulthood and my wedding, I still felt most at home in our fields. Though I only visited the rice paddies a few more times, the steady pace of our work made me relax. Talking with Maymie and the cousins about the weather, the crops and the animals brought on a sense of peace that I had never felt before at work. But I knew this life was ending. Mother had her course of action and she was sweeping me into motion.

As the end of 1946 drew near, my wedding date approached. I didn't actually know the date. Mother said so little about the details of the ceremony that I had no idea of the precise date or location until just ahead of time. I was expected to trust Mother and the matchmaker to put all the particulars in good order.

On December 17, 1946, halfway around the world, Charles Wong boarded a Northern Pacific train headed from Helena, Montana, to Seattle. A week later, he sailed for Hong Kong on board the American President Line steamship *Marine Falcon.* In addition to his personal luggage, Charles packed a large steamer trunk. In those days, traveling with a large trunk was a mark of stature. Practicality as much as prestige required his need for the trunk. All told, he carried 370 pounds of luggage. His travel documents specified the weight to the pound. He brought so much additional baggage that it cost him $2 in fees for excess weight, which seemed to me to be a large sum at that time.

Gifts for me made up most of his baggage. In Helena, Charles had special help in making the purchases for me. Amy Wong, the wife of Charles's friend Wong Sun You, did all the gift-buying at Charles's request.

Much later, when we opened the trunk after the wedding, I reviewed its contents with surprise. Amy, who was to become a close friend of mine in Helena, did not know my size, which hampered her purchasing. But she knew that I faced the severe change from China's heat to Montana's cold, so she bought a wool coat to protect me. Most of what filled the rest of the trunk was jewelry, cosmetics and lingerie. I remember the cosmetics—lipstick, cold cream, face powders and perfumes—were welcome items. Amy certainly had good taste, I thought. When I got to the lingerie, however, my opinion swerved on a different course. What are these frilly things, I wondered. All of it was so different from any clothing I had ever seen before. Charles later insisted that the purchases of women's undergarments were more Amy's doing than his. Months later, as I learned of Amy's sensible ways, I suspected Charles played a more significant role in the lingerie purchases than he ever let on.

With about two weeks to go, Mother finally announced my wedding date. It was to be January 15, 1947.

As Charles, his trunk and other bags were arriving in Hong Kong, Mother, Dorothy and I were on our way there as well—first on foot and then by boat. Florence, Joyce and Maymie remained at home because we did not have enough money for everyone to attend the ceremony and banquet. Weighing on me was the knowledge that I was leaving the only home I had really known. On top of that, I would not see my family members for many days; I remembered from Edith's wedding that the bride is separated from her family for at least three days after the wedding. In the future, I was to be only a visitor in my own home. For an immature eighteen-year-old, this prospect was troubling.

Once we reached Hong Kong, I finally came face to face with my husband to be. Mother and I met him at the dock where his ship landed. By tradition, we did not speak with one another. Naturally, he talked with Mother, as they had details of the ceremony to complete. He and I looked at each other but did nothing more than nod. To me, this lack of direct contact was a relief. I really did not know how to act when he entered the room. After all, I had never been around many men—much less one I'd be marrying the next day. As usual, I was much too reserved and nervous to say anything. No romance at all marked our first meeting; business talk between Mother and Charles about final wedding preparations filled the time.

What I do recall was how handsome, polished and well dressed in a coat and tie he looked. Certainly he seemed older than I expected. Yet, even the difference in age did not upset me.

To deal with my major expenses, Charles provided the money for my wedding dress and shoes. The dress was a delight for me. Much more painful, both in fit and fashion, were the shoes Mother and I bought. Awful was the only description to suit them. Even though I had no sense of style, I could see they were out-of-date and ugly. I probably had had only two outfits to my name and no more than two pairs of shoes in my life, but those new shoes reminded me of what I saw on the feet of old ladies. New or not, I knew I didn't like them.

By contrast, my wedding dress, once it was finished, was the most beautiful creation imaginable. Crafting the gown was no simple task. In Hong Kong in those days, you could not buy a dress to fit. Add to that the fact that I weighed less than 100 pounds—not much more than skin and bones. So we were forced to hire someone to make my wedding dress. We bought some material that I liked, and Mother rushed around to find a dress shop to do the job.

Wedding party of Charles Wong and Flora Lee in Hong Kong, 1947. Front row, from left, Charlie's sister Wong Gon Tilt, Charlie's brother Wong Jack Nin, Charlie, Flora and Flora's sister Dorothy. Far right front row is Flora's mother Chen Sun Ho. Others are unknown.

On the day before the wedding, my fitting revealed a dress still several sizes too large. Mother, Dorothy and I scrambled to resize it some more. When we completed the final work with only moments to spare, I surveyed the dress in the mirror and thought it was just beautiful. Made of brocade silk, it had soft hues of mauve and rose as its base colors. Intricate, delicate swirls added a rainbow of colors, including purple, navy, pale green, yellow, silver, crimson red and dark brown. I have saved it to this day.

By the time my wedding day arrived on January 15, 1947, my nerves took charge. Dorothy tried to calm my anxieties as I struggled into my dress, but she was at a loss to help. Only thirteen, Dorothy had little idea how a bride should look on her wedding day. Not that I had any better concept of what a bride's appearance should be. Mother had left us a bit earlier to attend to final details with Charles, so Dorothy and I muddled along as well as two novices could. After much fussing with my hair and my dress, we decided we had done all we could do. Mother returned and judged the details to be satisfactory. All three together, we whisked off to the wedding, but I must have looked a bit sad.

"Don't worry. We'll be fine," Mother said. "And you will be, too."

Our wedding followed none of the American traditions. No bridal showers, no church, no large reception. It was simple and quick. Flanked by Mother and Dorothy, I arrived by hired car at a Hong Kong restaurant. I remember its name, the Golden Dragon, but I can't recall its location. There I was in my dress, balanced on my unfashionable shoes and holding a large, gaudy bouquet of gladiolas. I remember feeling insecure despite my wonderful dress, new lipstick and freshly permed hair.

Charles's dapper appearance did nothing to calm my nerves. On this day, I am afraid the groom overshadowed the bride. As we entered the restaurant, he stepped forward, dressed in a dark, double-breasted suit. To this day, I can picture how very nice he looked—his suit immaculate, his tie tied just right and his shoes smartly shined.

In mere minutes, our ceremony began and ended. The marriage license already had our names on it, so the major event came as we affixed our chops, which are seals or stamps used in place of signatures in China, to the multicolored document. Charlie stamped his chop first, and I followed. My mother marked her chop as well. To close the ceremony, Charles presented me with a gold necklace and gold bracelet. No rings were exchanged; the practice was not a Chinese tradition. My new husband, knowledgeable about American ways, explained that we would have rings once we returned to Montana. With our marks on the document, the marriage was official.

Following the official business of the ceremony, everyone attended a small banquet in the restaurant. Our wedding guests consisted of fewer than twenty people seated around two tables. Even in such a small group, I knew only my mother and sister. Others included Charles's younger brother, his younger sister and other friends of his that I did not know.

As the festivities wound down and Mother turned to leave, she summed up her advice to me in two sentences.

"No looking back. You simply can't."

CHAPTER THIRTEEN

A New Life

OUR WEDDING FEAST CONCLUDED. My mother and sister departed. I was a newly married woman awash in feelings of freedom and fear. I was only eighteen and my husband was just shy of forty-one. Right then, I thought to myself: "This is it. You're on your own now."

Charles and I spent our wedding night in Hong Kong and remained in the city for the next two or three days. I was unenlightened and a bit frightened at being alone with my new husband. Just as many young brides of the time, I suspect, I was full of speculation but woefully lacking in any knowledge. Where I was anxious and fearful, Charles was composed and steady. He sensed my awkward feelings, and he did his best to help me relax. Charles and I seemed to get along well from the start. For whatever reason, the difference in our ages never seemed to be an issue.

Our honeymoon was brief. With the Chinese New Year celebration upon us, Charles wanted to return to his home village for the festivities. By boat and then on foot, we traveled from Hong Kong to Charles's village of How Voy. We moved into the house that had been in Charles's family for many years. How Voy looked and felt much like Lin Fong Lei. Here I saw the same crowded rectangle of houses surrounded by fields of rice and vegetables. Terraces of land, dikes and low hills made up a familiar vista. I felt at home.

Wong family portrait, 1948. Charlie, third from left in front row, holds adopted son Na Bing. Flora is seated at far left. This is the last portrait taken of Charlie's family.

As a dutiful son living in America, Charles (I learned then that he was called Charlie by his friends and family, but it would be two years before I would call him that) for many years had sent money home to maintain the family land and house. Charlie's younger brother, Jack Nin, and his wife, Sui Ying, lived in one end of the family home, while Charlie and I occupied the other. Jack Nin and Sui Ying had three very young children, Kent, Juana and Loo. Activity filled the house. My new house was larger than my family's home and sat apart from the surrounding village. Two kitchens, two bedrooms and a dining area filled the main floor, with more rooms upstairs, just as in my own home. Living nearby were Charlie's older brother, Wong Hay Nin, and his four children: daughters Leui May and Sau Han, and sons Na Dok and Na Moi.

How Voy village was a bit larger than my own. Its layout confused me at first, so I did not go out much alone. My formal relationship with Charlie's family added to my isolation. In accordance with Chinese social structure, they paid me respect due to my position as wife of Charlie, the middle brother in the family. They called me *thlom seem*, for "auntie number three," based on Charlie's third position in the birth order of his family. Because Jack Nin and his wife were younger, they ranked lower in the family hierarchy. They did not call me by my first name, Jong Hai, because, as Charlie's wife, I held elder title. So *thlom seem* was the only name people in our household called me. I referred to them by their first names; only when speaking to those with equal or lesser stature in the family would you use first names. Despite the formal arrangement, Charlie's family treated me well.

Even though we spent a lot of time together, I never grew close to Sui Ying. As much as I welcomed female companionship, she and I kept our distance. All my days in How Voy, she and I ate together. At the start, she cooked while I watched and tried to learn new kitchen skills. My sister Florence, with guidance from Mother, had always done the bulk of the family cooking, so my culinary skills were woefully undeveloped. I quickly learned that Charlie, too, had great talents in the kitchen. Even with these coaches, I made very little progress in those early days as a new wife. Before long, Sui Ying eased me out of the kitchen and I looked for other ways to keep busy. Between cooking duties and childcare for her three youngsters, Sui Ying had a demanding schedule. Though we shared the same house, she and I seemed to have little in common. Friction didn't build between the two women in the house, but we were content to be independent.

No one seemed happier to have more of my time than Charlie. Right away, I knew I was happy being married to him. He coaxed me into talking about my family and myself. By contrast, I had few skills to draw him out and learn about his life. I responded to his questions, but he gave me little information by which to understand him.

Apart from Charlie, I had little companionship, so I naturally began to miss my family. Although Lin Fong Lei was less than twenty miles away, the trip by foot required at least four hours. We did not make the journey very often.

To deal with all the extra time on my hands, I stayed inside most days, sewing, knitting and crocheting. Hunched in a low chair, I tried to build on the sewing skills I learned from Mother. To improve my embroidery, I watched others in Charlie's family.

In my first months in How Voy, sewing our clothing became my main activity. My everyday clothes around the house were simple tops and plain slacks, all in black. These ordinary designs were easy for me to make. Soon

I could turn out serviceable mandarin collars for our shirts. Our slacks were made of a thin, muslin-type material. The light material was just right for our climate. I had no buttons, so I used a simple fold and tuck technique to hold up our slacks. If I was less than first-rate in the kitchen, I reasoned, at least I was productive with a needle and thread. However, after a life of hard physical labor, I worried I wasn't doing enough around the house.

For a bit of excitement, Charlie suggested we take trips to Guangzhou. On these excursions, I exchanged the drab blacks for a few pieces of colorful attire I made. The styles were the same, but I selected fabric in pastels and floral prints. I quickly learned to be a pretty good seamstress, working entirely by hand with just needles and thread. My handiwork was one of the few areas where I began to build confidence early in my marriage.

Still too shy to meet other people easily, I kept mostly to myself at home and in my new village. Neighbors gathered occasionally with Charlie's family to talk and gossip. Lively conversations filled the house, but I stayed quiet. I fell back on my ability to listen, a skill I had practiced throughout my childhood. Just as in my school days, I wanted to fade into the background. Charlie prodded me gently to take a more active role in these exchanges, but I simply didn't know how. For me, after years of outdoor work, being cooped up inside seemed awfully dull. Charlie noticed my difficulties and plotted a new course.

৩৩৩৩

Early in 1948, about a year after our wedding, Charlie and I adopted a boy. His name was Na Bing, and he was three years old. He came from a family in a neighboring village. I had not produced a child in our first year of marriage, so Charlie thought we should adopt a son. It was the Chinese belief that you needed a first child to serve as the initial root to nurture your own family, the same course of action my family used when Nancy was given to a childless couple in Boston.

The decision to adopt Na Bing grew from discussions between Charlie, his brother Jack Nin and Sui Ying. I played no role in the decision. As had always been my way, I merely accepted events as they developed. Looking back, I can see that, even if I had been consulted, I would have had difficulty making my feelings clear. Still ill at ease in speaking up, I rarely

Flora Wong with adopted son Na Bing in 1948 in Guangzhou.

expressed my thoughts on important matters.

What a happy addition to our family Na Bing was. Almost immediately, the toddler created a pleasing balance in our lives, and Charlie and I took great joy in our new son. I took little Na Bing everywhere I went. Na Bing always behaved—certainly due more to his natural inclinations than any training I provided. He had a big smile and happy laugh. At each new phase in his life, Na Bing gave me new reasons to be overjoyed in my role as a mother.

Day by day, my boredom evaporated as I tended to our son. A child, I found, was a blessing in a marriage; and Na Bing was that good fortune in our marriage and a blessing to me. As my parenting abilities grew, so did my self-confidence.

Early in 1948, while I cared for our new son, Charlie made preparations for our return to Montana. Before his trip from Montana to Hong Kong for our wedding over a year earlier, Charlie had placed his eighteen-year-old nephew, Willy, in charge of his store. The youngest of four brothers, Willy was a hard worker, but having so much responsibility was new to him. Over time, Charlie grew concerned about being away from his store for so long.

Another matter required Charlie's attention. Starting in the spring of 1948, Charlie began contacting immigration officials to determine what clearances would be necessary for me to reenter the United States. Later, he made the same inquiries on behalf of our adopted son. Several troubling issues emerged. Although I was a U.S. citizen, I had no current documents proving my status. Na Bing had no papers at all and was not a U.S. citizen.

Wisely anticipating questions about his own citizenship, Charlie had resolved the matter before setting off for China for our marriage. On July 25, 1946, he became a naturalized citizen of the United States. His naturalization certificate showed him as a widower and a former citizen of China. Assured of his U.S. citizenship, Charlie came to China to meet me without fear of problems upon his return to Montana. But he knew enough about immigration authorities to be worried about me and our son.

My own citizenship should not have been in doubt. After all, I was born in Boston, a U.S. citizen from birth. But the subject of Chinese immigration to the United States had been a sensitive matter for many, many years. To compound my difficulties, I had no passport and my family had not saved any documents related to my citizenship. Restrictions on how many Chinese could enter the United States had a long history, since the passage by Congress of the Chinese Exclusion Act in 1882. The law established a policy of barring entry by all Chinese laborers to the United States and prohibiting Chinese immigrants from becoming naturalized citizens. Although Congress repealed the law in 1943, lawmakers left in place a strict quota system that allowed entry for just over 100 Chinese immigrants per year. If anyone doubted the harsh climate for Chinese immigrants, then the history of the Chinese Exclusion Act provided evidence of its severity. As we were to discover over many months, clearing up my citizenship status required time and lots of shuttling between Chinese and U.S. immigration offices. For many months, the process yielded only more confusion.

First, I needed identification from Chinese authorities. Next came the required clearance to enter America from U.S. officials. Along the way, we faced an uphill struggle to obtain papers for our son. Each step required various levels of official approval, which never came easily. Throughout most of our time in China, Charlie and I spent many hours chasing paperwork. Complicating matters was the fact that Mother had asked Charlie to help obtain travel documents for Florence, Joyce and Maymie. Charlie readily agreed to Mother's request. Many times my family looked to Charlie for help, and he always jumped into action.

In the summer of 1948, while we still awaited our visas, Charlie received a letter that threw our planning into further disarray. Willy wrote to say he had a new job offer that required him to move. Charlie was very worried about the fate of his store. He had been gone for more than eighteen months and knew the store required more than a caretaker overseeing operations. Charlie had already been absent months longer than his original plan.

Although my immigration status concerned both of us, Charlie and I agreed that he would return to Montana alone. As we hastily packed his belongings for the long journey, my husband assured me that he could assist in obtaining my and Na Bing's immigration papers from Montana. Over and over, he reminded me to take care of myself and our son. I couldn't resist the temptation to worry.

"We'll see this matter to the end," Charlie said. "We'll find a way."

CHAPTER FOURTEEN

Missing Charlie

O N AUGUST 3, 1948, Charlie and I walked down a long dock in Hong Kong, searching for his steamship, the *General Gordon*. I could hardly believe he was leaving. Pulled in two directions, Charlie worried about leaving his young wife and new son back in China, but felt concerned about the fate of his grocery store, the source of our livelihood. What we had to do, I told Charlie, was let him focus on his store while I worked with Mother to obtain final travel documents for me and Na Bing. Charlie knew his young family would face great challenges alone in China, but he knew we had no other choice. We lingered on the pier, saying a sad farewell. Then he climbed the gangplank, turned to wave and disappeared into the ship. His port of entry was to be San Francisco. From there, Charlie would ride the train to Helena.

For a very long time, I stood on that pier, watching as the *General Gordon* sailed out of view. A feeling of emptiness swept over me as I turned and walked back down the dock alone. As I journeyed back to How Voy, worries about travel visas as well as the separation from Charlie swirled in my head. I had worked so hard to make the adjustment from relying on Mother and my family to relying on Charlie. Now all I had was myself,

Charlie and Flora, 1947.

and a son who relied on me. But could I move forward without my mother's guidance?

My reprieves from loneliness came in the form of letters from Charlie. In all, we wrote forty-one letters to each other. Today, I still have every one of those letters. Charlie often addressed his letters to me as Congi, meaning "princess," and he always signed Mingzhu, his married name. In our region, when a man wed, he would choose or be given a marriage name. In most families, possession of a marriage name marked an important step in male adulthood.

He composed his first letter to me in the first hours of his trip. He wrote many more times during his two-week journey aboard the *General Gordon*. His letters arrived quickly and often, a very pleasant turn of events. He described life on board the ship, telling me what I could expect on my trip to America. Kenneth, who had left years before with Edith, had returned to China to marry on July 20, 1947. As Charlie made his plans to sail for America, Kenneth and his wife Joy decided to sail on the ship as well. But Charlie must have been lonely, as he let his emotions seep into his writing. His letters came so frequently that I could not keep up with my replies.

I read and reread his words over and over, in part so I could work on my return correspondence. In many instances, I had difficulty composing my replies, as putting my words on paper came slowly. Still, I looked forward to the task because I enjoyed his sentiments. I'd get up most mornings, take out a letter and sit to read it again.

Charlie's relatively smooth Pacific voyage allowed him time to send letters regularly. The *General Gordon* stopped at other Chinese ports, allowing him to mail several messages before setting off across the Pacific.

August 3, 1948

Congi my dear,

Three hours after I departed from Hong Kong all I could see has been the wide-open, borderless ocean. The weather has been nice and calm. The western food served on board is delicious. The ship is nice and clean, but it is very hot out. Since taking a bath is nearly impossible, I try to stay where it is cooler. It's hard to fall asleep at night. The cabins for females are on the top deck, which is cooler than the men's lower deck. It is stuffy in the room, so I spend most of the day on the deck or in the big hall, watching operas or playing cards.

There are quite some Chinese women in first and second class on the ship. Too bad you are not with me. A lot of people on board are couples traveling together, which saddens me and makes me miss you even more. When you travel to the U.S. by yourself, you are sure to meet some ladies who know English and can help you order food. So don't worry about that. The staff on board is also very helpful. Our ship gets to Shanghai at about noon. I am not planning on getting off.

Regards,
Mingzhu

In a letter written over several days as the *General Gordon* steamed close to Hawaii, Charlie described the rocking of the ship as it crested large waves. I had no experience with ocean travel and I wasn't sure how I would handle it. Better news was hearing how the crew kept the ship so clean. He assured me that on my voyage I would find other passengers who knew English and could help me take care of necessities during the journey. Thoughtfully, he advised me that I would need to take walks on deck to avoid seasickness.

August 13, 1948

My dearest Jong Hai,

It is the night of the seventh and the sailing has been smooth with cool breezes. The nighttimes are lonely and it is hard to go to sleep. I think about you often. I saw a couple holding hands going to the dining room. I felt lonely without having you with me. When I get to the U.S., I will make every effort to get the papers done so that you can join me and we can be man and wife.

Kenneth's wife got seasick and she was very pale. She doesn't listen well. She is supposed to go to the upper deck and walk in the fresh air, but she doesn't do it. Everyone on the ship should walk outside each day. Tomorrow is the 12th and we should land in Hawaii. I am also feeling some seasickness and need to go for a walk.

Mingzhu

As I had feared, our separation was difficult. But Charlie's romantic messages and thoughtful advice cheered me. His letters usually contained money. In addition to directing how the money should be handled, Charlie offered advice and direction on how to proceed with our immigration papers. I finally enlisted the help of Mother, and together we called on many officials, seeking the proper clearances not only for me and our son but also for Florence, Joyce and Maymie. Our difficulties in obtaining all the official approvals soon became clear.

August 25, 1948

Jong Hai, my beloved wife,

I arrived in San Francisco on August 19. We had to go through customs which took until the 21st of August. I ended up taking a car to Helena. I was going to write to you in San Francisco to let you know, but I left in a hurry. I will be sending a cashier's check of $250 U.S. When you receive the money, my brother should get $100 H.K., my nephew $50 H.K., your *mother $50 H.K. and the rest is for you. I am planning to see the lawyer as soon as possible. The lawyer does want you to go to the U.S. immigration office in Guangzhou when the papers are complete. Maymie's papers are not complete and our adopted son's papers are not ready.*

Wish you well,
Mingzhu

P.S. I know you are six months pregnant. When you come, I will buy you a first class ticket.

Your loving husband,
Wong Yin Nin

His postscript baffled me. How Charlie guessed I was pregnant, I never knew. Perhaps he talked about it with my mother, or maybe he guessed on his own. For my part, I had only a vague understanding of the word "pregnant." In my comprehension, pregnancy was a period of time before the arrival of a new family member, much like an adoption. I understood adoption: This was how my sister Nancy had left and how my son Na Bing had arrived. But my lack of education left me completely in the dark about the natural process taking place in my own body. My ignorance of biology and vocabulary would bring consequences soon enough.

Two days later, Charlie sent another letter saying that the paperwork for Joyce, Maymie and our son was complete. Charlie had hired a Helena lawyer who apparently placed a call to the immigration officials in charge of our village district, but the poor phone connection limited the exchange. To keep the immigration process moving, Charlie wrote with new instructions—this letter was all business, not much romance.

August 27, 1948

Jong Hai, my beloved wife,

Yesterday, I sent out a letter with $250 U.S. I went to the lawyer and he said that on July 17 he sent a letter to the immigration office in Guangzhou. The paperwork includes Joyce and Maymie's information. Maymie's paperwork does not need to go back to the U.S. Immigration. Our adopted son's paperwork is complete. Make sure to bring his birth

*certificate and visa back to Guangzhou immigration office. Take the law-
yer's letter and tell the office that they have all the necessary paperwork.
It has taken a month to get all the papers there. By then, you and our son
can come together. The lawyer did call to the village on July 17, but the
call did not go through.*

*It is too bad that since I was in China at the time, but did not receive the
letter until after I left. I should have received the information in August
and then I could have gone to the immigration office while I was there.
The lawyer did not hear from me and couldn't wait, so he called my
brother to let you know to go to the U.S. immigration office to get your
passport. The lawyer said that time is short.*

*The lawyer says that he got a letter from your mom about Florence's birth
certificate. The Lee family has also asked for help but says that it is not
urgent.*

*About your passport, you can come by boat. No matter what, we have to
wait three to five days. Let me know as soon as possible what you decide.*

Business is a little slow. I'm doing fine. You take care.

Mingzhu

September 4, 1948

Jong Hai, my dearest wife,

*I heard from the lawyer shortly after I arrived home. The lawyer wrote in
English to inform the U.S. immigration office in Guangzhou to get your
visa, Joyce's and Maymie's and also your birth certificates. Our son's papers
should be at the U.S. immigration office. They are waiting to hear from
you. They have been waiting day and night to hear from you. It worries
me that you have not contacted them.*

*I did hear from your mother twice. She writes that they only use U.S.
money on the boat. When you come, make sure you have U.S. money. I
was in first class on the boat, which was $15: $5 for food, $3 tip and $7
for room service.*

*Wish you well,
Mingzhu*

Thus began a shuffle between Chinese and U.S. immigration officials in Guangzhou and in the countryside. In reality, most of the hurdles came from the U.S. side. Long before Charlie's return to America, he started untangling travel papers and records for all of us. Yet, after many months of effort, we were no closer to having the proper passports for me, our adopted son and my sisters. Despite all the advice flowing back and forth, what remained unclear was which immigration office to contact. In a series of later letters, Charlie tried to help us sort out the problems. In one letter, Charlie would advise a visit to the office close to our village. In another, he would send me to Guangzhou. The conflicting advice and the delays, compounded by the long distances separating us, made what was already a maddening process even more difficult. By mid-September, I found I had to apply for a new identification card and a new visa. This meant retracing my steps back and forth between both immigration offices.

Somehow, at least some authorities knew that I was pregnant. They asked how far along I was. I did not know how to respond. Despite not comprehending my condition, I understood that their questions related to my family status. Although lack of practice showed in my calligraphy strokes, I eagerly wrote a string of letters to Charlie. In the first, I described my feelings at his departure. A later letter wondered whether my still mysterious condition might get immigration officials to speed up the review of my papers.

September 11, 1948

Mingzhu, my dearest loving husband,

I received your letter and the check of $250. As you requested, I have given each member of the family $100 H.K. You do not need to worry. I hear that you have safely arrived, which makes me happy. When I received your letter, I was at my Mother's house and they didn't let me know that the letter was waiting at your brother's home. That is why you didn't hear from me on August 6. Your brother phoned and asked me to come home and gave me the letter. You asked that I take our son to the immigration office.

Thinking back to the time when you left, I have the memory of seeing your boat leave. You were on the boat, but I couldn't see you. It was hard to see the boat sail away. I stayed until the boat moved and disappeared. It took my breath away. I felt you had the same feeling. Talking about man and wife, there is no end to our love. The sooner I arrive to the U.S., then we will be reunited as man and wife. I will be careful and hope you do the same. My wish for you is good health and the business is going well.

Your loving wife,
Jong Hai

September 15, 1948

My dearest beloved husband,

It has been a month since you left and it seems like a year. I don't know when we will be reunited again. It makes me feel very sad. I can't believe that we are so far apart.

In regards to going to the immigration department, I had to go through the governor to get the correct forms and identification, but I have not received it yet. The immigration office wants me to get back home fast to reapply for a new one and then return to the immigration office so that it can be sent to the U.S. Let me know soon when you book the tickets for the ship so that I won't be worried. I heard on the news that the U.S. ship is on strike. Don't know that this is true or false.

As far as I know, you didn't find the family photo. I know I put it in for you. Maybe when you were in Kowloon going through security, it got lost. There is tension in the country. The Chinese dollar is 75 cents to the Hong Kong dollar.

I wish you well. Next time when you send a letter, send it to Guangzhou. I am fine so don't worry.

Your loving wife,
Jong Hai

September 19, 1948

Mingzhu, my dearest husband,

It has been over a month since you departed. I still think about you often. I think about the good times we had and then it is hard for me to fall asleep at night. We are now so far apart. I hope I can get to the U.S. soon. Then we will be happy again.

Na Dok [one of Charlie's nephews] *is in school. The books cost $95 H.K. Na Moi* [another nephew] *did not want to go back to school. He just wants to stay home and goof around. It is not right. You should write him.*

I got your letter today with the $10 H.K. and the lawyer's letter. I had to wait until I got back to have a friend read it for me and then go to the immigration office to apply for my visa. I have already done so, so don't worry. They didn't ask me any questions. They just had to check my identification before they can start working. They did ask me about my being pregnant. How far I am, I am over four months. I think you sent a letter to the lawyer about it. Maybe the lawyer had informed the immigration. Maybe that is why they ask me how far along I am. Maybe they will work on my paper quicker, you think?

I can leave for the U.S. in October. If I can, it will make me really happy. We are all fine at home and wish you well. Take good care.

Your loving wife,
Jong Hai

Fall, usually my favorite time of year, came at me differently in 1948. I had so many worries over my travel papers that I wasn't looking forward to the season. Mother and I remained busy with our calls on immigration officials, so much so that we did not talk at all about personal matters. We should have. More time passed and that word "pregnant" came up again in my letters. Still, I did not connect the term to my own condition. As for the number of months, well, that calculation changed all the time and never made any sense to me. I never asked Mother about the word; she never took time to explain.

CHAPTER FIFTEEN

Back To Mother

A S MORE TIME PASSED, I suffered from the distance separating me from my husband. I realized, too, that we needed to put more pressure on the immigration authorities. Despite the help from Charlie's brother and the Montana attorney, too many formalities blocked my path. To depart from China in October, as I hoped, I needed wise counsel followed by action. I returned to Lin Fong Lei and Mother.

True to form, Mother stepped in with her usual determination. Mother immediately enlisted the help of a family friend, Tong Mon. He lived in a nearby village, had friends in government and understood how best to approach officials. She also made plans for the two of us to travel to several immigration offices for personal meetings. Reuniting with Florence, Maymie, Joyce and Dorothy also buoyed my spirits.

Charlie continued to send money, as he had all along. He wrote often, filling his pages with personal messages and advice. When I read Charlie's words, I felt a sense of peace—my doubts about the future eased. Mother, too, came to rely heavily on Charlie's strategies.

On my own with all the rules and regulations, I toiled to little effect. But with Charlie and Mother advising, I never had any thought that we might fail.

Charlie wrote often in his gentle, reassuring way.

September 23, 1948

Jong Hai, my dearest loving wife,

I sent out a letter to you yesterday. Maybe you have received it. Since I left you, I think of you often. It is hard to sleep at night. I keep dreaming of you. I get up but it is hard to keep going since I keep thinking about you. I think you have the same feeling. Everything will be okay, so don't worry.

When the time comes that you are on the boat, there will be a doctor to take care of you. When I came over, there were one thousand six hundred passengers. Of those, seven were newborns. I hope you take care. When you travel between the towns, make sure you are with your mom. Wish you well and take care.

Your loving husband,
Mingzhu

September 25, 1948

Jong Hai, my dearest loving wife,

I received your letter. I know the love you have for me and it makes me miss you even more. I don't know when we will be together again. When we do get together, we will be very happy. But right now, one day feels like three seasons. I am thinking that you are feeling the same way. Our deepest affection that we have for each other as husband and wife will last forever, even when we are apart.

We got married over a year ago. My heart is alone. I hope that you get the papers complete so that you can come to the U.S. and we can be reunited as husband and wife. That would make me happy.

When you are on the boat, be careful. Keep an eye on your belongings, especially your clothes and jewelry that is worth $300 U.S. You should put the jewelry in the suitcase. You will need to be aware of the other passengers and their jewelry. One or two jade rings are not important. Don't carry the jewelry in your pocket since you might be searched. The jade rings are up to you to bring back to the U.S. It is up to you as *to how many you want to bring back. Buy $50 to $60 for each ring. Don't buy the expensive one. Buy five, ten or twenty. It is okay. Don't put all in one place, spread it around. Buy some herbs, lokyee [antelope antlers] and ginseng. If they search you and see the herbs, tell them that it is for your own use.*

There is more to talk about, but that is all for now. I will write again. My feeling for you is no end. I will continue next time. Wish you well.

Mingzhu

October 4, 1948

Jong Hai, my dearest loving wife,

Since I left you it has been two months. It is like a knife cut. Thinking of our love and being lonesome for you. It is really hard to fall asleep. Even when you want to write there is no ending. The love I have for you will not end. I think you know my feelings. I will do my best and get you over here. We will begin our love and I will sing for you. That is my wish.

I talked to the lawyer about the date October 31 and if you can be on the boat from Hong Kong that departs on November 7. The lawyer called the Guangzhou immigration to inform them that you will be on the boat on November 7, but it is not sure. I will let you know as soon as I can. I got the letter from my sister that she talked to you about Willy. He wants to get married to Dorothy.

I have just bought a new home. It is big and beautiful. On September 30, I moved in some furniture. When you arrive, you and I will live together and enjoy our new life. When you come, you don't have to bring my pajamas and shirt, but make sure to bring my first wife's photo and my sister's family photo. I want to keep my first wife's photo for memory. The love I had for her is the same love I feel for you. It is all in my heart with the thoughts of a happy family. The photo we took in Hong Kong and our wedding photo. Make sure to bring them. If you have time, will you buy a pair of embroidered pillowcases? It is for our bedroom. I know I can buy it here, but I like it from China. That is my wish. My father in law will come here to help me so that I can come out to San Francisco to pick you up. I can't wait. My love for you will never end. Take good care of yourself. I wish you well.

> *Your loving husband,*
> *Mingzhu*

Two of his announcements caught me off guard. First was Willy's interest in my youngest sister Dorothy. Here was a matter to discuss with Mother, but the topic could wait while we worked on our current passport problems. Second was his request for his first wife's photo. His interest in the picture surprised me at first, but I knew Charlie was sentimental, so I understood.

Days sped past with no progress on official immigration procedures. My fears spilled over into my letters to Charlie. I suggested pushing the Helena attorney to contact immigration officials directly, believing pressure on U.S. officials might encourage action. In his response, Charlie said I would soon receive another letter from the Helena lawyer, including a visa for me and our son. Charlie added another twist, suggesting we seek help from our village leaders as well. Right away, Mother and I talked to several people, but nothing seemed to smooth the way for our departure. Still no progress, still no papers. I remained stranded in China.

Mother and I had another concern: a Chinese economy facing ruin from rapid inflation. Mother, for her part, had been reluctant to mention our financial situation because she knew how generous Charlie had already been. I chose not to mention this new worry to Charlie.

In other letters, Charlie kept me informed about events in Helena and his store. Willy and his mother, Charlie's oldest sister, had moved back to San Francisco. Back to managing his store, he must have been encouraged about prospects, enough so that he purchased a new home for us. His description sounded wonderful. He wrote that he figured the cost for my boat ticket would be $400 for first class. He reassured me again there would be someone on the ship who spoke English so my Chinese could be translated for easier communication.

By mid-October, concerned that we still had no response from the immigration offices, Mother took control. Although money was scarce, she rented a home in Guangzhou, a step that would enable us to get from office to office more readily. Mother recognized we had to push hard to get

Portrait of Mother and her daughters, early 1948. Chen Sun Ho, seated. From left, daughters Maymie, Dorothy, Flora, Joyce, and Florence.

action out of the two governments. Charlie sent more letters and funds—business was going well at the store, and I was anxious to see the new home he had purchased for us—and Mother stood resolutely by my side. My hopes began to rise.

October 18, 1948

My dearest Mingzhu,

It has been a long time since we've seen each other. I think a lot about you.

Even though I hear from you often, when I read your letters it makes me miss you more. My love for you is deep as I feel your love for me. Now we are far apart and I dream that we will be together soon.

Right now everything is expensive. Hong Kong money is high, almost like the U.S. dollar. Even if you have money, you can't buy pork or beef. If you want to buy rice, you have to pay black market of $80 U.S. for a bucket. Now it is beginning to look like fall. It is getting colder each day. My wish is that you take care of yourself. I'm doing fine, so don't worry. Keep writing to me. All for now, til next time. Wish you well.

Your loving wife,
Jong Hai

As our personal turmoil swirled, China's civil war flared and its economy floundered. Even the purchase of basic items such as rice and vegetables required handfuls of paper money. Meat cost so much we no longer could buy it. Mother, I knew, kept a wary eye on her financial resources at all times. Skyrocketing inflation must have frightened her, but she kept her commitment to me and my sisters. Forced to choose between rent in the city and more resources for herself, she pressed forward on the immigration front, never saying a word to me about the expense.

Charlie's regular financial contributions offered critical assistance throughout these days. Many nights, I didn't sleep. During the day, I had trouble concentrating with so much going on—and so much going wrong. My only comfort came in the constant stream of letters from Charlie.

October 19, 1948

Jong Hai, my dearest loving wife,

I received your letter that you sent on the 13th. It really makes me frustrated and gives me a headache that we can't be together right now. Reading your letter makes me worry more. After receiving your letter, I went to the lawyer right away to see how things are proceeding. He says it may take one or two days before he knows.

Today I also got a letter from my brother saying you were going to Guangzhou. He also stated that his wife was three months pregnant and miscarried. She is pretty sick. Everyone is very sad. You mentioned that your mother rented a house in Guangzhou to make it easier to hear from immigration. I don't know when that will be. Joyce and Maymie went to the immigration office last June. We just have to wait. In a few days, I will talk to the lawyer again and then will let you know. Wish you well.

Your loving husband,
Mingzhu

October 22, 1948

Mingzhu, my loving husband,

I received your letter and a check for $100 U.S. Don't worry. I know that you have bought a new home. That really makes me very happy. Too bad your sister and Willy had to be back to their home. Now you have to take care of the business and cook for yourself and eat by yourself. It makes me unhappy thinking that you are alone. As I was reading your letter, I know and feel the love you have for me. I want you to know the love I have for you is so deep. Soon we will be reunited again as man and wife. We will be as happy as can be, so don't worry. Okay? When we get together, we don't have to talk about our lonesomeness.

I am living in my Mother's home because I am six months pregnant. It is not easy to travel. We do a lot with my sisters and our son. It won't be long until we hear from immigration. So don't worry. If I can make the boat on the 11th it would be great. If not, I don't know when I will see you. That makes me unhappy. I wish God can help us get together so that we will be happy like before. In love as man and wife, that is my wish.

About Willy's mom wanting Dorothy to marry Willy. Mother says she is too young. Hope she forgives us. Lately so much has been going on. It is hard to fall asleep. I'm glad you always send me letters. They comfort me. I'm doing fine. Our love will never end. I will write to you soon. Wish you well and my love.

Your loving wife,
Jong Hai

Although I mention my pregnancy, specifically the term, I remained unaware of what it all meant. All that was going on—and much of what was to come—remained a strange mystery to me for some time.

What my reply omitted was news from Mother of a possible shipping strike, a new development that threatened my voyage to America. Charlie had read in the papers about the internal tension in China as the Communist and Nationalist forces continued to fight each other. And he had gotten word about the potential strike. His worry and frustration were reaching new heights.

October 23, 1948

Jong Hai, my dearest loving wife,

It has been three months since I left Hong Kong. Your documents still are not complete. This makes me really unhappy. Every time I go to the lawyer, he says he hasn't heard anything. It really makes me want to blow up like a burst of fire. I just want you to get back to the U.S. as soon as possible so we can enjoy our life together. I won't be at peace until we are together. I will do what I can to get you over here. Right now the boat is on strike. Maybe that is why the immigration office is not in a hurry or is lazy. Maybe I will have some news to let you know so you can go get your passport.

I want you to go back to the home village. I will let you know when to go back. You are pregnant so make sure you take care of yourself. I always worry about you. Right now the ship is not selling any tickets. You have to go through the bank with your passport before they will issue. Your mom is with you now. When you go back home, our son will be with you. Take care. I will write to you soon. Wish you well.

Your loving husband,
Mingzhu

In a separate letter, Charlie wrote that his local attorney had contacted U.S. officials. When Mother heard this news, she determined that we, too, should meet again with American officials in Guangzhou. On a surprisingly hot, humid fall morning, Mother and I walked to the U.S.

consulate once again. Mother stopped at a couple of doors, asking for the correct department. Finally, she found what appeared to be the visa office; we knocked and went in. Inside, we walked up to the lone U.S. immigration officer on duty. Mother stepped to the desk, introduced herself in respectful Chinese, and began to make her case.

"My daughter is Flora Lee, married name now Wong, and I am here to get her papers to leave for the U.S. She is a U.S. citizen. There should be no more problems."

"Does she have her passport, her visa," the man said.

"No sir, we came here, as we have before, to get them from you," said Mother, her impatience overriding her usual reserve.

"So you have no papers for your daughter," he replied.

"No, they are lost. Her husband is in Montana and we are here in Guangzhou working to have them replaced."

The officer said to us, "Then here is what you will have to do." He handed us a list of instructions, the same inventory we had studied before, and told us to wait at home until we heard further word from his office.

Mother argued, "No, we need action by you now. Her husband waiting for her back in America says the same thing. Her citizenship is in order and papers should be ready."

"But I am here in front of you and here is what you have to do. Follow those instructions. Wait until you hear from us. I can do nothing more for you now," he replied.

As Mother began to mount her next argument, the man waved us away.

"That is all I can do for you now," he said, ending the discussion.

As we walked out the door, I asked my mother to explain what the man had said. Though the conversation was in Chinese, I had missed many points in their rapid exchange. I wanted to know what had gone wrong. Why were we leaving empty-handed again?

"Our talk started very nice," she said. "He listened to me very politely, but he did nothing at all. I wanted to say to him: I will try another office but I am afraid there will be more people exactly like you. People who talk and do nothing."

I was a bit surprised by Mother's outburst. For a brief instant, she stood up very straight before that official and spoke her mind in a way I had not witnessed from Mother.

"Then, I decided it was better to say nothing more. I must stay calm."

"What do we do next?" I asked.

"Well, we will see what Charlie has to report."

Immigration laws, Mother recognized, were complicated matters. It would require her pushing from inside China—which she had done in this instance—and Charlie's pulling from America. Mother had the practicality to judge when she could prevail and when she could not.

Mother's measured, persistent conduct throughout our visa disputes taught me about her tough spirit and endurance. I did not like to ask so much of my mother, but I needed her help. Where I was anxious and afraid, Mother was resilient and tenacious. To succeed in life, I saw I had to become more like her.

Throughout that fall, I had many recurring spells of doubt as government turmoil in China worsened and travel papers eluded us. My torment was not misplaced. Many Chinese families in our region told stories of young brides separated from their husbands in America for years at a time. In some cases, the couples never were reunited. I hated the stories. Would this be my fate?

Perhaps sensing my growing despair, Charlie wrote again: "We are apart and I miss you more. I know the feeling when you really love someone. I understand and know that this is your first time. I left you and I know it is hard for you with the deep love we have for each other, but soon we will be together as man and wife. We will celebrate our deeper love like a beautiful blossom. I think your mother understands. Make sure you listen to her and take good care of yourself."

His next letter carried hopeful news. For some reason, Charlie's lawyer believed we were just a week away from getting our visas approved. Charlie made tentative plans for me to travel on a boat departing November 7. If that did not work out, he wrote, there was another boat leaving on December 11. Mother was thrilled, but I was afraid to get my hopes up, only to have them dashed yet again.

In the letter, Charlie also acknowledged the grim news we had tried to ignore for months. By then, Charlie and I both realized that obtaining a passport and passage for Na Bing to the United States would be impossible. Charlie decided the best choice for our son was for me to send him back to live with the Wong family in How Voy. With no travel papers and no American citizenship, his entry into the United States was not to be. I knew Charlie was as heartbroken and devastated by the idea as I was; we had longed for the three of us to be reunited as a family.

The letter went on. Travel documents for Maymie and Florence were held up for unexplained reasons. At that point, Charlie concluded, only clearance for me and Joyce seemed workable.

Despite his assurances, I remained anxious about my status. I wrote to him on October 31:

About my documents, they still are not complete and it is worrying me. Some things can't be helped and that makes me unhappy. So every day I am hoping that the immigration office will inform us to go and see the American immigration office. I don't understand the delay. They are not in a hurry to do their job. I am always thinking about you. I will take good care of myself. I always want to hear from you. I wish you well.

Your loving wife,
Jong Hai

By November, as each visit to his Montana attorney yielded no steps forward, Charlie's patience reached its end. He had written earlier of wanting to blow up like "a burst of fire." When I read his annoyance, I responded with words of encouragement.

November 8, 1948

Yin Nin, my loving husband,

It has been over three months since you departed from Hong Kong. I always think about our love and the love we had together. I miss you deeper than the deep blue sea. I dream about you and then get lonesome for you. I know you have the same feelings. I just wish the immigration would hurry up and get my passport ready so I can be on my way. How happy that would be, us together again as husband and wife.

To get upset is no use. Just take care and I will do the same. Our love is always there. There is no end. All for now. Until next time.

Your loving wife,
Jong Hai

Determined to find a way to clear away my immigration problems, Charlie embarked in a new direction—one that finally found success. He called on Mike Mansfield, then a U.S. representative for Montana, to ask if Congressional intervention would help eliminate the obstacles. In response, Representative Mansfield wrote a letter to the Immigration and Naturalization Service, asking them to look into my case. Congressional interest in my situation must have swayed the correct officials. Soon after Representative Mansfield's office contacted immigration officials, bureaucratic tangles seemed to loosen.

Through the efforts of Charlie and his lawyer, my mother and me and, finally, Representative Mansfield, we were able to pry open the door for my return to America. Representative Mansfield—who would serve five terms in the U.S. House of Representatives before being elected to the U.S. Senate where he also served as Majority Leader—acquired two lifelong supporters in Charlie and me.

Finally, Charlie wrote to notify me the good news was official: my papers were ready. This time he sounded certain, as certain as he could be.

November 13, 1948

Jong Hai, my dearest loving wife,

I have heard from the lawyer. He informed [the U.S. immigration office in Guangzhou] *that your papers are ready. They want you to see them so that they can issue your passport.... Maybe you haven't heard from immigration. As soon as you hear from them, you have to get out there so they can get the paperwork done.*

Wish you well,

Your loving husband,
Mingzhu

Our letters must have crossed because I had written to Charlie on November 10, explaining that I had heard from the lawyer advising me to take five photos to officials in order to process my passport and visa. Charlie wrote right back, saying I should come by plane, not ship. Despite the higher cost, he recommended the airplane as the faster and more reliable alternative.

Mother and I shuttled between offices to pick up passports, visas and plane tickets. By the end, the cost of our tickets more than tripled, jumping higher with China's inflation. Through all the last-minute commotion, I settled down a little. I could see, at long last, a clearing of the obstacles in my path to Charlie.

November 22, 1948

Yin Nin, my dearest loving husband,

It has been almost four months since you departed. I have been thinking about you a lot. I hope you are doing well and that everything is going well with you. That is my wish.

Good news. My paperwork is all done. I have received my passport from immigration and I have my ticket. The plane leaves on December 4 from Hong Kong on China Airlines. I hope you can come early to pick me up. It won't be long now that we will be united again. How happy we will be. You won't have to worry anymore. Take care of yourself, okay? I will send you a telegram on the first or second to let you know.

Florence and Joyce's papers are also done. Joyce will travel with me. Maymie's visa and birth certificate are still at U.S. Immigration. I hope you can hurry them to send it back to Guangzhou immigrations so she can be ready to travel with us. Since November 10, I haven't sent you any letters because I was supposed to leave on the 23rd. They didn't have a seat for me. My airfare is $2912 Hong Kong. I am doing fine and our son is also doing well. Don't worry. Soon we will be face to face to talk. All for now. Wish you well.

Your loving wife,
Jong Hai

In her drive to get her daughters out of China, Mother now had final documents for Florence, Joyce and me. She arranged tickets for Joyce and me on a flight in late December and coordinated a flight for Florence about a month later, in January 1949. Unfortunately, Maymie's visa and birth certificate remained caught in the inner workings of the U.S. immigration process. Officials had no good explanation for the holdup in Maymie's case, but my family knew we could do nothing about it immediately. Maymie's predicament undercut my own joy; it was very painful to leave behind the sister who had been my constant companion my entire life. I still held out some hope that Maymie's documents would be approved in time so she could join us. But the many months of delay had taught me that I could not wait or take any chances on my travel plans. I had to be ready to go, despite the fact the airfare had by then increased to nearly 3,000 Hong Kong dollars.

There was still so much to worry about. Over those frantic four-and-one-half months, Charlie and I exchanged forty-one letters expressing our feelings for each other and frustrations with officials. Reviewing our words years later, I marveled at my ability to write with such feeling, as I had barely finished more than a few years of primary school. Of course, I took a long time in replying. Dipping my brush into my ink, I carefully crafted my responses. Quite often, I did not understand some of the words or passages that Charlie used in his letters, but I had a practical solution. In many instances, I simply copied words and phrases Charlie used. For my envelopes, I used the same technique. With my brush, I duplicated words Charlie used to address the envelope. My envelopes read the same: to Mrs. Charlie Wong in Helena Montana. How was I to know what that word "Mrs." on the envelope to me meant?

In many letters, Charlie continually cautioned me to be careful because I was pregnant. When I wrote back, I copied that same word exactly, never understanding what it truly meant—neither in English nor in Chinese. All this time, Mother and I had never discussed childbirth, neither its cause nor its effects. To me, pregnant meant to expect the arrival of a baby at our house, almost as if it would be a delivery from the stork. In fact, I was carrying our first daughter. I felt no different, gained very little weight and had no morning sickness. How would I know what the word meant if my condition wasn't evident to me? In fact, I would later have several more pregnancies before I had even a vague understanding of how best to prepare. It would be another month or more before both we learned I was carrying our first daughter. How that fact would change our lives was a surprise we were yet to face.

One adjustment confronted me directly. My sadness leaving my mother and sisters behind in China throbbed inside. Yet, knowing that my mother was pushing me to go tempered the ache. As Mother continued in her whirlwind of action, I suspected evacuation for Maymie and Dorothy would not be far behind. Clinging to a family that was dispersing so quickly would not be wise. I could see that my mother's choice for me was inescapable.

None of these details lingered as I packed a few items for my trip. My thoughts were already across the ocean with my husband, gone now for more than four months. My bags were ready, and my travel papers, tucked away for safety, showed all the necessary approvals. All was in order. Safely packed were the twenty-five letters Charlie had sent me while we were apart. Words on paper would soon be replaced by Charlie in person.

CHAPTER SIXTEEN

Leaving China's Turmoil

Anticipating my first airplane ride on the morning of December 4, 1948, I should have been anxious. But I was simply too excited to think of being scared. My sister Joyce and I were leaving China—a land gripped in chaos for so long—for America. Joyce's trip would take her to Nebraska, where she would meet her future husband, Bill Chinn. I was finally closing the distance between Charlie and me. The prospect was so thrilling that I failed to see how my journey would also take me away from my mother.

When the time came to say goodbye, Joyce and I parted with Mother and our sisters in the village. While I believe my mother understood the consequences of our going away—she had planned for it and taken great care to make it happen—she had little to say to either of us. I can't remember any specific words we shared in these final moments. In the Chinese way, showing emotions with hugs or tears was not proper. Mother kept her quiet demeanor and composure, as always. Probably a wave of the hand or a nod of the head was all that passed between Mother and daughters.

Once we were on board the shiny airplane, I sat back in my seat, paying only slight attention to my surroundings. My mind churned with questions, not about travel but about my future. Would I like Montana? What was Helena like? What prospects lay ahead? What I needed was Charlie, so I could feel reassured. As our plane took off, my thoughts spun again, this time to the past. Would I see my mother and sisters again? Would I ever return to China? In the disorder of my final months with Mother, we never talked about these matters. In all our days, we spoke little about any important topic. As the airplane propellers hummed, I returned to thoughts of Charlie and Montana.

Hop-scotching across the Pacific, our flight made its first U.S. stop in Honolulu. Although we did not go through customs there, I recall that the officials put Joyce and me through a thorough inspection. They confiscated some food treats—salted prunes—I had packed. I believed, at the time, that I was never far from unfriendly representatives of the government.

Before long, our next flight climbed into the air again, headed for San Francisco. I remember most vividly my happy feeling that we were almost officially back in the United States. Although the last leg of the trip was uneventful, our flight had been a long one, lasting nearly two full days.

Some hours before we reached the mainland, I felt chills, followed by a fever and a terrible headache. From long experience, I knew it was a relapse of malaria. As I had many times in the past, I pushed the pain and fatigue away. If I could work through illness in the fields, then I could make it through this flight.

On December 6, 1948, our last flight landed in San Francisco, and Joyce and I stepped into the customs office. The line outside the door was long, so we settled in for a wait. After more than a decade, we were back on our former home soil with our papers in order. Still, we had to wait. When we reached the front of the line, the officers herded Joyce and me into a small room, where we were questioned and held for what eventually became two days of detention. Late on the first day, they moved us to a small room, which had just enough space to sit, sleep and eat. I learned later that Charlie waited for many hours outside the customs office, but at the time I did not know he was there; we were not allowed to communicate in any way. Throughout our stay, we had a supply of water to drink and small amounts of boiled cabbage and rice. Fear that some new legal obstacle might send us back to China gripped me. Outside, Charlie paced. I had crossed the Pacific Ocean to be reunited with my husband, but rules and regulations still kept us apart.

When he left Helena to pick me up, Charlie left his store in the hands of his first wife's father. Soon after we were married, Charlie shared with me the details of his first marriage. Her name was Minnie; they were married on December 20, 1939. In the pictures Charlie shared with me, Minnie was young and pretty. Sadly, early in their marriage, she fell ill and died at the age of twenty-six in 1946. Over the years, Charlie and Minnie's family remained friends.

Growing upset and impatient at the slow pace of our clearance, Charlie made several attempts to jolt the immigration office into action. He called his nephew Bill, who lived in San Francisco, to see what might speed up the process. It may have helped, for we received our clearances shortly thereafter. Finally, on December 8, 1948, officials stamped our new passports and released us from their custody. Joyce and I walked out of the building together. Still reeling from the symptoms of malaria, I was overjoyed to have Charlie by my side again.

We held each other close in a joyful reunion. With little time to spare before our trains departed, the three of us caught a cab to the station. Perhaps because I had just completed a grueling trip across the Pacific, and felt ill and worn down by the uncomfortable entry process, I parted from Joyce without much emotion. Where you might have expected hugs and tears, we parted with few words. Maybe I still carried resentments from her childhood mocking of me and what I viewed as her sense of superiority. Charlie was hesitant to linger on the platform for fear of missing our train. Joyce, too, wanted to be sure she caught her train for Nebraska. I don't think she looked back as she walked away.

Charlie and I surveyed the depot gates to find our train for Helena. When we reached the doorway, Charlie helped me up, gave the tickets to the conductor and walked me to our compartment. Without another word, I sat down and pressed my head into the seat to sleep. I was tired and sick. After months of frustration and separation, we were overjoyed to be back together, but I would have to enjoy our reunion later. A rumbling from the train, very faint and low, barely reached my ears as I drifted off to sleep.

Later in the day, Charlie woke me so our conductor could make up the bed. My husband, thoughtful as always, had arranged for a sleeper car compartment. Instead of dozing upright in our seats all the way to

Montana, we would enjoy a comfortable ride by day and a bed at night. I knew these tickets cost a lot more, but I was pleased Charlie looked after me so well. As regular as clockwork, our porter came each night to convert our seats into beds. It was heaven after the long plane ride and the days at the immigration office.

Every mile on the train took me through landscapes unlike anything I had seen before, but it passed in a haze because I was so ill. The train rumbled past dark forests and high mountains, and Charlie pointed to wintry scenes—so beautiful after more than a decade in a tropical climate. Charlie warned me to be ready for bitter cold in Helena, well below freezing. He said the thermometer registered 8 degrees below zero on the day he left Helena to meet me in San Francisco.

Freezing air and a biting wind tore at us as we walked out of the station in Helena on December 10, 1948. Covering everything in our path was a deep layer of snow, probably a foot or so. I am sure I saw snow as a young child in Boston, but stepping through it in Helena seemed like a first. Despite the cold, so different from Lin Fong Lei, I felt happy to be in Montana. Before taking me home, Charlie took me to one of his favorite restaurants to sample Chinese food, Helena style.

At that very moment, events taking place in China made it clear how lucky I was to escape when I did. On the same day, December 10, Chiang Kai-shek, president of China's Nationalist Party, had extended martial law in all Nationalist-controlled areas of southern and eastern China. He strengthened government powers to head off the growing Communist rebellion. In retaliation, Communist troops marched to within fifty miles of Nanking, the Nationalist capital at that time. Helena's newspaper carried the news on the front page.

Many Americans watched closely as the events unfolded in China. Since the end of World War II, the lengthy rivalry between Communist forces and the Nationalist Army had become bloody, marked by fighting in far-flung areas around the country. The hostilities had a long history, beginning in the late 1920s. By 1927, the Chinese government had splintered, with warlords, the Chinese Communist Party and the Nationalist regime contending for power.

From 1928 to 1937, the Nationalist government, led by Chiang Kai-shek, declared themselves the new central authority and made their greatest strides.

Over this decade, Chiang's administration stabilized prices, built roads and railroads, improved health care facilities and assisted industry and farmers. About the time my family moved from Boston to China, Chiang Kai-shek's government reached its peak influence. Far to the north at the same time, Communists had consolidated their power in the rural provinces of Hunan and Jiangxi. Although the two groups cooperated in the conflict with Japan, the Communist and Nationalist fight ignited again after 1945.

Growing up in Guangdong Province, I had little concept of the continuing civil war and what eventually became a favorable tide for the Communists. Most of the party's victories in the early years had come in the north, far away from my village. Had I been able to read English when I arrived in Montana, I could have followed events in China's internal war more closely in Helena's newspaper than if I had been back in Lin Fong Lei. Americans who followed the developments in China likely knew more about what was going on than many Chinese living in the villages. Helena's paper, like others around the United States, featured on the front page almost daily coverage of the escalating civil war. Opinions on editorial pages warned that there was little blocking the Communist Army of the Communist leader Mao Zedong on its march to control China. Most writers reported that this Communist takeover, in alignment with other Communist forces in the region, painted a bleak picture for future U.S. interests in Asia. Many Americans were worried. I read none of this, so gave the situation no thought at all.

On my second day in town, December 11, 1948, the *Independent Record* carried a front-page story on the Communist encirclement of Nationalist forces in Nanjing. Several weeks later, the action shifted to Tianjin, where the news was the Communist seizure of that city. According to the story, the battle brought a "crowning blow" to Chiang Kai-shek and the Nationalists. Over the next several months, the Communist advance gained speed, first taking over Tianjin on January 12, 1949, then Beijing in February, Nanking at the end of April and Shanghai in late May.

Later in 1949, persistent rumors pointed to a Communist advance on Guangzhou. Earlier, shortly after my own departure, conditions turned so bleak that many people who were able to travel started to flee my home region. Ships and trains into and out of Hong Kong were booked beyond capacity for weeks in advance of their departure dates.

Leading up to my trip, Charlie, I am sure, read these accounts regularly in the newspapers and discussed their meaning with his friends in town. China's deterioration surely fueled his efforts to get me out of the country. Once in Helena, I was too sick to take any notice, and he did not share any developments with me.

In my first weeks in Montana, my condition remained so fragile that I barely got out of bed. I left the house perhaps once or twice. Charlie and I were happy to be together again and, although I was weak, I wanted to enjoy our reunion. Later, when the weather warms, I told myself, I would be ready to explore my new town.

Over a span of months in 1949, revolution began to transform China. If Charlie filled me in on any of the details, I have no recollection of it; I suspect he said nothing to me. He would not want me to be troubled about Mother. By the fall of 1949, most major Chinese cities passed from Nationalist hands to Communist control. In most cases, the cities fell with little resistance.

Nationalist forces moved south and established a new capital in Guangzhou, where they hoped to hold off the Communist advance. On October 1, 1949, Chairman Mao proclaimed the formation of the People's Republic of China. Then, on October 14, nearly ten months after my flight out of Hong Kong, the Communist Army entered Guangzhou. The Nationalist Army retreated again, blowing up the Haizhu Bridge, one of the Guangzhou's major Pearl River crossings, as they fled the city. By October 29, the Communists controlled all of Guangdong Province, including the region of my home village of Lin Fong Lei.

In early December, almost a year after the date of my flight from Hong Kong, Chiang Kai-shek's Nationalist government fled the mainland for the island of Taiwan.

Because of the tireless efforts of our mother, the rest of my sisters were able to flee the country just in time. Florence departed in January 1949. Maymie left that May. Dorothy was the last to escape, in August 1949, just before the Communist troops took over the region. Aware of the upheaval and possible danger, Mother stayed in Hong Kong after arranging for Dorothy to leave. Relying on friends to compose her letters, Mother corresponded with Florence and Maymie as the Communist shadow settled over the country. For a time, Mother remained in Hong Kong, now a haven for many refugees. She waited, considering what to do next.

Florence and Maymie wrote to her several times—something I learned many years later—telling her that family in America could raise money to bring her back to the United States. Florence encouraged Mother to remain in Hong Kong until a plan could be devised for her to travel. Florence and Dorothy even considered arranging a marriage for Mother as a means to aid her escape.

Many years later, Florence told me, "We tried to get Mother over here. Like having somebody pretend to marry her so she can come over here, then we'd break it off."

She continued, "We tried to get her to come to the U.S. I said to her, 'Don't go back to the village.' I said, 'Stay in Hong Kong. We will help you return to the U.S.'

"When I got her letter, I wrote her back right away. I said, 'Don't go back there to Lin Fong Lei,' but someone wrote to her from the village, telling her to return. Well, she worried about the land, so she went home."

Florence told me, "We all said, 'Don't go back to the village.' I wrote, saying each of us will send money, so stay in Hong Kong. But she went back there and it got her."

For reasons known only to Mother, she ignored pleas from Florence and Maymie to wait in the safety of Hong Kong. On her own, she returned to Lin Fong Lei before anyone could arrange for her return to the United States. We would never know why. Did Mother believe immigration laws blocked her escape? Was she motivated by a feeling of duty to protect the family home and land holdings back in our village? Sometime in late 1949 or early 1950, she decided to return to Lin Fong Lei, facing alone what this new era of Chairman Mao and his followers would bring.

No news of these developments reached me. I heard nothing from Mother.

CHAPTER SEVENTEEN

History, Helena and Charlie

ALTHOUGH MY HEALTH remained fragile that first winter in Montana, I made time to get reacquainted with my husband. Exploring my new home of Helena would have to wait as I fought off my fever, rested and tried to regain my strength. Charlie told me more about history, his own and Helena's.

Charlie Wong had been drawn to America, and to Helena, by the same attractions that appealed to many other Chinese men of his generation. They left South China for the west, looking for jobs, money, education and opportunities not open to them at home. Railroads and gold mines were the main reasons they came.

Over time, I discovered my own journey back to the United States followed what had become a well-worn passage. Over the span of more than half a century, many Guangdong Chinese, almost entirely men, had made the same voyage eastward across the Pacific.

In the 1870 census, nearly 2,000 Chinese residents lived in Montana, 10 percent of the territory's official population at that time. Later census numbers showed 300 Chinese residents in Helena in 1900. My home province, Guangdong, had been home to most of the Chinese immigrants coming to Canada and the United States in the 1800s. Hoi Ping, now commonly known as Kai Ping, the Guangdong county where my village and Charlie's were located, was a major source of many of these immigrants.

Before 1949, China had no national spoken language. Hundreds of dialects were spoken throughout the nation, making it difficult for people from one region to communicate with those from another. Charlie and I spoke a version of Taishanese (although we did not know it by its name at the time), a dialect related to Cantonese. So many immigrants came from our region that this dialect became the common tongue in many West Coast Chinatowns.

Charlie had shared fragments of his family history with me when we were first married. His parents were both Chinese citizens. His father, Wong Shee Lung, a native of How Voy village, grew up when our section of the Pearl River delta was even more isolated. Born in the same area and era, Charlie's mother, Chew Shee, also went by the name Nui Gam, or "Golden Girl." Her family came from another small village called Kor Doy. Charlie knew very little about his parents' earliest days. Even the dates of their births and deaths were unclear. Charlie's brothers, Hay Nin and Jack Nin, of course, were very familiar to me, but I knew little about his sisters. Years before, older sister Wong Dung Yuen moved to San Francisco, eventually marrying David Fong. Younger sister Wong Gon Tilt, who had been part of our wedding party, immigrated to Canada and lived in Vancouver, where she married her husband, Gat Chow.

When Charlie arrived in Helena in 1922, the Chinese population had been declining steadily in Montana for decades. Many factors drove the change, primarily the Chinese Exclusion Act, the law restricting the number of Chinese citizens who could move to America. Another issue was the small number of Chinese women in Montana, influenced largely by these same immigration limits. As a result, over the years fewer new generations replaced the early Chinese settlers, and numbers dwindled. In the 1920 census, the number of Chinese residents in Montana dropped below 900, out of a total state population of nearly 550,000 people. The true number of Chinese residents may have been higher because not all immigrants were comfortable registering in any official survey.

At age fifteen, Charlie set out for America. He departed from China with his older cousin, Houang Jen Shew. Both carried little luggage, but they had big plans for their lives in America. On January 15, 1922,

Charlie and his cousin stood on deck as their Japanese passenger vessel, the *Shinyo Maru,* docked in San Francisco. When he filled out his registration for immigration officers, Charlie wrote his name as Houang Yin Him. Although he planned to find work, he requested entry as a student. Where the form required his father's name, Charlie wrote in the name of his traveling companion and cousin, Houang Jen Shew. His cousin had family living in Helena, and the pair believed those U.S. ties would make entry into the country relatively easy for the older boy. Charlie's situation was different. He was relying on a common strategy to get around immigration limits of the Exclusion Act. Following the plan they adopted before departure, Charlie portrayed himself as the son to his cousin, a so-called "paper son." It was a ruse of paperwork many Chinese men used to gain entry to the country.

U.S. border officials accepted the story, and Charlie and his cousin were cleared into the country. Charlie's family name had been the Chinese version of "Wong" all along, but he adopted the "Houang" version for this one instance. Despite the different spelling on his entry papers, Charlie soon went back to using "Wong," but he never pinpointed for me exactly when he made the change.

After a short stay in San Francisco, Charlie and his cousin set out for Helena as planned, likely by train. At first, Charlie worked on his uncle's vegetable farm north of Helena. He used his wages to put himself through school, attending Warren School in the valley north of town. On June 27, 1929, at age twenty-three, Charlie received his eighth-grade certificate from the Helena school system. He never told me how he felt attending school with youngsters, but I know he valued his education, something he would not have received in China.

Before completing school, while still eighteen, Charlie began working as a waiter at the Yat Son Noodle Parlor in downtown Helena. It was a job he held until 1939. For the next fifteen years, Charlie held down two jobs, working days on the farm and nights at the Noodle Parlor. His days were long, but he didn't mind the pace. At a young age, he began to put savings aside regularly. Those fifteen years were good to him, Charlie often said. He not only learned about hard work but also developed the business skills at Yat Son that later helped him in his store. Out of his paychecks, he sent a good deal of his money back to his home village in China to support his

Helena friends, from left, Jerry Wong, Charlie Wong, Din Wong and Tommy Hom.

family, the same practice he used to help me and my family after our marriage match was made.

In late 1939, at age thirty-three, Charlie became his own boss when he purchased the Wing Shing Grocery. The store had occupied the storefront at 136 South Main Street for at least a decade before Charlie's purchase. Charlie relished the idea of running his own business. Practical and conservative, he set about improving the store, one small project at a time. Located in downtown Helena's southern end, the area had a reputation for roughness, but Charlie saw potential for the neighborhood.

Soon after purchasing the store, Charlie married his first wife, Minnie.

From his years in Helena and his work in the downtown area, Charlie had come to know a lot of people. He liked his neighbors and he wanted to do more for his town. Soon, Charlie found new endeavors in Helena. Because of his command of English and Chinese, many Chinese neighbors sought his translation skills and advice on personal and business matters.

Some years after our wedding, Charlie told me how much he loved Montana, a sentiment he repeated often. Yet, he sensed our small Chinese community faced challenges in achieving economic well-being and a place in society. In part, he told me, these concerns encouraged him to take on duties beyond his store.

Eager to use his understanding of America and China, he looked for opportunities to build connections between his former homeland and his adopted country. He saw the importance of unity between the two nations because he believed they occupied similar positions in the world and shared common political beliefs. Many Chinese leaders, he liked to point out, were educated in the United States and understood Americans and American culture. Charlie felt he could help link Helena's white and Chinese populations, and he set out to find ways to do so.

Even before the Japanese attack on Pearl Harbor in 1941, Charlie helped organize fundraising dinners to support Chinese war efforts against Japan. Once the United States entered World War II, Charlie volunteered for the Helena Chinese Relief Committee and served as president. For several years in the early 1940s, Charlie used his own address as the official address for the committee. As Japan's role in the world war escalated, Charlie reacted as Japan's army moved through China and the Far East. Once Japan attacked Pearl Harbor and the United States declared war, Charlie spoke before area civic clubs about the need for China and the United States to cooperate in defeating their common enemy.

In one speech in February 1942, Charlie addressed members of the Helena Rotary Club. His talk covered a bit of history about the Chinese Civil War and Japan's invasion of China. Then he rallied his audience to China's cause in the war. In a newspaper account of his remarks, the *Independent Record* reporter quoted Charlie's words about the ties between the United States and China. Charlie said both nations were unprepared for war with Japan, but that history and circumstance had created a partnership for both nations. Even though he had been gone from China since 1922, Charlie conscientiously followed its internal politics and the conflict with Japan, so he knew the history.

"America must be willing to sacrifice its riches just as China is to sacrifice her manpower," he told his lunch audience.

"Both nations made the mistake of trying to avoid the war, but now that they are in it, they must go forward united so that we can have peace and develop our nations along peaceful lines. Both nations, peace loving as they are, must give their utmost for the war now that they are in it.

"The true heart of America has been shown by its support of the United China Relief campaign last year. The Chinese government has found in the United States' declaration of war against Japan a Magna Carta to free the world of totalitarian tyranny. We all seek the best for our lands and we must move fast to get it."

On that day, as club member William Brown introduced Charlie to the audience, he added his own historical context to the topic of the speech. "The Chinese have been fighting the Japs for four years and have not been conquered and they will not be conquered in the future," Brown said. "China has been a football for ambitious nations throughout the centuries but never has been conquered."

For a several years, Charlie worked with the Helena United Relief Committee to sponsor dinners to raise money to support China's war efforts. Local clubs and civic leaders banded together to host what they called "rice bowl" dinners, banquets with Chinese food, decorations and entertainment. Helena's first rice bowl dinner attracted several hundred supporters on July 23, 1941. Charlie and Minnie, along with other members of the Chinese community, organized the food preparations for the first event.

In a newspaper interview, one of the committee organizers, Mrs. William Fitzsimmons explained the purpose of the event: "It is a gift from Helena to innocent people in distress. The point is the terrible need to help and the idealism that prompted Americans to give."

This project and others kept Charlie busy for several years.

By the time I arrived at the close of 1948, many of Helena's Chinese families had moved on. Only 100 Chinese residents lived in Helena by then—the town had a total population of approximately 17,000—but the city phone directory still listed fourteen different Wongs. To Charlie, the small Chinese community and the relative tolerance exhibited by Helena's other residents made him feel welcome. Charlie assured me many times how much I would come to enjoy his adopted hometown, just as he did.

I had seen bustling cities and towns in my part of China. To me, Helena moved at a slow, steady pace. By contrast to my village, Helena, though much larger, seemed peaceful. No dirt, no mud, no noisy animals. I liked the way my new home came at me in a size and pace I could understand.

Bessie Arrives

A FEW DAYS AFTER MY ARRIVAL in Helena, Charlie introduced me to his friend Amy Wong, the woman who purchased his trunk full of gifts for me. She came by our home to meet me one day when I was feeling better. In our first conversation, she gave me a warm greeting, a brief description of Helena and some helpful tips for adjusting to my new setting. Before long, I realized Amy would become one of the most important people in my new life in Helena. She and Charlie helped me adjust to my new setting and to the language and culture of Montana. I understood only a few simple words of English and I could read none at all. Meeting Amy, with a similar Chinese background, brought instant comfort. Over the next several years, Amy was my best friend and guide.

I was not to see my new friend again for many weeks. My weak health confined me to bed and I did not want visitors. Time passed slowly. Mostly, I sat in bed, wondering why I suffered such pain. My condition, I continued to believe, was the product of my malaria and the stress of leaving China. In truth, I had another medical concern, totally separate from malaria and stress. She would announce herself just twenty-five days after I stepped off the train at the Helena station.

Although Charlie and I had written in several letters about my pregnancy, I had no concept of what the word meant. Neither of us really knew what was to come, so we made no preparations whatsoever.

Thoughts of seeing a doctor never entered my mind, neither in China nor in Helena. Visits to physicians and hospitals made Charlie nervous. After the unexpected death of his wife Minnie in the hospital, he developed misgivings about medical treatment. Looking back, I suspect his doubts, combined with his own lack of knowledge about childbirth, left him completely unsuspecting about all that pregnancy entailed. Since I relied so much on Charlie, I, too, did not realize that our baby was ready to enter the world at any moment.

On January 3, 1949, I awoke early with an unusual, painful stomachache. I awakened Charlie to ask what I should do. Trying to be helpful but unsure of the situation, he suggested that I go to the bathroom. Neither of us was prepared for the chain of events that took place next.

As soon as I closed the bathroom door, our first daughter decided she was ready to be born. I called out to Charlie. He came in, realized immediately what was happening and ran to call Dr. David Berg, a local M.D. By the time Charlie rushed back to help me back to bed, I was very nervous. I don't remember how much time passed before the doctor arrived. Perhaps the combination of the stress of childbirth and my weakness from malaria hit me, because I must have passed out. The chain of events became a fog. Lucky for our baby, Charlie and me, Dr. Berg appeared just as our daughter was about to be born. Later, I heard our baby was halfway into the world when Dr. Berg arrived.

Before I could comprehend anything, Dr. Berg summoned an ambulance to carry us to St. Peter's Hospital, thankfully only ten blocks away. Once there, I regained enough awareness to feel Dr. Berg gently place our daughter in my arms. In my haze, I had only the scantest idea how she arrived and no time to enjoy holding her. Weighing fewer than five pounds, my little girl required immediate emergency care, a fact that had the doctors and nurses hovering all around us. Within moments, they swept her off to another part of the hospital. At the foot of my bed, Charlie and Dr. Berg conferred quietly in words I did not understand.

As it turned out, I would not see my baby again for a month. Born prematurely, my daughter required special equipment and attention at once. Hospital personnel kept her on another floor of the hospital. Meanwhile, due to my weak condition compounded by the lingering malaria, Dr. Berg confined me to my bed, no exceptions allowed. After putting their heads together, the doctor and other hospital personnel quarantined me. No one entered my room without full gowns, masks and gloves. Nurses provided me with my own set of dishes and utensils, sterilized and stored in my room. Worst of all, I could have no contact with my daughter.

Through January and into mid-February, I did not venture beyond my hospital room. My malaria symptoms remained severe, with high fevers followed by extreme shivering. I am sure recovery from childbirth added to the strain on my system. When I had the shakes, I trembled so badly that my whole bed seemed to rise and rattle in fits that lasted for an hour or more. I weathered bouts of joint pain and vomiting. The fever and sweating episodes, which seemed to attack every few hours, soaked my bed and covers. Outside, Montana was locked in a record-setting blizzard for weeks. Inside, my mind swirled like the weather gripping Helena.

What an ordeal my stay in St. Peter's Hospital became. I was so weak I could do nothing for myself. Still, I desperately wanted to see our baby. Yet even after several weeks, the nurses still did not permit me to see my daughter, not for even a moment. All this time, Charlie had his hands full. When not caring for his wife and daughter at the hospital, he looked after his store. Because he worried my system was not adjusted to American food, Charlie brought me soup and rice each day. When not in my hospital room, he was upstairs checking on Bessie (the name we had given our daughter soon after her birth). His reports were my only connection to my newborn daughter. I learned she was monitored carefully by medical personnel due to her small size, but for me the news wasn't enough. Charlie told me Bessie cried a lot during this time in the hospital. As a new mom struggling with all the apprehensions about how to care for a child, I cringed at the reports of her condition. Confined and miserable in my room, I tried to concentrate on improving my own condition—but all I could think about was Bessie.

Finally, after nearly six weeks at St. Peter's, we were discharged from the hospital, and proud father Charlie brought us back to 108 South Main. Bessie was still only five pounds. Holding her was her anxious twenty-year-old mother. As I left the hospital and round-the-clock nursing care behind, I had to get over my nerves right away. Charlie and I learned to care for our baby together. Here was our first step in the family adventure Charlie and I wanted.

In my first months at home, my transition to poised mother came slowly. When Bessie cried, I often cried, too. I was so unsure of how to soothe her. I had cared for Na Bing, but little Bessie was another matter. I knew just where to turn for help. Soon after I left the hospital, Amy came by to offer her advice and encouragement. Amy and her husband, Sun You, had a two-year-old daughter, and Amy was pregnant again and due within months. She possessed competence and experience, which she shared graciously. From Amy I learned about diapers, formula and baby ailments. Most important, she taught me how to quiet Bessie's cries.

Whenever she visited, Amy brightened my spirits. If I fretted that parts of my job as a mother were beyond me, then I would hear Amy's advice ringing in my ears, providing a bit of confidence. In my young life, I had often observed that you must take whatever life tosses at you and apply your best efforts. I thought I knew some of the steps.

So it went with my education about bearing a child and raising a newborn. Looking back on my daughter's birth and her first months, I realized you have no choice but to carry your child until her time comes, whether you are prepared or not. Hampered by my lack of familiarity with my condition, I moved along as I had for years—no special care, no change in diet, not even a call to the doctor.

Amy, by this time a regular presence in my life, was so many things that I was not. A skillful teacher, she was serious but understanding, tolerant of my mistakes and enthused by my successes. Her Cantonese dialect nearly matched my own, meaning we conversed with ease. Almost as important, Amy spoke English with precision, a reflection of the British version she learned as a youngster in China. Over several months, Amy taught me the meanings of some English words I encountered, from street signs to baby formula labels to newspapers.

Amy now had her own family of two young daughters: Lelan, born in 1947, and Letah, born just months after Bessie, in the spring of 1949. Relying on her head start in motherhood, Amy showed the self-confidence I needed. When my parenting skills, whether in boiling baby bottles or testing the formula temperatures, fell short, she helped me until I got it right. Even if I had Bessie's day organized pretty well, I found that things could go disastrously wrong, or so it seemed. Amy did her best to prepare me. Amy knew how to balance life, impressing me with her ease in shifting from infant care to cooking, from clothing to world issues. On important matters, she wasn't one to joke or make light of life. Yet she had a sense of humor and knew when to use it to make me laugh.

Springtime after Helena's cold winter produced a delightful transformation. Bright days and warm sunshine lured me out of our home and the store most days, and I would push Bessie in our baby buggy. By April, I felt much better, but the time in the hospital had left me weak. Never in my twenty-year life had I been so inactive for so long, as my lack of vitality demonstrated. Conditioned by steady chores in the rice paddies and fields throughout my early years, I normally enjoyed a strong constitution, which I was determined to regain. After a winter of Helena's subzero temperatures, I set out to rebuild my strength. As the sun warmed the town, I came back to life.

By May, Bessie and I had covered most of my new neighborhood terrain by foot and baby buggy. My renewal accomplished many purposes: I learned my way around Helena, my liveliness returned and Bessie blossomed in my care.

Summer brought heat and dryness to Helena. I expected the heat, but I was used to the high humidity of Lin Fong Lei, with rain running off my hat and moisture soaking my clothes. In the Rocky Mountains, the wind blew frequently and everything dried out quickly. Helena's air carried the smell of sagebrush, pine and other crisp fragrances. In place of the steaming dampness of my village, I found pleasant warmth that brought all my neighbors out to enjoy it.

Our short walks outside were a time for me to take in the new landscape, so much different from my vistas in China. The low hills of dull-colored brush and bamboo beneath hazy skies of my village now gave way to a totally new and beautiful landscape. To the west, the slopes of Mount Helena rose right above our neighborhood. Off to the south were more hills covered by green trees and brown grass, divided here and there by narrow gulches. Best of all were Montana's open, peaceful spaces. Its sky seemed bigger, spreading out to the horizon. When I looked out my window, I saw blues, greens and browns.

Some of my favorite memories in these early Helena days revolved around gatherings to eat and socialize, activities that also made Charlie cheerful. Usually on Sundays, Amy and Sun You came to our house to talk and cook. To my delight, we ate pretty well. For dinners, we prepared either a roast, spareribs or a special Chinese feast. Faced with my limited cooking skills, Charlie acted as the main chef, mixing together meals of Chinese and American foods. He functioned without any recipes, but when he needed advice, Amy knew just how each item should be prepared. Watching the two of them, I began to learn to cook.

Our Sunday gatherings were highlights of my early years in Helena. Because the town and the culture were so new, I did not take an interest in many people or activities outside my narrow world. A big event to me was a walk to Amy and Sun You's home, just a few blocks from where we lived. Sometimes, we drove around in Amy's car, a maroon Studebaker. Often we gathered the children and visited the park in the center of town for a picnic.

Although Charlie provided some of our daughter's requirements from our store, Amy guided me through the department store, the drugstore and the supermarket. So many choices confronted me—very different from my little village, where we grew our own food and sewed our own clothes. Amy continued to tutor me in English, though we conversed almost entirely in Chinese. Charlie and Bessie, Amy and Sun You were my constant companions—my only companions really.

Slowly I discovered the skills to be a mother, but Bessie's early days were not easy. Different scenes from this chaotic time remain clear in my memory. For a time, I could not grasp the concept of diapers. Growing up in my small village in China, diapers were unknown, and the mothers I saw used split pants for their babies. These garments were designed so mothers could hold their little ones with legs apart to go potty, which seemed to me to be a simple, practical solution. As they got older, toddlers learned to squat down to take their bathroom breaks everywhere and anywhere. As I faced similar duties in Helena, I found that fitting and pinning diapers on Bessie created only headaches. How could I fasten a diaper on my squirming daughter without sticking her with a pin? I also faced Bessie's second diaper test, all the dirty ones to be cleaned. I was truly tempted to try split pants for her. Only strong persuasion from Amy convinced me otherwise.

"No. What we did in China won't work here in America," Amy said.

"Too bad," I said. "But I see you are right."

"Your neighbors won't understand squatting children," Amy replied. And that was the end of that.

CHAPTER NINETEEN

My Spinning Top Stops

Now that we had our daughter, a home and our small business, Charlie and I felt life was good for our little family. Wing Shing, our grocery store, required a great deal of Charlie's time, but he didn't mind. He enjoyed the work of running a store: greeting and serving customers, working with suppliers and salesmen, keeping precise inventory and doing the bookkeeping and accounting. He kept meticulous accounting records, relying on his abacus for the calculations and noting figures in his beautiful handwriting. Charlie loved visiting with the salesmen, who would share a few tall tales, area news and gossip and stories from the local business world. Charlie collected their yarns, most of which he shared with me late in the evening after closing time. These tales were my window to a wider world, the one beyond the confines of our home and store.

When Charlie came home at the end of the day, he took great pleasure in holding or playing with Bessie or visiting with me. I looked forward to our talks, a time to make a few plans or hear about the world as Charlie saw it.

As much as I wanted to help Charlie in the shop, my shyness and flawed English held me back. I knew I wasn't equipped to work the front counter of the store, at least not yet. I worked for short stints, but only to allow

Charlie a momentary break. I would always call him back to help a customer whose request left me confused. My days, spent mostly at the back of the store in the kitchen area, limited my contacts with other people.

At first, I gave little thought to more children, but Charlie seemed eager to add to our family. He did not seem to have a specific number in mind. "Just lots," he said. I wanted more children as well, but, even after Bessie's birth, my idea of how children were conceived was still largely a mystery. Charlie, I should have guessed by this time, was too private or proper to consider having such a conversation with me on the topic. He concluded, incorrectly, that I had a minimal understanding of female biology. I didn't. And by the end of my first summer in Helena, we were headed for another family surprise.

By late August, I suspected something might be amiss. My strength slumped again. I felt tired and gained a little weight. Because I had no fever, no shakes and no aches, I guessed malaria was not the cause. Looking back, I am sure most women see pregnancy and all of its signs clearly—not in my case. Once again, we both were woefully uninformed and unprepared for a new arrival.

Sure enough, I was carrying our second child. Once again, I never really figured out what was going on and I didn't visit the doctor. With no sense that I was about to have a second child, we were again completely surprised by my sudden labor in October 1949. Charlie rushed me to St. Peter's Hospital. Alerted to the situation, Dr. Berg met me at the door and cared for me throughout the delivery. While in labor, I could barely make out what was happening all around me. When the baby came out, Dr. Berg said, "It's a boy." Our first boy was born October 16, only ten months after Bessie's birth.

Next came a flurry of activity among Dr. Berg and the nurses. Because our son arrived prematurely, the nurses whisked him away to the incubator before I could even hold him. Despite the commotion all around me, I had no inkling of any complications for my new son. Charlie joined me in my room after the delivery. Although we talked late into the evening, Charlie did not let on that we might be facing serious complications. To this day, I don't know if Dr. Berg said anything to my husband.

Charlie and I were proud. We immediately decided on his name, Charles Junior. As I drifted in and out of sleep, my husband assured me our growing family would mean health and prosperity for all of us.

"And a boy, this time." he said. "A sign of good fortune for us."

When I woke up very early the next morning, I noticed Dr. Berg lingering outside my door. As soon as he saw I was stirring, he came in. His face, with its sad eyes, alerted me at once that something was wrong. At first, he spoke so quickly that I did not comprehend his meaning. Seeing that I did not understand, he repeated himself, this time more slowly.

"Your little top stopped spinning this morning," he said. "He stopped turning."

I didn't comprehend his words. I sensed his serious meaning, but his roundabout sentences only confused me. Finally, he spoke bluntly.

"Your top has stopped turning. Your son, he died last night. He was too tiny to survive."

In that instant, the full force of his words hit me. In fact, it was my world that stopped turning. I feel it now as I felt it then. It hit like a weight on my chest. I came to the hospital knowing my child and I would be cared for; I never even considered that death could be an outcome. As I searched my physician's expression for more explanation, I found none. In this single, desperate moment, as pain creased Dr. Berg's face, my tears streamed out. I did not know how to break free from the grip of his unfamiliar words. Once their meaning became clear, all I could do was turn away from the doctor to face the wall of my hospital room, silent except for my sobs. Dr. Berg was still, not knowing what to say. Moments later, he departed quietly.

Soon, Charlie came to my side. He struggled to comfort me, but he, too, reeled from the loss. "Our son is gone," he said.

"I know, I know," I said, as I again lost control of my tears.

For the next few days, perhaps a week, I remained confined to my hospital bed. My thoughts were dark, and nothing I did seemed to shake the feelings. For a long time, I was not myself—I slept more than usual and wanted to be left alone. How strange it was to feel this way. Charlie worried constantly, but I think he realized there was nothing he could do for me, except let me grieve. Worst of all, I wondered if our son's death was my fault. If only I had known he was about to be born, I would have been better prepared. Why had this happened? What could I have done differently? I found neither answers to my questions nor comfort from the pain.

As I lay in bed day after day, my thoughts turned to our adopted son

Na Bing in China, memories that brought more tears. Over time, I had come to grips with the knowledge that I would never see him again. But now, as I stared at the ceiling, I thought about the misery of losing not one, but two sons. When I fled China, we had arranged for Na Bing to stay with Charlie's brother and wife, but he did not respond well to the change. He often ran away to go back to his natural parents. When forced to return to How Voy village, he soon disappeared again. In the end, Na Bing ran away for good and no one sent us any more news about him. News that he was gone, when it eventually reached us, brought further heartbreak to Charlie and me. We harbored hopes that we would eventually bring our adopted boy to live with us in Helena.

Life's hardships had made me resilient, but I had found the limits of my strength. No matter how hard I tried, I could not force myself to climb out of bed or walk through the halls. If a nurse came in with a cheery word, I didn't want to hear it. What was there in the world to enjoy?

Charlie struggled with his misery, too. He had lost his first wife, now his first son. To occupy his mind, he turned to funeral preparations, starting with ordering a small coffin for our son. When he met with the funeral home, he arranged to have Charles Junior buried in the cemetery at the foot of Minnie's grave. Both of us were too shattered to make plans for a public memorial service. While I was still in the hospital, Charlie arranged for a private burial. By the time I came home the following week, our son had been laid to rest in his grave. So bleak was our outlook that Charlie and I could barely talk as we mourned.

How well Charlie and I would cope with this pain concerned me a great deal. When faced with life's challenges, I had always reasoned that you have to will yourself to keep going. However, strength of mind, a trait I learned from Mother, would not be enough by itself to see us through the loss of our son. Grief gripped us, and it would take its time in leaving.

My life's newest lesson arrived like a destructive wave washing upon the shore. In the past, I tried to remain steady, much like a rock, so stable that even the larger waves would not move me. Now, I could see that even the larger, stronger stones around me, such as Charlie, might be at risk. In time, he reassured me and tried to restore my confidence, but I was uneasy all the same.

And so the fall of 1949 and the next winter passed. My energy came back slowly, while the ache lingered. For me, this time was a blank.

CHAPTER TWENTY

Opportunities

IT WAS AROUND MIDSUMMER of 1950 when I finally emerged from the worst of my pain. Charlie sensed my renewal and welcomed me back to the store. Watching my daughter, I noticed how her playfulness and growth rekindled my own interests; as she was awakening to her world, I found new enthusiasm in my daily tasks. Soon, I discovered I was pregnant again. We greeted the news with joy.

Another bright spot was the arrival in Helena of my youngest sister, Dorothy, who came in August to live with us. Now sixteen, Dorothy had left China the previous August, just ahead of the Communist takeover. At first, she stayed for a year with Florence in California. When she decided to join us, Charlie arranged a bedroom of sorts for her in the front part of our home. Next, we contacted the local elementary school, and the teachers held a spot for Dorothy. After assessing her skills and past education, school officials placed her in the sixth grade at Emerson School. She was older and smarter than her classmates, but her English needed polishing.

Having her with me after the loss of our son proved to be a great comfort. She pitched in with housework and Bessie's care. Most of all, Dorothy brought me more stories of Mother, remembrances that kept my spirit on the mend.

Mother-and-daughter outing in Helena, Montana, 1954. Flora Wong, left, with Amy Wong. Daughters, from left, Lelan, Gloria, Letah, Thel and Bess.

Dorothy related her story about escaping just ahead of the Communist drive into our province.

"I got out just in time," she said. "I think my papers were ready, but we had no money for my trip. Family in America sent money, and Tong Mon helped Mother buy the tickets. I think the family sent money, $750 or $800."

Mother made sure Dorothy left in time.

"I left in August and the Communists came in October. Mother pushed me out."

Dorothy stayed with us for two years, a period of time where I shared my enthusiasm for Montana with picnics, family outings and walks around town. Dorothy left Helena in November 1952 to move to Denver, where Joyce and her husband, Bill, lived.

The start of 1951 brought number-two daughter, Gloria, to our family. Now, my days revolved around the care of two lively youngsters. Try as I might, I continually fell behind in looking after Bessie and Gloria, even with Dorothy's help. I was overwhelmed with washing diapers, doing regular laundry and feeding the girls. Pots of water for sterilizing bottles and heating milk filled the top of my stove. As they grew, I came to discover a new and discouraging arithmetic that strikes most new mothers, I am sure. My math skills were imperfect, but I was sharp enough to see that, in this instance, one plus one equaled more than two. Both were happy babies, but they kept me constantly on the move.

Finally, I realized my situation: One single child can pin down an adult so that when the next one arrives, you are fated to fall further and further behind. The difficulties in balancing competing family needs would come to me over and over as Charlie and I added members to our family. Each new youngster, it seemed, made for more than a doubling of work for me. How much better did I appreciate my own mother as I tried to raise my children.

So it was that the responsibilities of caring for Bessie and Gloria left me on edge at times. Luckily, Charlie cooked the meals almost every night. And Amy continued as my guide.

"Remember, Flora, a mother's love is natural. You don't have to teach it and you don't have to learn it," Amy reminded me after one strenuous day.

"Diapers, yes, you learn how to handle those. Food, yes, you have to learn how to prepare it. But not care and love. Those are part of you."

I found much to admire in Amy. A petite, slender, almost bird-like woman, she struck me as well educated and wise to so much of the world that I did not understand. She was much stronger than her small stature would suggest. Her stylish, round-eyed glasses matched her elegant attire. At times quick to laugh, Amy also observed all that happened around her with a critical eye. Her assessments were often sympathetic, but she could be very tough and disapproving when the circumstances required. A speedy judge of people and situations, she was self-assured in her perceptions. With Amy at my side, I developed my own self-assurance and a better understanding of life in America.

Amy had arrived in America after her own long and tormenting journey. Over our many months together, she related the bits and pieces of her story. She was born in another small village in South China, less than twenty miles from Lin Fong Lei.

"You are so lucky you are born in the U.S.," she said. "You didn't have to go through all I did to get here to Helena."

Fresh from my own trials at reentering the United States, I was tempted to talk about my experiences. But as I learned all the details of her hardships and her difficult escape from China, I held my tongue. Her life and times in China, along with many other similar experiences, perceptions and sympathies, helped seal our friendship over the years.

Amy and I had a link from the past. It came by way of the parents of Wong Sun You, at the time Amy's future husband, that Charlie purchased the grocery store. Sun You's family wanted to return to China in the late 1930s, but they had to sell their store first. Someone told them Charlie might be interested. He met with the couple, discussed his options and quickly concluded the sale of the business. Located at 136 South Main, the store occupied the first floor, with an apartment on the second floor. For the next ten years, Charlie rented the building, living upstairs and running the store below. About this time, Sun You and Charlie first met.

Sun You and his older brother, Sane Foke, both went to high school in Helena. Later, Sun You attended Cornell University, graduating in 1939 with a degree in water conservation. Right out of college, he worked as an engineer for the Montana Water Conservation Board. When his parents set out on their mission to help China with its wartime challenges, they urged him to travel with them. This trip, they suggested, was a well-timed opportunity to put his college training to work to benefit his family's home country, so Sun You went along, landing in Hong Kong for a time. Soon after his arrival in the British territory, friends introduced Sun You to Amy.

The two grew very close quickly and, soon after their meeting, they were married in 1941. Casting about for a way to use his training to help China, Sun You contacted the Nationalist government at a time when it faced great challenges in rebuilding its roads and railroads. Almost immediately, Sun You found an assignment as a transportation engineer. For a time, Amy remained behind in Hong Kong. Before long, the government transferred Sun You to various locations in southern China, eventually assigning him to a transportation post in the interior region, near the cities of Chongqing and Kunming. As soon as the job appeared to be more than short-term, Amy decided to follow him.

Her first leg of the trip from Hong Kong to Guangzhou was uneventful. Amy noticed the destruction from years of fighting with Japan, but the waterways and roads of southern China remained open and passable. Once she began her 600-mile journey northwest from Guangzhou to Chongqing on the Yangtze River, Amy's travel turned hazardous. Many roads, marked by potholes, deep ruts and the pockmarks of bombs, were nearly impassable. In dry spells, the hard grooves in the surface jolted passengers. When hard rain hit, the channels in the surface quickly changed to soft, sticky mud.

Amy's immediate problem was how to find her way hundreds of miles across several provinces—no simple matter in a passenger transport system that had disintegrated in the years following the Japanese invasion. To make her way farther north and west, Amy used a patchwork approach, traveling on foot, by small cargo truck and sometimes by sedan chair, a single chair carried on poles by porters. Later in her trek, one truck driver assured Amy he could deliver her safely to Sun You at his camp high outside the city in the mountains. Before long, the truck broke down, forcing Amy and two other passengers to hike farther up the road into the hills. After miles of walking and with darkness coming on, they came to the home of a farmer, the first possible refuge they had seen all afternoon. There, the trio bought food and settled down to wait for repair or rescue, not knowing when either might arrive.

"We were lucky the farmer agreed to help us, and there was nothing else we could do," Amy said, describing her adventure years later.

When the wait stretched into seven days, Amy began to consider her options. She was in a very remote spot, leaving her just two choices: walk back down the road, or head deeper and deeper into the mountains to where Sun You was living. Then, looking out the farmer's door one morning, Amy noticed a figure coming down the road. As the man walked closer, Amy realized it was Sun You. Knowing her route and the difficulties it would present, he had grown anxious when she did not arrive as scheduled. He waited a couple of days, then set out on foot to find her himself.

Their happy meeting, of course, delighted Amy. Unfortunately, Sun You had ominous news. Just days earlier, while Amy waited at the farmer's house, the Japanese had attacked the United States at Pearl Harbor. Of more immediate concern to the couple, the Japanese also had invaded Hong Kong, right after Amy started on her trip. Sun You told Amy she had escaped the city with only days to spare. The escalating Japanese attacks made the pair even more anxious to reach their destination farther inland as soon as they could.

By walking and finding rides on passing vehicles, they reached Sun You's temporary home in Kunming, only to find that the Nationalist government had reassigned Sun You to Yunnan Province. After they relocated, the couple lived in a two-room house in a small country town Amy remembers as Shaguan. Sun You continued his work as an engineer on highway projects, but the commotion and disorder in the area made progress on his tasks very difficult.

Amy's home in Shaguan had no running water or toilet. Her communal kitchen, an open-air charcoal fire, sat in the dirt fifty feet from her front door. Keeping house was hard enough, but staying healthy was beyond what Amy and Sun You could manage. They seemed to be constantly sick with one ailment or another.

Within a year, Amy and Sun You moved again, this time to Guilin, to the east and closer to Guangzhou. Here they rode out most of World War II, as Sun You continued his work for the Nationalist government. A couple months before the war ended, Sun You began coughing up blood and running a high fever. Amy recognized the symptoms as tuberculosis, a serious, infectious disease and one of the leading causes of death at the time in China. She knew Sun You needed skilled medical care right away, so she moved him to a hospital in Guilin.

"I put my husband in bed. There was no quality care, no medications." Amy said. "He needed milk and all I could find was goat's milk. So we made do with that."

Alerted to the crisis, Sun You's family tried to intervene, suggesting that Sun You come to their small village. Amy would have none of that idea.

To deal with Sun You's condition, she felt they had to stay in the hospital, even a poorly equipped one.

"You go there and you know you will die," she said. "Conditions there were even worse than in Guilin."

By great good fortune, Amy heard about help nearby. Dr. Everitt A. Tunnicliff, a veterinarian from Bozeman, Montana, lived in this same corner of China. Sun You and Dr. Tunnicliff, who also was a professor on the Bozeman campus of Montana State University, were well acquainted from their Montana days. They first met when Sun You studied for a short time in Bozeman and rented a room from the Tunnicliff family. Years later, the Nationalist government hired Dr. Tunnicliff, an expert on animal infections, for a special assignment to develop programs to care for a range of domesticated animals.

After learning the facts about the veterinarian and his friendship with her husband, Amy urged Sun You to contact Dr. Tunnicliff for help. Aware that his health appeared to be declining, Sun You eventually agreed to write his friend, describing his condition and circumstances. As soon as Dr. Tunnicliff received the letter, he hurried to visit Sun You in the Guilin hospital.

Reacting to the seriousness of his friend's condition, Dr. Tunnicliff immediately searched for help. First, he sought out his contacts with the Chinese and U.S. civilian governments, and later the military, in an effort to assist his friend. By wrangling with various offices of the American government across southern China, he arranged a flight for Sun You, an American citizen, on a U.S. Army plane making the run west from Guilin to Kunming. At first, the Army blocked Amy from boarding the flight because she was not a U.S. citizen. Heated arguments broke out, with Dr. Tunnicliff standing firmly by the couple. In the end, Dr. Tunnicliff, with persuasion and a bit of bluff, convinced officials that Amy needed to ride along to care for her husband.

Recounting the story years later, Amy credited Dr. Tunnicliff with saving both their lives at that point. Sun You obviously needed improved medical care, and Amy would have been in danger on her own.

"If I had been left behind, I would not have been able to leave Guilin," Amy said. "In that case, I would have been left in the hands of the Japanese at some point. The Japanese would probably just shoot me. There is no doubt about it. I was all by myself before Dr. Tunnicliff helped out. There was no one to help me move my husband from the hospital and no one to look after me at all.

"The Japanese at that time could pretty much do as they pleased. There was no protection from the Chinese Army. Even if I had somehow survived the war, there is no way I would have made it out of China and on to the U.S. without his help each step of the way."

Along with the flight he organized, Dr. Tunnicliff orchestrated hospital care in Kunming, where Sun You's condition improved slowly. But Amy recognized that her husband, who continued to lose weight and cough up blood, required more skilled medical treatment in order to survive. Although the hospital had been affiliated with the British and was better equipped than most others in the area, the war had left it disorganized and depleted, with little modern equipment or medicine and few trained medical personnel.

"It was nothing more than an old country hospital," said Amy.

Again, Dr. Tunnicliff intervened. In this instance, he called on his connections in the Army to coordinate yet another flight, this time to carry Sun You all the way back to the United States for further treatment. However, nothing Dr. Tunnicliff did would convince the Army to put Amy, a Chinese citizen, on the plane with Sun You. In the middle of war in 1944, with disaster raging all around them, military officials had no time or resources to help a lone Chinese woman, even if her husband was American.

The couple, who had been through so much, had to part. During his evacuation, Sun You landed first in Calcutta, India, where he remained hospitalized for three months. Next, Army officials found a bed for him on a Red Cross ship headed for California. Some time later, he made his way back to Montana.

Left behind in Kunming, Amy worked for a time as a teacher, instructing first graders in Mandarin. She also applied to the consulate in Hong Kong for a visa so she could travel to the United States.

As 1944 drew to an end, Dr. Tunnicliff prepared for his own return to Montana. Before his departure, he made another round of calls, hoping to help Amy find a way to America. In one of his last acts before boarding his flight home, he finalized transportation and tickets for Amy to the United

States on a winding route around Asia. She was to travel south through China, overland across Southeast Asia and eventually to India. From there, she had a ticket for her final leg to the United States. With all the necessary papers in hand, Amy planned her exit for mid-August 1945. Up to that point, Amy had been sure she would be left behind to face the unknown in China, but now she had more than hope. She had her actual tickets in hand. On August 15, the night before she was to depart, the Japanese surrendered. Good news for the world, but the peace accord blocked all the transport plans Dr. Tunnicliff had mapped out. Amy felt trapped again.

"I could wait where I was, but that offered no answer," Amy said. "Instead, I decided to go back to my home village in the south of China and see what I could work out. In Kunming where I was living, I knew no one. In my village, I knew at least I could wait and see what could be arranged in familiar circumstances."

Her choice carried high risks. She still had a visa, but its expiration date was just three months away. Finding a travel route without help presented immense difficulties and uncertainties, particularly in the aftermath of the war. Even more troubling was the immediate legal hurdle threatening to block Amy's path. In Washington, D.C., lingering immigration controversy limited options for all Chinese citizens seeking entry to the United States. In 1943, U.S. lawmakers had repealed the Chinese Exclusion Act, but this opened the door only slightly. Under the new quota system, the U.S. government allowed only 105 Chinese to immigrate to the United States each year. Amy and all other new immigrants faced considerable odds against admission.

Amy applied for entry as soon as possible. To her surprise, she managed to obtain one of those few immigration openings. She always believed that Dr. Tunnicliff had a hand in her selection.

"I was one of the lucky people, just one of 105, to get into the country in 1945," Amy said. "How could that be? I could not have qualified on my own, so I always suspect that someone else—I am sure it was Dr. Tunnicliff—must have helped me."

Ultimately, clearing all the barriers required another year of effort on Amy's part. She spent three months waiting in her village, trying to press her case from her remote village. To deal with the unpredictable details of tickets, visas and passports, Amy eventually moved to Hong Kong, after the U.S. consulate began to function again. Continually pressing her case with officials, Amy kept her bags packed, ready to leave on short notice when her chance arrived. Whatever lay ahead, Amy was all set.

"After the war, China needed lots of imported material, so one day this cargo ship arrived carrying railroad tracks and grain," Amy said. "The ship was from New Orleans. It belonged to the Lykes Brothers Steamship Lines and was named S.S. *Kendall Fish.* The name, I think, came from this Mr. Fish, an American pilot. He died in the war and this ship was named for him."

Amy found passage on this ship. The vessel, one of sixty-four built near the end of the war, measured 450 feet in length and traveled at fifteen knots. Although the trip lasted thirty-six days, Amy had no complaints, enjoying the conditions on board the new ship and sailing closer to Sun You with each passing day.

Amy explained to me: "The ship was on its way home to New Orleans through the Panama Canal. As a cargo ship, it did not carry many passengers, only twelve, so I was lucky to find a spot on board.

"My roommate was a British lady who spoke good English. She made sure that I had good food at each meal. Many of the other people were seasick, but not me. Every day, I walked on deck to get fresh air. I did not miss one meal the entire voyage. My roommate always made sure to give me the best food when we ate.

"I also learned a few more words of English. It was a pleasant trip."

As the *Kendall Fish* pulled up to the New Orleans dock, relatives greeted her. After a short visit, Amy headed for Greenville, Mississippi, where she had an uncle and several cousins. After two weeks there, she traveled by train for three days and nights to Helena. There, in 1946, she finally reunited with Sun You, ending their nearly two years of separation. While his condition had improved with medical care in the United States, he still remained in the hospital for more tuberculosis treatment. So Amy lived for a time in a spare bedroom of the apartment over Charlie's store. Eventually, Amy and Sun You were reunited and moved into a house not far from us. In November 1952, Sun You died unexpectedly. It was tuberculosis and he went quickly at the end. Amy stayed in Helena for two more years and then left for the South where she had relatives, taking her daughters Lelan and Letah with her. The departure of my close friend stung.

When we reunited many years later, Amy reminded me of her ordeals during the war: "You can say that I'm pretty tough. At that time, I didn't know I was tough. You just do what you have to do. It was much the same for all us in China during the war. We had no one really to protect us. You just had to keep moving if you wanted to survive."

She often told me how fortunate I was to be born a U.S. citizen. "So lucky you were born in the U.S.," Amy would remind me. "You didn't have to go through all this."

CHAPTER TWENTY-ONE

Learning

FOR CHARLIE, WHO WOULD ALWAYS be my best teacher, Amy's advice to me came as a welcome addition. Charlie had answers to most of my questions, but he appreciated Amy's female sensibilities in her advice to me. My husband was generous in his insights on our neighbors, local businesses and the character of the city. Putting some of my shyness aside, I was becoming more comfortable helping in our grocery store. My English progressed to the point where, with some prompting from Charlie, I could point people toward what they wanted on the shelves.

In the early 1950s, our family flourished. Ten short months after Gloria was born, I delivered daughter Thel early in 1952. When Thel was born, I had reached a point where I was coming into my own as a mother. I was getting good at handling most every situation. Next came son Poy in 1954. Then, in 1955, we celebrated the birth of daughter Nancy. With four girls and one boy, our family felt complete. In just six years and ten months, I had been in and out of the hospital for six births. We still grieved over the death of Charles Junior, but we were thankful for a big family of lively, thriving children.

Despite his long days in the store, Charlie felt content. He easily blended work and family life. Even before the kids reached school age, he assigned

Wong family in living room of South Park Avenue home in Helena, 1956. Front row, from left, Gloria, Bessie, and Thel. On parents' laps, from left, Nancy and Poy.

each of them jobs at the store. Charlie taught them to help dust the shelves, sweep the floor and restock the groceries. His patience rarely faded despite the added attention they required for most of their designated tasks. For Charlie, our large family was important. He savored the time in each day to share work and play with his children.

Although I had learned all sorts of lessons from Charlie and Amy, I recognized my weak English skills still held me back. This constraint kept me from getting out in Helena to learn more about the community around me. Most of my days revolved around the children, leaving little time for developing new talents.

A new adventure materialized in 1952, when I learned to drive—with encouragement from Charlie. Perhaps driving is a simple talent for many.

To me, it was a big move and the learning was not easy. This new skill gave me a measure of freedom, self-reliance and confidence.

But self-reliance wasn't the primary reason for my driving lessons. At first, Charlie used my driver's training as a means to fend off a persistent salesman. A local car dealer, Cray Painter, stopped by our store frequently. A natural at sales, Mr. Painter enjoyed visiting with Charlie, but he rarely missed an opportunity to make a pitch about our need for a car. He pushed, and Charlie dodged. Our budget did not have much room for such purchases. Running low on objections, Charlie tried a new delaying tactic to hold off Mr. Painter. When asked what it would take to finally close the sale, Charlie replied: "When you teach my wife how to drive, then I will buy a car. Not before."

Charlie figured his strategy perfectly. I still could not speak more than a few words of English, which would stall any purchase for a while. Needing the sale, Mr. Painter decided he could bridge the language barrier. And so my driving lessons began.

What an odd pair we were. Mr. Painter spoke no Chinese, and I spoke little English. Through a curious mix of trial and error, sign language and some pictures, he somehow taught me how to drive. As you would expect, we did everything behind the wheel slowly. At first, we practiced in an open parking lot, where I wouldn't have to worry about hitting anything. To master the mystery of the car—its pedals, steering wheel and other controls—I tried copying all the moves Mr. Painter showed me as he drove.

At my first lesson in the car, I confess I wasn't at all enthusiastic about any part of driving. The car seemed so big, its controls so foreign and its turns so fast. But once I got the feel for the gas pedal and brakes, I looked forward to mastering all the techniques.

When my turn to drive on the streets came, Mr. Painter tried to teach me the rules of the road. Using very simple English, most of which I did not understand, he explained signs and traffic rules. Most days, I had my first three daughters, Bessie, Gloria and baby Thel with me. Piling them in the backseat was a significant distraction. Mr. Painter, still determined to make the sale, paid little heed to the girls. Driving class was a great adventure for the youngsters, who had never been in a car before.

After two weeks of careful instruction and practice, Mr. Painter decided I was ready to take my driver's test.

Off to the motor vehicle office we went, with Mr. Painter standing by as my interpreter. Before I got behind the wheel, Mr. Painter took the driving examiner aside to suggest a modification in driver test protocol. He told the official he needed to ride along to test his instruction techniques. Without waiting for a reply, Mr. Painter jumped in the back of the car as the official examiner slid into the passenger's seat to put me through my paces. Nervously, I tried to understand the examiner's directions, setting off on an unknown course around Helena. At least this time, I told myself, I don't have my three children in back to distract me.

Even before we arrived for my test, Mr. Painter had explained his special strategy to me. So it was that at each turn of the course, I was guided mostly by finger pointing from Mr. Painter. He noted the examiner's directions and, to tip me off to the directions, gave me hand signals from his spot in the back seat. I listened to my passenger in the front seat, checked the mirror for my signals from the back seat and drove along the streets. As the two men conversed in English, I nodded as if I understood completely. I am sure the examiner knew precisely what we were doing, but he seemed unconcerned about my language deficits.

Best of all, my examiner decided not to test me on my two greatest fears: The parallel parking test or any written examination. When the exam was complete, I waited in nervous anticipation. The examiner checked his paperwork, looked up and gave his verdict. I had passed. I couldn't believe it. As I stood holding my new driver's license in my hand, I thought: If I can do this, I can learn anything.

A deal was a deal, so Mr. Painter stopped by shortly thereafter to deliver a new, pale green, 1952 Chevrolet four-door sedan, a car our family enjoyed for many years. To my amazement, I became an eager driver, putting both my driver's license and our new car to many tests. I became a regular fixture on the streets of Helena, driving to the store and taking spins around the neighborhood when I really could have walked. I drove as often as I could. Soon I was confident enough to "tootle," as I called it, most anywhere in town.

Charlie, too, liked to take the wheel. Late in the evenings after the store closed, we loaded Bessie, Gloria and Thel in the Chevrolet and headed to the A&W for a root beer or a soft swirl ice cream cone. Other times, Charlie drove to the airport, where we parked to watch the big airplanes take off and land. Gazing up as the planes lifted off the runway always fascinated him.

Amy and I regularly packed the kids in the back seat and went for drives. Sometimes, we drove to Hill Park, near the Helena Civic Center, where our children would romp around on the grass. Other times, when we felt more daring, we drove as far as McDonald Pass. To Amy and me, that two-lane mountain road was scary. The winding trip up the mountain pass went fine, but our return back to town on Highway 12 always tested our courage. The steep downhill grade and many narrow turns took my breath away. I wasn't always sure I could trust the brakes, or my skills, to slow the car. Whenever we took the sedan to explore, Amy and I chatted away about the scenery and our lives.

One summer day in 1952, we set out on a drive for a picnic in Butte, taking along our girls, Lelan, Letah, Bessie, Gloria and Thel. Added to our group were three college-age girls from Taiwan, Nancy, Emmy and Marion, all foreign-exchange students at Helena's Carroll College. They made lively additions to the outing as they conversed about college classes and events in China. How we managed to fit all ten of us in the car, I don't remember, but we did it.

Driving around Butte, we found a park with some trees and a bit of shade. There we enjoyed a nice summer picnic with our kids. Just as we were getting ready to leave, a policeman approached us. Hostile from the start, he told us we must clean up after ourselves before we left. Amy and I felt his lecture and tone were unnecessary. We were two responsible people who knew very well to clean up after our picnic.

The policeman's treatment of us mystified me. Amy smarted over the incident. She reminded me that we clearly were cleaning up well before he arrived to chastise us.

"He was not nice," I said. "He did not have to tell us how to behave."

"I am sure he was showing his prejudice against us," Amy said. "He said all that to us just because we are Chinese. No doubt in my mind. This man, with his small view, he singled us out because of who we are."

Here, in my first encounter with discrimination, I did not share Amy's anger, but I knew the policeman's treatment did not feel right. Despite his intrusion, Amy and I were happy at how the rest of our big Butte adventure had gone. I drove all the way without a hitch.

Discrimination and bigotry were real concerns for some Chinese in Helena, as I learned over time. Some Chinese neighbors shared their personal experiences with racial intolerance. A couple of neighbors on Main Street told me of their early days growing up in Helena and riding the trolley out to a popular swimming hole on the outskirts of town. Once there, however, only the white children were allowed to swim, while the Chinese children had to stand on the shore and watch. In another discussion, a woman related stories about her children walking home with their white schoolmates. As the group arrived at one home, all the children except the Chinese students were invited inside for hot chocolate. The Chinese children turned and walked home.

One of my Chinese neighbors said that if you were white, life was easier. Some even advised their children to check the "white" box indicating race on official documents such as applications for a driver's license—if their physical features allowed them to do so. For me, thankfully, experiences with discrimination were very rare. Nearly all of my Helena neighbors greeted me with open minds and open hearts.

What most got in my way at this time in Helena, whether it was greeting neighbors, shopping or finding my way around, were the basics of the English language. I should have been eager to improve my English, but shyness still held me back. Amy and I communicated just fine in our version of Cantonese. I looked forward to our chats in a language where I felt at ease, but our practice meant I was making no headway in English. I still strained at anything beyond a handful of simple sentences. Each time I watched Amy converse fluently with others, I regretted that I was unable to speak in what should have been my native tongue. Perhaps my success driving the Chevrolet truly gave me the inspiration, because soon after getting my driver's license, I set out to speak English.

As a practical matter, I faced certain stumbling blocks. Although I learned some English long ago in Boston, the words had vanished from my vocabulary. In our home, with only our children around, Charlie and I spoke to each other solely in Chinese. Our children learned Cantonese long before they learned English. And my shyness made me falter when speaking new words in English; I was very self-conscious about my awkward attempts.

But Charlie had a plan. Late into the evening after we closed the store, he walked me down the aisles as he repeated the English names of items on the shelves. At first, he concentrated on the simple words: candy, bread, milk, eggs. As I progressed, anything in our inventory was fair game. When he felt comfortable I had learned some of the fundamentals, Charlie helped me to put words into sentences and to respond to questions. Before long, I managed a few more words and phrases.

Then, without telling me, Charlie enrolled me in English classes at Helena Business College. When Charlie surprised me with this development one evening at the store, I greeted his idea with fright and a little rebellion.

"Classes are a good step for you," he said.

"No, it's too late for me. I can't sit still for studying. I am too busy with the kids and the store," I protested.

"No, it's time for you to learn more," he said.

I wouldn't listen. "School was never good for me. Now it's too late. I'm too old."

"Oh, you're young. Look at me, I'm much older and I still learn new things all the time," he said.

"But I never finished grade school. I would like to learn more, but it's too hard to catch up. I never liked to study," I continued.

"You must accept that you will work harder at it than the others," he said. "Remember, learning is a gift that will follow you the rest of your life."

If I was stubborn about staying out of the classroom, I should have realized Charlie would be even more persistent. I was going back to school, no more questions asked. A part of me was glad Charlie pushed so hard. Without his prodding, my wariness about school would have held me back. As usual, Charlie cleared the way, and I eventually had the good sense to follow.

Soon, there I was: enrolled in the Helena Business College for six months, attending language classes one hour each afternoon. In a roomful of classmates, I was the only one studying English. The others took the business classes offered by the college, which had just one classroom. From time to time, I listened to the other lessons around me, but to little effect. What I heard seemed too complicated, so I turned back to my own lessons.

Lucky for me, our teacher, Esther Huey, noticed my exertions right away and devoted special attention to me. I suspect Charlie had already warned her I would need extra help. I was slow but persistent. At Charlie's direction, I also began working with a tutor. Dorothy Kendrick, a schoolmate from his early days in Helena, dropped by the house to give me extra lessons.

During my six months in class, Mrs. Huey and Miss Kendrick emphasized vocabulary, grammar and spelling. In the process, we got to know each other. A great teacher and a bundle of energy, Mrs. Huey enjoyed my young daughters, so I often loaded Bessie, Gloria and Thel into the car to drive over to her house for extra English lessons. As Mrs. Huey and I sat in the kitchen, practicing my verbs and nouns, the girls played at our feet.

Later at night, Charlie patiently checked my writing lessons, noting spelling progress as well as errors. Although my Chinese calligraphy came easily, my English writing came slowly. I remember one word particularly baffled me: "eleven." For years, I wrote that word in my check register so that I could go back and carefully copy it whenever I needed it for a check.

Mrs. Huey and Miss Kendrick were much more than tutors. They became good friends. For many years after my lessons, we made family visits to their homes at Christmas. However, I never called them by their first names. Teachers, in China, were highly respected, and tradition dictated formality.

CHAPTER TWENTY-TWO

Wing Shing Company

OVER THE YEARS, Charlie described his history in Helena to me, filling in more pieces of his story. I knew he had worked at several jobs and set aside savings, eventually accumulating enough money to purchase the original Wing Shing Company in 1939. The building at 136 South Main Street, which he rented, housed his store and apartment for nearly a decade.

Just before my return from China, he purchased another building a few doors down the block at 108 South Main. Here was our big and beautiful new home, just as my husband had described in his letter to me. As promised, Charlie waited for my arrival so that we could make the move together. Although it served as home to us initially, Charlie eventually planned to convert the site into our next store.

Around 1952, we purchased a duplex located across the alley from our home. Soon, we moved into the larger portion of the duplex, with room enough for our growing family, and transformed our former home into our new Wing Shing Grocery. With these moves complete, Charlie gave up the lease on his original store site and set up shop at 108 South Main. Now we had our own store property and a separate home.

"Now we really are in charge of our future," he told me. Ownership was important to Charlie.

Wing Shing Grocery on a snowy Helena morning in the late 1960s. Son Poy is shoveling snow.

As he worked on the store renovations, Charlie divided the space into three sections: a larger retail space at the front of the store with more room for shelves and counters, a storage area in the middle and a kitchen space at the back. I spent most of my time in this rear area, a large space where we added some comforts: a stove, sink, kitchen table and couch. We had a small bathroom off to one side. Charlie arranged it so we could sit at the table, watch the front counter through a small window and take care of any customers who came in. Despite the fact that our family home was just steps away, across the alley, this corner of the store served as the center of family activities. Over the years, we had many lively dinners with family, neighbors, friends and Carroll College students in the back room. All the years we ran the grocery, the back room was my regular station. There, I watched my kids, minded the store and cooked many meals.

Across the narrow alley, our duplex faced South Park Avenue. A square, flat-topped brick and wood building, it sat at the corner of Park Avenue and Wall Street. We lived in the larger north section and rented out the smaller unit. Our new home had six small rooms: a kitchen, a dining room, a living room, one bathroom and two bedrooms, all shoehorned into about 700 square feet. To us, it seemed spacious, all the more so because we spent so much of our time in the store.

When we first moved into the duplex, we were a family of five, with daughters Bess, Gloria and Thel. Charlie and I had one bedroom, separated by a curtain from the other bedroom where the children slept. Bessie had a single bed in the corner; Gloria and Thel shared a double bed. The arrival of Poy and Nancy soon pushed the bedroom to its limits. To cope with the crowd, we added a toddler bed for Poy in one corner and later wedged Nancy's crib behind a door to the dining room. What a crowd in that tiny space of a bedroom.

As the children grew, we adapted the porch to serve as a third bedroom for Poy and Thel. Space and privacy were luxuries no one in our family knew. As the youngest, Nancy had it toughest. She had to sleep in that crib until she was eight or nine years old. We simply did not have any other place for her to sleep. Only years later did my youngest daughter tell me how embarrassed she was to have friends come to the house. She dreaded they would learn she still slept in a crib.

Having just one bathroom for seven of us required creativity on my part. Our mornings followed a routine. First, I pulled on the string to turn on the light suspended in the middle of the bedroom. The children recognized this as their wake-up call. One by one in order of age, they hopped out of bed and lined up at the bathroom door. Usually, they waited quietly, awakening slowly and rousing themselves for the day. Everyone wanted to get to the head of the line, where a small gas heater at the bathroom door provided a bit of warmth on chilly mornings. Because we had no sink in the bathroom, Charlie usually waited next to the bathtub, washcloth in hand, to wipe faces and hands. Next, he collected the children alongside the tub so they could brush their teeth. Five kids in the procession made for quite a wait most mornings. If we could keep the assembly line going, we had everyone dressed on time. Then, the children gathered at the kitchen table for breakfast, usually cereal and toast, or fried eggs on special mornings. And, at last, they went out the door to school.

Despite its tight quarters and tiny rooms, I loved our little duplex. I don't think I have felt quite the same about any other home I have ever lived in. Not in Boston, not in China, not at our other home in Helena. When I think of what home means to me now, my thoughts return to this small house between Park Avenue and the alley in Helena. Our large family packed our small house, but we seemed very happy in those days.

Although it was a quarter the size of our home in China, our duplex had a snug feel to me.

I planted a small garden in the back yard. In time, my enthusiasm made the most of this tiny plot. I grew peonies in spring, gladiolas in summer and chrysanthemums in fall. When I raised snapdragons, the kids picked off the heads and snapped them at each other. Part of the yard became my kitchen garden, where I harvested cilantro, kohlrabi, bok choy and mustard greens, all of which reminded me of China and spiced up my special Chinese dishes.

Our store and duplex were situated in a busy section in downtown Helena. Another grocery store, Weggenman's Market, was just across the street. Farther south on Main were two restaurants, Yat Son and the House of Wong, with Bakke Drug and the Corr Café on the next block. Atop the nearest hill, a large fire tower guarded downtown Helena and our neighborhood.

Early in the 1950s, our store did well financially, but I learned to sew to help stretch our family budget. With five kids, money for new clothing was in short supply. As a young girl in China, I had learned very simple stitching, but I found the patterns here to be confusing. I puzzled over how to make them into clothes.

One day, I asked Pearl Fawcett, a neighbor and regular customer at our grocery store, for her help. Pearl and her husband operated an upholstery shop up the street from the store, so I figured she could give me tips on the essentials of sewing. A large, tough woman, Pearl had a striking, memorable appearance. Her usual outfit included a plaid wool shirt, a white turban wrapping her curly red hair and bright red lipstick. As an experienced seamstress, Pearl had a well-used sewing machine and work-hardened hands to go with it. After just a few lessons, I had learned some of the basics of how to use a sewing machine. Next we turned to reading patterns, where my language problems slowed me down. To keep it simple, Pearl had me work from the pictures alone; before long I learned to cut the outlines and make dresses for my daughters.

As my capabilities developed, Charlie purchased a sewing machine. We set it up in the storage area of the store, where I could sew while keeping watch for customers at the counter. My sewing turned out to be an enjoyable task for years. Sewing also introduced me to American holidays. At

Wong family Christmas portrait in 1963. From left, Poy, Flora, Thel, Charlie, Nancy, Bessie and Gloria.

Easter and Christmas, I made identical dresses for each of the girls and one for myself. I saved many pictures of my girls dressed up in matching Easter outfits holding their little Easter baskets. My favorites at Christmas were red felt skirts, with different appliquéd decorations for each daughter.

As the girls grew older, they, too, learned to sew. They gradually improved their skills to the point where they made their own clothes.

Always proud of his family, Charlie liked to show off my handiwork. Several times a year, usually on my birthday, Mother's Day and Christmas,

Charlie made a big production of taking the kids for a walk downtown. To prepare, we dressed all the girls in identical outfits and sent father and kids out the door, usually with Charlie and Poy in the middle of the pack. Outside the house, they would stop, look back at me and wave. To me, they were a happy sight as they walked down Main Street, all hand in hand.

Although I stayed behind to run the store, I knew the goal of these excursions was something special: a gift for me. Charlie usually led his troop to Fligelman's, Helena's main department store. To this day, I have saved many of the gifts from these family shopping trips, including an emerald-green three-quarter-length winter coat and a pink quilted robe with embroidered flowers.

As my sewing expertise expanded, I moved on to more intricate, precise tailoring projects, making my own coats and suits. Word got around about my work and I started doing alterations for some of the neighbors. Soon, I had customers for everything from simple projects to complete outfits. Later in my sewing career, one of my favorite customers was Elsie Jones, the cook in the governor's residence across town near the State Capitol. Elsie introduced me to Montana First Lady Betty Babcock, the wife of Governor Tim Babcock; she became one of my most famous customers and I did alterations for her from time to time. I remember Mrs. Babcock as an extremely nice person, very charming and easy to work with, but also very business-like. When I met her, she was still new to Helena. Like me, she loved the community.

In addition to his family parades through town with all the children, Charlie regularly took Poy to the barbershop. Usually on a Saturday, whenever hair length required it, Charlie took his son by the hand and the two of them walked to Burrell's. It was easy to spot, with its traditional revolving barber pole spinning next to the door. Once inside, Charlie and Poy watched the other patrons get their haircuts. As they waited, they took in the male banter of the barbershop. As part of these trips, Charlie quizzed Poy on cars: the various models, their equipment and related car facts. Other customers added their opinions and details, so Poy learned quite a bit about cars and mechanics. By age four, Poy could name nearly every car you might see on the streets of town. In later years, Charlie said lots of conversations went beyond cars, but I didn't ask for details.

Charlie enjoyed business so much that, when the store seemed to be

succeeding nicely, he started looking for other opportunities. On Main
Street, just a block south of the store and behind the AA Garage, sat a
group of eight small cabins, known as the Cole Cabins. In the spring of
1955, Charlie bought the parcel of land and its collection of one-room
rentals. These small structures, little more than bunkhouses, needed work.
For days, Charlie and I cleaned and painted the exterior stucco walls. On
the inside, he scrubbed walls, floors and windows and added a new coat
of paint. When his renovations were complete, Charlie became a landlord;
his clientele were exclusively single men, most of whom were living precar-
ious lives, financially and otherwise. Charlie kept his rents low, knowing
the men could not afford to pay much.

At rent collection time each month, Charlie loaded the kids in the car
and drove to the cabins. Charlie's rules for the kids were strict: wait in the car
while he made his rounds. They peered out of the windows as Charlie went
from door to door. Charlie never explained to me his purpose in taking the
kids, but I suspected his reasons. Maybe he wanted to show the residents he
had a family he was supporting. Maybe he wanted his children to see that
running a business required close attention to detail. Perhaps he wanted
to teach his youngsters there were others less fortunate than themselves.
Charlie, I am quite sure, saw these trips as educational for his children.

Charlie knew some of his renters pretty well. And he was sympathetic
to their financial troubles. Some fell behind on the rent from time to time.
Others came to the store in need of groceries, but alerted Charlie they
couldn't pay until their monthly checks came in. When the situation war-
ranted, Charlie extended credit to them as he did for some other store
customers. Charlie was kindhearted and generous with those tenants who
deserved such treatment. In turn, some of the men became good and loyal
customers at the store.

A good businessman and bookkeeper, Charlie kept meticulous records
on amounts owed, both on rent and at the store. He seemed to have a
knack for determining just how much credit to extend and when to draw
the line. Month by month, he made the rounds to collect rent and persuade residents to bring their accounts current, whether rent or groceries. Charlie knocked on each door, discussed necessary financial matters
quietly and moved on. Charlie kept this part of the business to himself,
so I never knew the details. My only job was to record any grocery credits

accurately in our books. I learned enough bookkeeping to know that Charlie collected on most debts with only a few slipping by.

Many of the renters and customers must have appreciated Charlie's generosity. When Poy was an adult, he was approached by an older patron while enjoying a beer at the Red Meadow Bar on Rodney Street. The man offered to buy him a second beer.

"I remember you," he said. "You worked at Wing Shing Grocery. You're Charlie's boy, right?"

When Poy nodded his head, the man pushed the beer to Poy. He went on to tell Poy how much Charlie had assisted the man several times in the past.

"Your father lent me a hand when I came to Helena," he said. "He was a good man. He didn't have to help me out, but he did."

CHAPTER TWENTY-THREE

Life on Main Street

SIGNS OF HELENA'S ORIGINS and early history were everywhere in our neighborhood. What began as a rough-and-tumble gold mining town became the capital city. Main Street, also known as Last Chance Gulch, acquired that name because it was thought to be here, in what was then a stream, that four desperate miners finally found gold and staked their claims in 1864. Our duplex sat within steps of this site.

When word of the gold discovery spread, Helena became a boomtown almost overnight. As the town grew and mining thrived, a large number of Chinese miners moved to town, joining a contingent of men from around the country and world who sought their fortunes here. By the late 1800s, the Chinese population reached an estimated 3,000 men. A "Chinatown" developed in the area of South Main Street, opposite what became known as Reeder's Alley. Early descriptions noted a large number of laundries and noodle parlors, operated mostly by Chinese immigrants.

By the early 1900s, gold mining had slowed and many miners had moved on. Census records show that Helena still had a Chinese population of about 300 at this time. Many worked as gardeners or operated noodle parlors, laundries or silk shops.

When Charlie first arrived in Helena in early 1922, the town had a number of Chinese businesses: a laundry, at least four restaurants, and at least three groceries. Members of the Chinese community formed the Chinese Benevolent Association, a service organization formed to represent the interests of Chinese Americans.

In the early 1920s, a number of Chinese families lived in town: four Wongs, two Yees, one Yung, one Lee, two Fongs and two Chings. If they weren't involved in running their own businesses, the men usually worked as cooks, waiters, gardeners or janitors. Few women worked at careers of their own. Most supported their husband's business ventures and cared for their children.

When I arrived in 1948, I was introduced by Charlie to two restaurants, Yat Son Noodle Parlor and the OK Café. Both prepared good Chinese food at reasonable prices for an appreciative audience. We did not eat out much, but when we did, these spots were our favorites. They sat within a block of our store, one to the north and the other just across the street. Charlie knew the owners, distant cousins but from separate Wong families. Along with Amy, they became friends early in my Helena life.

Yat Son Noodle Parlor, originally owned by Thomas Young, opened in the early 1930s. The OK Café, jointly owned by Dick Wong, Gar Wong and Kim Ming, started business in 1937. Fred Wong bought it in 1947. Fred eventually closed the OK Café and bought Yat Son, running it with family members at several locations. Much later, Jeff Wong moved Yat Son to East Helena. At 3 South Main, Jerry Wong started another Chinese restaurant, House of Wong, in the late 1940s.

Some considered our south downtown neighborhood a little rough. With a bar on every other corner, it could certainly get rowdy from time to time. Our section of Main Street had at least three bars. On our side of the street was the Central Bar. Across the street were two more bars: the Bison and the Blue Moon. Within a few blocks to the north you came across the Midway, the Palace and Tracy's Lounge, which was something of a nightclub.

Tracy's, at 11 North Main and the site of a former Chinese restaurant called the Golden Dragon, had very nice décor and seemed tame. Even here, though, you could find a taste of the Wild West. On July 23, 1949, my first summer in town, a cowboy rode his horse through the front door of Tracy's, sent patrons flying out of their chairs and rode back out into the street. Crowds out on the town for Helena's Golden Canyon Days celebration scattered in the street as he galloped away.

Although Charlie warned me that our block had some tough characters, our kids had no other place to play, so I allowed them to use the sidewalks of Main Street as their bicycling spot. I worried about the effect this environment might have on the children, but we had no choice. Whenever they were out on the street, Charlie made sure our kids knew they were not to look into the bars as they rode or walked by. I can still see the kids walking in front of these drinking establishments, necks craned stiffly in the opposite direction. As instructed, they avoided even a peek at the saltier side of life within. Even Red's Cycle Shop, a motorcycle shop run by Paul "Red" Drennon several doors down Main Street from our store, attracted a colorful crowd. Red's bunch was so lively that I was a little worried about the lessons the kids might learn from him and his buddies.

The northern stretch of Main Street, away from the cluster of bars, was the bustling center of city life. Banks, large stores and offices congregated along this stretch of the street. After a city ordinance in 1953, Main Street acquired the official designation as "Last Chance Gulch," taken from the narrow valley linked to the early Gold Rush days. We used both street names interchangeably. As Helena grew and businesses came and went, the street itself changed. Dust and dirt mixed with congestion when Main Street was torn up for repaving in 1958. When the project was complete, the old brick paving and streetcar rails disappeared, replaced with asphalt pavement.

The AA Garage structure, located at the south end of Main Street, had a history that traced the changing times in Helena. Originally built as a stable for horses, the building later became the barn for the streetcars that served Helena's downtown. Then, as automobiles became the main form of transportation, it became the AA Garage for auto repairs. That was the business I knew when I came to Helena.

North of our store and still on Main Street were many other prominent businesses. I remember Fligelman's Department Store, Globe Clothing, Main Street News and Confectionery, Eaton-Turner Jewelry and many others.

A favorite place in my memory was the Parrot. In a small building tucked in the middle of the block, the Parrot was a candy store with endless delectable treats. It first opened for business on April 20, 1922. Before our time in Helena, it had moved a few doors north and added food service.

In my day, the Parrot was a much-loved stop for our kids; they enjoyed cherry Cokes and tamale macs, the Parrot's special offering of the traditional Mexican dish.

Another building, so much larger and grander than anything I had seen in China, caught my eye. The Placer, a large, square brick hotel at the corner of Main and Grand streets, first opened its doors in 1913. I remember it for its blocky, substantial presence in downtown. Since Charlie and I did not go out much in the evening, we rarely stopped at the hotel, but it was the central gathering place for Helena's residents and visitors alike. For many years, the Placer served as the unofficial headquarters for Montana legislators. When they took time off from working at the State Capitol, located a mile or so to the east, most lawmakers headed for the Placer and its lounge, Cheerio. I remember thinking that Cheerio had something to do with breakfast cereal, until Charlie explained that this Cheerio was far busier at night than on any morning. People told an old story about gold being discovered at the bottom of an elevator shaft in the hotel. Charlie told me not to believe it, because nearly every location around our neighborhood had been the topic of similar stories. Even our kids ran home from time to time tightly gripping what they thought was gold, only to find it was a piece of fool's gold.

During the 1960 presidential campaign, the Placer Hotel hosted then Senator John F. Kennedy, along with his younger brother Ted Kennedy, during their tour of the state. While he was in town, Senator Kennedy spoke to the convention of Montana Democrats at the Marlow Theater. Having a presidential candidate in town was big news for Helena. Charlie thought about attending one of the campaign events, but eventually decided he had to mind the store.

Several other grocery stores stood just north of our location on Main. Closest was Weggenman's Market, a full-service store. It occupied the ground floor of the Colwell Building, a distinctive structure completed in 1887, according to the date etched above the main entry. The stone on the three-story building had a yellow tint, prompting my kids to call it the "banana building." Weggenman's storefront opened onto Main just as our store did, but it had a much larger selection of goods than we offered. Close to Weggenman's was another market, Jorgensen's, which also carried a full line of groceries. At the south end of our block was Heiser's Store, a small family-operated market like ours. Across the street from our store was a fresh produce market.

∝⊙⊚∽

As the proprietor of a typical small operation, Charlie worked every job: manager, cashier, stocking clerk, meat cutter and janitor. Charlie kept the books, stocked the shelves, dusted and swept. To restock his inventory of fresh produce, Charlie drove the car, with kids packed in the backseat, to suppliers around the area. A regular stop was a farm located a few miles northeast of town on York Road near Warren School, where he bought potatoes by the 100-pound bag. Often his next stop was Montana Brand, a large warehouse owned by Dick Sherwood and located in the Kessler Brewing Building on the west side of town. A tall, thin man with wire-rim glasses, Dick usually came out front to greet Charlie. While the two men conducted their business, the kids, with Dick's permission, explored the back warehouse, filled with large sacks of potatoes and assorted other grocery goods. Dick apparently looked the other way when the kids made a game out of going in and out of the huge produce cooler room.

Whenever I could, I tried to share in the fun of these buying trips. During vegetable harvest season in late August and September, before opening the store in the morning, Charlie and I stopped for fresh tomatoes at another farm a few miles outside of town. As a special treat, the owners allowed you to eat as you picked. I was careful not to eat too much, but my kids were another matter. I checked on them early and often. They sometimes seemed so engrossed in eating the juicy tomatoes that they forgot the purpose of the trip was to gather tomatoes to take back to the store and to our own kitchen.

Fun had its place at the store, but in our family operation everybody worked. Weekends and after school, Charlie assigned chores to the kids, from sweeping floors to restocking shelves to taking orders from customers. Charlie could be meticulous, directing that canned goods be dusted on top and turned so all labels faced forward. In Charlie's inventory system, the lightest items—such as toilet paper, paper towels and tissues—went to the top shelf at the front of the store. To restock this uppermost spot, the kids made their own assembly line system. First, one unloaded the box in the supply room and tossed the item to the doorway. There, a second worker caught the package and threw it down the aisle, where another pair of hands waited. From the aisle, the item went to the last person in line, who placed the article on the top shelf. When the stocks ran low, the children turned restocking into a game. Charlie enjoyed watching the ingenuity of his pint-size work crew.

When a customer needed an item from the top shelf, Charlie reached up with a yardstick, flicked the merchandise lightly and caught the item as it dropped. Soon enough, several of our kids mastered this skill and challenged each other to catch the falling product before it hit the floor. I tried it, but never perfected the practice. "Reach higher, Mom. Farther to the side. That's not the right one, Mom." I stepped aside and left the retrieval game to Charlie and the kids.

For its special customers, Wing Shing Grocery offered delivery service. Typically, at least two of the kids made the trip. One regular customer, Mrs. Ruth Berg, lived just south of us on Park Avenue south of Reeder's Alley. Mrs. Berg loved visits from the kids, and they returned the sentiment. Another delivery, for a single woman living at the foot of Mount Helena, was not so much fun. By distance, it was a very short walk from the store, but the rugged road eventually turned into a rocky trail, transforming the trip into a small expedition. Charlie and the kids drove the car as far up the road as was safe. Then, they unloaded the groceries from the trunk, repacked everything into large boxes and carried their loads the rest of the way up the steep incline. Most of her groceries consisted of cans of cat and dog food, so Charlie usually slipped a bit of extra human food into her order whenever we made the delivery.

At the top of the list of tough assignments for the kids in the store was slicing lunchmeat. We sold bologna, salami, liverwurst and head cheese, all from large loaves stored in a refrigerator in the front of the store. We handled each order individually as it came in, usually with the customer standing there to observe. Charlie cut and wrapped the meats precisely, so customers were happy. Over the years, he tried to teach the children, but only a couple really mastered the technique. His instructions were exact: use the large Chinese cleaver to cut thin, even slices, then wrap carefully in brown butcher paper. It was harder than it looked, especially for small hands. You had to be very careful to guide the cleaver for uniform cuts. In most cases, the kids' slices were anything but even—too thick on one end and too thin at the other. To add to the pressure, Charlie and the customer watched each step. Of all the kids, Poy and Thel probably stood out as the best slicers.

To Charlie, family time at dinner was very important. Evenings were our times to be together, and he never liked anyone to be absent from the table. Of the few times I saw Charlie's mood darken, the cause usually was someone's late arrival for dinner. Around our table, each family member had their assigned seat. We ate our evening meal Chinese style, with rice bowls and chopsticks. I cooked several dishes, usually soup, stir-fried vegetables and a meat dish. We used chopsticks and bowls, no silverware and plates. I took on the task of instructing the kids in the etiquette of Chinese dining, just as my mother had taught me. I made sure the kids selected a single piece of meat or vegetable from the plate directly in front of them. "Don't be rude and reach for something in front of someone else's plate," I would say. I also told the kids how to hold their chopsticks and eat in proper fashion.

"Don't hold your chopstick near the top end," I said. "If you do, you will move far from home. Hold them at the bottom near your food and you will stay close to home. Eat everything in your rice bowl. If you don't, you are sure to marry someone ugly."

Meals were lively, as the kids chattered back and forth in English about their day in school. When the children grew older, Charlie encouraged them to use their Chinese, often saying, "gong hong-wa," meaning "speak Chinese." Quiet ruled for a few moments as the kids stopped talking entirely. But before long, they were back to regular conversations, still in English. Charlie seemed to forget his instruction as he listened contentedly to his family.

Over the years, our dinners expanded to include more faces. One regular group of visitors came from Carroll College, the private, Catholic college located not far from Main Street's north end. On many nights, we welcomed two or three Chinese students to our home. As with many college students, they seemed to figure out early on that dinnertime was a good time to visit. I always appreciated the extra company. Although they usually spoke a different Chinese dialect, our guests were talkative and well-educated. They spoke English and Chinese, brought new viewpoints and gave my children a better look at the world around them.

Over time, as my children expanded their perspectives on the world, so did I. By the late 1960s, I found I was much more comfortable meeting new people. On several occasions, I spoke to local groups about China—the countryside and its customs. Before a gathering of Campfire Girls and their leaders, I described my early childhood in South China. I took along a collection of clothing I wore when I was young, pictures of Lin Fong Lei village and Chinese money. Their interest in my early life in China made me want to share more and more of my stories.

In late winter 1967, I displayed a number of Chinese handcrafts, including my hand-stitched clothing and samples of art objects, at a social tea for the American Business Women's Association, a group I had recently joined. For this adult audience, I was happy not to have to make a formal speech. Simply answering questions from the audience taxed my English skills, but the women were appreciative and I felt comfortable. For my audience, I am sure the event was a regular affair. To me, my ability to speak and answer questions marked a valuable personal milestone.

My children's school activities also pushed me into the community. Through the local parent–teacher association, I met other mothers. As an active member of the group, I helped pass a bond measure in a local school election. When I received a commendation letter from Hawthorne School's Principal Gerald Roth for my role, I felt honored. More exciting to me was the fact that I could read the letter, with just a little help from Charlie. My English really was improving. When he saw my delight, a smile crept across Charlie's face.

Charlie was right to be pleased. Life on Main Street had proved to be happy for his entire family.

CHAPTER TWENTY-FOUR

A New Homecoming: Shirley and Pocky

C HARLIE'S COUSIN EARL WONG became a frequent visitor at Wing Shing Grocery. Earl's nickname was "Pocky," a shortened version of his Chinese name, which sounded something like "pock." Pocky was the only name I called him for many years.

We shared very similar experiences in leaving China and building new lives in Montana. When I first met Pocky in Helena, he was working as a cook. Mature and determined, he reminded me of Charlie. Loneliness also marked Pocky's life. He had a young wife still trapped in China. In their story, I gained new appreciation for my own good fortune.

Born in Helena, Pocky was the eleventh child in a family of thirteen kids. His father, a Helena restaurant owner, immigrated from Guangdong Province, like many other Chinese residents in Helena. Immediately before the Japanese occupation, Pocky returned to China with his father and several family members. After World War II, Pocky met and married a young Chinese girl. Pocky was nineteen; his wife, Jue Suet Yang, was just seventeen.

Theirs was an arranged marriage, like my own to Charlie. The bride did not meet the man who would be her husband until just before their wedding in Guangzhou. Not long after their marriage in 1946, Pocky returned to the United States with two of his brothers, Gene Wong and Jimmy Wong, and his sister Sally Wong. Their father remained behind in China, as did Jue Suet.

And, like me, Jue Suet became trapped in a maze of immigration laws that kept her in China. Though Jue Suet had married a U.S. citizen, a step that should have qualified her for entry into the country, she still faced many hurdles. She had to persuade the Chinese government to allow her to leave. Yet another obstacle was the disruption caused by China's ongoing civil war. As the Nationalists and Communists battled, she wasn't sure which government to turn to for travel papers.

As soon as he returned to Helena, Pocky worked to clear the way to bring his wife to Helena. What should have been fairly straightforward—he was a U.S. citizen, she was his wife—would stretch across years.

Pocky faced two major obstacles. His most immediate challenge was how to convince the U.S. government to allow his wife to immigrate. While U.S. laws had eased slightly, strict quotas on Chinese entrants remained. Problem two was the cold relationship between America and China. After the Communist takeover in China, official contact between the newly formed Communist government and the United States were infrequent and cold. When the Korean War broke out in 1950, communication all but ended.

By 1950, after several fruitless years of trying to gain passage for his wife to America, Pocky turned to two powerful allies in Helena: Judge John Harrison, an associate justice on the State Supreme Court, and Howard Ellsworth, a retiree from the Northern Pacific Railway. Both men offered their help.

Judge Harrison made at least two trips to Washington, D.C., to discuss the situation with State Department officials. He spelled out their case and asked the U.S. government to intervene on behalf of Pocky and Jue Suet. Despite the judge's efforts, one setback after another continued to block Jue Suet's path out of China.

"I had very little official evidence to prove that we were married," Pocky told Charlie and me. "All I had was one document, my marriage license, with only Chinese characters. Judge Harrison warned me the license was not enough to convince the State Department to act to help us."

Even so, Judge Harrison kept working on Pocky's behalf. For years, he wrote to officials in Washington and in the Far East.

Soon after the Communist government took control in 1949, Jue Suet realized her peril was growing, so she started her own search for admission to the United States. First, she went to authorities near her own village, showing them the evidence of her marriage to Pocky. Always her question was the same: When will I be allowed to leave? She never got any definitive answers. No answer meant no departure.

By the mid-1950s, after nearly a decade of work, Pocky's bride remained trapped. Jue Suet decided to skirt official pathways. She secretly met with the owner of a small fishing vessel and discussed a plan to escape to Hong Kong. Jue Suet had become desperate. Merely speaking to the skipper was a risky step; she didn't know the man at all. He might help her in her quest, or he might go to authorities, exposing her plan. If her intentions reached the wrong ears, she could be punished harshly and even imprisoned. Yet waiting for government approval to leave seemed pointless. Jue Suet decided to act.

On a blustery, rainy night, she met the skipper as agreed at a small port on a tributary of the Pearl River. Climbing aboard his fully loaded boat, she quickly hid amid the barrels, boxes and fishing gear on the deck. Braving the weather and severe consequences if she were detected, Jue Suet set off down the river and along China's south shore. Throughout the night and into the next day, the boat picked its way, crossing a stretch of open water, finally reaching the relative safety of Hong Kong, which was under British control.

In Helena, Pocky had no idea his wife was risking such a perilous course. When Pocky received Jue Suet's account of her adventure and ultimate success, he was elated that she had reached Hong Kong, by then a safe haven for many refugees from China. He thought for a time that their reunion would come soon. But her hazardous voyage to refuge in the British territory proved to be only the first leg of a drawn-out trip to Helena. Jue Suet faced more official barricades in her journey back to Pocky.

Several more years passed, and Jue Suet supported herself by working in a shirt factory. She and Pocky wrote regularly to one another, but immigration approval for Jue Suet appeared to be blocked. Finally, late in the 1950s, Pocky's Helena supporter Howard Ellsworth intervened. On a business trip to Hong Kong, he first located Jue Suet and then, at the request of Judge Harrison, met with U.S. consulate personnel. Armed with advice and paperwork from Mr. Ellsworth, Jue Suet formally requested a visa allowing her to come to the United States. The initial answer came back: "No."

"I can't understand why our government won't help us," Pocky told us at the time. "Without the voices of Judge Harrison and Mr. Ellsworth, I would be nowhere."

His desperation showed as he added, "I thank them for listening to me and I thank them for their help. I also tell them: Please tell me there is progress."

In February 1961, Mr. Ellsworth again flew to Hong Kong. He made a new approach to U.S. officials on behalf of Jue Suet and Pocky. When he returned from that visit, Mr. Ellsworth had more encouraging words. The U.S. consulate in Hong Kong said Jue Suet would eventually be allowed to enter the United States, but final details needed to be concluded. As expected, Pocky was jubilant at this development, but he remained cautious. More months passed as the workings of government churned slowly, and still Pocky received no official notice that Jue Suet was on her way.

Then, without notice, in late September 1961, Pocky received a telegram from the U.S. Consular Services. Here was the long-awaited approval. Jue Suet's papers were ready, and she was free to leave for America. All that was required was the money for her transportation. Finally, some fifteen years after his wedding day, Pocky was on the verge of bringing his wife to Helena. Pocky immediately wired the plane fare. On October 9, 1961, Jue Suet climbed aboard a jetliner at the Hong Kong airport, headed for Montana.

We had never seen a more contented look on Pocky's face as in the days leading up to Jue Suet's arrival. Flanked by a happy throng of his friends, Pocky greeted his wife at the Helena airport when her Northwest Orient plane touched down the next day.

Telling her story to a Helena newspaper reporter days later, she relied on Pocky as her interpreter. She knew about Americans and their manners, she said, from watching U.S. movies and seeing American tourists in Hong Kong. Her job in a Hong Kong clothing factory sewing shirts for shipment to American buyers helped her learn about western fashion tastes. When she arrived in Helena, she was surprised not to see gun-toting cowboys and Indians with feathers, as she had anticipated. She said that she immediately liked Helena "because it was so quiet as compared with Hong Kong."

Their apartment, at 3 South Jackson Street, stood around the corner from our store. Pocky brought his wife by often to see us, so I got to know Jue Suet right away. She began to go by the name Shirley, the American version of her Chinese name. Shirley spoke no English. Our conversations were a good refresher course for my Chinese. The stories she told of her escape reminded me of my family's experience in China, and her questions about Helena sounded so much like my first days in town. A small woman, she had a bright face that lit up in a radiant smile whenever she talked. I found her to be very shy, courteous and soft-spoken. I had great difficulty picturing this tiny, reserved woman engineering her secret marine getaway from China.

Pocky and Shirley usually joined us in our kitchen at the back of Wing Shing Grocery. On most occasions, Shirley and I cooked while Pocky and Charlie talked. For special meals on Saturdays and Sundays, Pocky and Charlie managed the kitchen duties. Both were accomplished cooks, and they created great dinners together. From his work as a cook at George's OK Café, another downtown restaurant owned by Charlie's cousin George Wong, and House of Wong, Pocky had mastered a number of Chinese specialties. With so many cooks, new dishes to try and plenty of food, our feasts were memorable.

Soon, the couple started their own family of four children: Earl Junior, Howard, Poy and Irene. They named their second born after Mr. Ellsworth, who had so diligently pursued Shirley's immigration case in Hong Kong.

Over the years, I often thought about Shirley's courage. Would I have had the daring to flee by boat? I did not think so. Though, facing the fifteen years of delay that she endured, I, too, might have found a way to escape. Yet, I doubted I had so much boldness.

CHAPTER TWENTY-FIVE

The Wild West

JUST AFTER 9 P.M. ON A WARM Thursday night, August 9, 1962, I put my youngest kids to bed, as usual. Then I waited for Charlie to come home from the store. When it neared ten o'clock, I thought I'd better check in on him. Normally, he would call me as he prepared to close up for the night. I waited a few more minutes. When I still had not heard from him, I dialed the store. After several rings and no answer, I grew concerned. It was not like him to ignore the phone, even if he had customers.

I had good reason to be troubled: Just two years before, a knife-wielding thief took $700 from our store. In that confrontation, the assailant thrust the knife in Charlie's face, forcing him to hand over the money from the store cash box. Thankfully, Charlie was not injured, but the experience terrified us. I tried to push those frightening memories from my head as I ran across the alley and through the back door of our grocery to check on Charlie. As I stepped into the dark of our back room, from out of nowhere someone grabbed me. Before I could say a word, I felt his dirty, sweaty hand clamped over my mouth. At my throat, he held the point of a knife. I was too scared to fight back or scream. I looked down to see Charlie tied up and sprawled on the floor near the kitchen doorway. To my relief, he was moving.

Across our back room, I saw another man in the shadows near Charlie.

Before I could get a look at my attacker, he released me. One of the pair yelled, "Get out of here, quick." Out through the back door they ran. As they dashed away, I did not even think to yell or look to see which way they headed. My only thought was my husband.

Bending down to untie Charlie, I worked at the knots, my hands trembling so that I fumbled at the task. As soon as he was free, Charlie jumped up, ran to the phone and dialed the police to report the crime. Coincidentally, within minutes of his call, three girls walked into the downtown police station to describe two men they had seen running across the Marlow Theater parking lot, located just north of our duplex. The girls told police the men headed west on Edward Street. Helena's police department immediately sent out officers and called other police agencies for assistance. While the Helena police chased after the suspects, the state highway patrol and the county sheriff's office sealed off the downtown area with roadblocks.

Even before the police responded, the fast-moving drama caught the attention of our neighbor Red Drennon. Red and two of his friends, Doug Dandro and Bob Olson, had been talking in front of Red's motorcycle shop, a few yards down the street from our grocery. Outside enjoying the summer evening, the three heard Charlie's shouts coming from our store. They rushed to our front door to check on us. By this time, Charlie was off the phone with the police, so he gave Red a quick description of the robbers. Red ran back to his car and grabbed his single-shot .44 caliber pistol. Scanning the street, he spotted the two men running north away from the store. Red chased after them on foot while his two friends jumped in their car. Just then, a shot rang out from the direction of the fleeing robbers. Inside, I heard the loud bang. Afraid the sound was gunfire, I felt a tingle of dread run through me. Outside, Red heard the sound, too, but paid no heed as he ran after the culprits. Seeing this band on their trail, the robbers split up.

In the gathering dusk, one robber climbed quickly up a steep hill west of the store. He appeared to be heading for an escape route into the foothills of Mount Helena, where rougher terrain and trees might give him cover. Red, still below on Park Avenue in front of Eddy's Bakery, ran to close the distance between them.

As the robber scrambled higher on the ridge, Red called a warning: "Stop now or I'll shoot."

The man did not slow his pace, so Red fired a shot. He aimed "high into the air" above the suspect as a warning, Red said later. Still, the man kept running upward, so Red reloaded, leveled his pistol again and fired. This bullet hit the man in the left shoulder, spun him around and dropped him to the ground. Almost immediately, police officers caught up to the wounded suspect and captured him.

Meanwhile, a few blocks away in downtown, other officers tracked the second robber. He had made his getaway down a side street, taking refuge in a hedge across the street from the bus depot. When the suspect thought it was safe to move, he began to walk quickly toward his car parked near Wall Street. By this time, the police had him encircled by their barricades around the city center. At 11:09 P.M., Helena police sergeant Ed Porter and Officer Vic Sandru arrested the second robber just a few blocks from our store at Bob Abel's Texaco station.

One wounded robber went to the hospital with a flesh wound to the shoulder. Taken into police custody, the other suspect eventually led officers to a .32 caliber automatic Beretta pistol dumped in a clump of bushes. Later, police identified this as the weapon one of the gunmen pointed at Charlie during the robbery. When questioned by police, the second robber said it had fired accidentally as he tried to put the safety on while running from our store. Police examined the gun carefully. In the magazine, which had a capacity for eight cartridges, investigators found six unspent rounds, while the chamber held one empty shell. When police checked their records, they found the gun had been stolen in a gas station holdup in Three Forks, Montana, just weeks earlier.

Back in the store, Charlie and I missed all the action: the chase, Red's shots, the captures and the search for the gun. Charlie stayed near the phone. My hands continued to shake. Charlie, too, showed the effects of his ordeal, pacing back and forth as we waited for the police. Neither of us said much as we struggled to regain our composure. About the time we settled down, several officers knocked at the entrance to the store. Still stunned, we sat there trembling and holding onto each other as Charlie recounted the story for the officers. Charlie spoke; I merely nodded in agreement with his statements to the officers.

Charlie said he was starting his nightly routine to close the store when two young men came through the front door, looked around briefly and approached the counter. Suddenly, one pulled out a gun and ordered Charlie to hand over his money. They reached over the counter, grabbed some cash from our box and began to shove Charlie to the back of the store. In the back room, they pushed Charlie to the floor, took off his belt and used it to tie him up. All the while, one

Paul "Red" Drennon aboard one of his motorcycles.

robber waved the pistol at my husband. The man said repeatedly he was not afraid to use the weapon. Charlie thought one of them went back through the store to look for more money or valuables. As the robbers continued to threaten Charlie, I walked in the back door, and they grabbed me.

In his recounting of the ordeal, Charlie said he thought he recognized one of the men as the robber in the holdup of the store two years earlier. While the officers finished with our statements, they received a radio report about the capture of both suspects. Shortly after hearing this news, they departed, telling us to lock up the store, go home and be ready for more questions the next day.

We felt exhausted and overwhelmed. Charlie and I sat down in the back room to collect our thoughts. Finally, I told my husband we had to go check on the children. Since it was a warm, summer night, some Carroll College students were at home watching TV with our older kids. Once we sat down to tell them what had happened, I was happy to hear they had heard none of the activity.

By the next day, the robbery, Red's roundup and the police hunt were big news. The front-page headline that ran across five news columns in the *Independent Record* read: "Two Brothers Apprehended In Helena Holdup Attempt, One Wounded In Gun Fire."

Other particulars fell into place quickly in the lengthy newspaper story.

The account covered much of the front page and ran on an inside page as well: Big news in our small city. Arrested and held in jail were the two Best brothers from Willow Creek, Montana. Younger brother Richard, age twenty-one, was the wounded robber, arrested on the hillside. Older brother Ralph, age twenty-three, led police to the gun after his capture downtown. Questioned later, Ralph Best told police investigators this was his second robbery of our Wing Shing store. He had returned to rob again, he told police, "because it was so easy the first time." When the dust settled—literally, it seemed to me at the time—the Best brothers, Ralph and Richard, were behind bars and our nerves were shattered. Charlie had been correct; one of the men had robbed our store before.

Red told police he didn't think twice about running after the suspects because his own store had been robbed six months earlier. In that break-in, Red lost $800 and his sports car. He flew into action this time, he said, because he had his eye out to protect his neighborhood and he did not want another robbery to occur.

Wary and on his guard after the motorcycle shop burglary, Red had warned Charlie to be careful as well. Red promised, "Charlie, if anybody bothers you, you just yell and I'll come running." That night, Red kept his word.

At their August trial, the Best boys were in the courtroom of Judge Lester Loble. Charlie had to testify, and he told the court he believed Ralph Best had been the man who robbed him at knifepoint back in 1960. On the witness stand, Ralph, the older brother, told Judge Loble that he had stolen the gun used in the August 9 robbery of our store. He also admitted to the judge that he had robbed Charlie at knifepoint back in 1960. Even before the trial reached its conclusion, the men pleaded guilty to the August 9 attempted robbery.

On the morning of Friday, August 17, 1962, Judge Loble handed down stiff sentences for the brothers. Ralph Best received a twenty-year sentence, while Richard Best received a ten-year sentence. From the bench, Judge Loble sternly lectured the two.

"It is by the greatest good fortune that someone wasn't killed and, had that been, you would have faced the gallows or life imprisonment. This is the unconscionable stickup of a defenseless man such as Charles Wong and his wife, who are supporting five young children, struggling to make a living.

"It means nothing to you or men like you that hours of honest toil accumulated these few dollars for when you, in place of working, decide you want some money. You take a revolver and threaten their lives at gunpoint."

Before concluding his remarks, Judge Loble lectured the Helena police department about the need for foot patrols in the neighborhood around Red's shop and our store.

"Since this robbery attempt occurred, there have been ever increasing applications to me, which I have readily granted, by business people of the South Main Street to obtain permits to carry guns for their protection. People of…this area are entitled to a foot patrolman," the reporter quoted Judge Loble as saying.

"If this area were patrolled from 5 P.M. until morning, it would be a great prevention of these offenses. The very presence of a uniformed man, his ability to recognize known criminals, his dropping into places where they gather, all could be a great step forward in law enforcement and criminal prevention."

Judge Loble's decision ended the trial—the men were tried and sentenced just eight days after the robbery—but more time had to pass before Charlie and I got over the fright. Immediately, we changed how we ran the store. In place of our previous 11 P.M. closing, we locked the door at 10 P.M. We watched more carefully who came in to shop, particularly late in the evening. Slowly over time, we got over the nightmares brought on by the violence of these armed robberies.

For me, the crime left its mark. Always a bit fearful of strangers, I observed everyone who entered the store with apprehension. Though the robbers were in jail, my natural instinct to trust people would not return for years. Left alone with your fears, you find a way to remake your confidence and faith in others. The change requires time and, in my case, several years passed before I felt comfortable around people I did not know.

Some good did come from the attack that night. What a loyal friend and neighbor we had in Red, and he became our family's hero. A lanky, agile man with a shock of red hair, Red fit my image of a cowboy perfectly. I knew him as a hearty character, full of stories, bravado and action. His response in our emergency came as no surprise to Charlie or me. His daring feat, tracking down armed robbers with gun in hand, was just what we might have expected from him.

Red and his brothers were born in Missouri and joined the Navy during World War II. After the war, Red moved to Helena, where he cut a dashing figure with his good looks and long hair. His business, Red's Cycle Shop, down the block from our store, shared our alley. To my dismay, my daughters saw Red and his motorcycle buddies as very romantic figures: young, energetic and full of pranks. The young men tinkered with their motorcycles and exchanged loud talk with anyone who passed by. As a mother, they worried me because of their uncombed looks and the interest they generated from my daughters. However, as I got to know them, I found them likable and fun. And after the robbery, of course, Red could do no wrong so far as I was concerned.

To pass the time, Red and his friends occasionally raced their motorcycles up the steep hillside above Park Avenue. Most times, they rode up partway, only to back down when they couldn't reach the top. My kids loved watching their exploits. Poy especially liked hanging around the cycle shop, and Red and his friends looked after him and taught him all about motorcycles and mechanics.

Some years later, Red moved his shop several blocks north, but still on Main Street. A hunter and skilled outdoorsman, Red later worked as a wilderness guide, after he closed his cycle shop. His daring showed in all of his interests: flying, skydiving, skiing and snowmobiling. I knew Red as a good-natured, kind-hearted neighbor, a gentleman who also could be very tough when the circumstances demanded it. I remained grateful for his friendship for many, many years.

Our holdup and Red's heroic role had all the elements of a real Western tale: gun-toting robbers, a chase with guns blazing and talk of the gallows in the courthouse. For our mostly quiet, tranquil family, the robbery was too close, too real and too frightening to be of any amusement.

CHAPTER TWENTY-SIX

A Family Broken

I N 1950, NEWLY COMMUNIST CHINA, led by Chairman Mao, joined North Korea in a war against South Korea and the United States. For my family and most people everywhere, the Korean War and the Communist Revolution effectively cut off normal communications with China. Far away in Montana, I had no idea what this upheaval meant for Mother and our village. Later, when we learned how China had been transformed and how our mother was affected, my family endured a staggering blow.

Looking back at these events is not easy. This part of our family's past carries too many terrible memories, and brings with it a great deal of pain. My telling of what happened to Mother is second-hand, passed along from others. By the time my family and I returned to the village many years later, few traces of our lives remained. The old days were gone and, with them, nearly everyone we knew.

Before I was a mother, before I became a Montanan, before I left China behind, I was my mother's daughter. From my earliest days in Boston, I looked to Mother as my truest guide, someone I watched accomplish many tasks with her sheer will. As painful as it is, I knew Mother's story needed retelling because she shaped the lives of generations of her family.

The Communist Party's land reform campaign, aimed at taking private lands and handing the acreage to farm laborers, reached its peak in the early 1950s. In the northern sections of China, the farm restructuring had largely been completed in the first years of Communist rule. By 1952, party leaders turned their attention to the task of extending their land redistribution plan to the vast area of China south of the Yangtze River, a large region containing most of the nation's most productive agricultural lands and large private holdings. Communist leaders had delayed moving into the south for some time because they viewed the population there as more resistant to the proposed conversion.

The party's goal was clear: take land and other assets from the landowners and give them to poorer farmers. In the story related to me, in Lin Fong Lei, as in many villages, an active peasant association developed. Encouraged by the Communist party, these rural councils evolved into a form of local government. By 1952 in our region, party members and local association leaders enthusiastically embraced land distribution and pressured landowners to hand over their property. Throughout China, I later learned, this period became known as the time of "settling of accounts." All across China, the seized properties were known as *dou zheng guo shi,* literally, the "fruits of the struggle." For many villagers without land holdings, these "fruits" might mean a new beginning with land and farm tools they could take from others and put to use. For my mother, on the other end of this ruthless equation, these same "fruits" had a far different connotation. As a landowner, she became a target of attacks. I was completely unaware of the anger and devastation facing Mother.

China's new government sharpened the divide between the social classes, creating distinct divisions of friend and foe, informant and those informed upon. Communist leaders targeted many "rich peasants" opposed to China's progress as objects for ridicule, or worse. Neighbors began to regard neighbors with fear, mistrust and even hatred. In the Communist political culture, a localized sense of rage became a potent tool for social action.

For a time after the civil war, Mother's village and the surrounding region remained peaceful. Soon, though, teams of party workers came to make arrangements for redistributing the land. In its first stages, this plan did not attack landlords directly. Instead, the initial phase concentrated on organizing poor farmers and laborers. Before long, Communist party leaders incited the locals to attack landowners and take away their property. What

Flora's father, Lee Sing Kim, and mother, Chen Sun Ho, approximately 1936.

followed was an atmosphere of public trials, mass accusation, terror and, often, executions.

The Communist Party ushered in an era in which if you had money or valuable land, your neighbors viewed it as a crime. And the Communists gave people the means to act. The first tool was humiliation, followed by severe beatings. Large, public meetings were held, and selected landowners were beaten, often to death. This scene, occurring over and over, was about to come to Lin Fong Lei.

If you were poor and had little of value, you were usually safe from the harm. But if you had money and property, you became a target. If you appeared to have lots of money and land, some sort of attack by the Communist Party was almost certain. At the direction of the government, party members went village by village, organizing for mass campaigns of workers, youth, women and students.

In the story that reached my family years later, every time the Communists organized a demonstration or attack against landowners in Lin Fong Lei, people aimed their anger at Mother. By this time she had little money left, but their main objective was her land. Starting with humiliating public attacks, villagers first dragged her from our home, gathered around her in the village center and made her the centerpiece of their demonstrations. Echoing Mao's call against the rich, they could assail Mother without fear. Within a short time, the people who had been my neighbors took everything my mother owned—her furniture, her clothing, her remaining animals, her small supply of money, her position in the village. Everything.

Once they had taken her remaining assets, people began to torment her physically. One day in 1952, the mob took violence to its final, brutal end. The story of Mother's final days did not reach me or my family for a long time, but the accounts related to us were too cruel to comprehend. So horrible was the story that my family and I could not speak of it for many years. To this day, few of us can discuss what happened.

In towns across China at this time, similar scenes were reported. Communist Party leaders gathered a crowd together in a so-called "struggle" against a villager identified for abuse. Once a large group congregated, the defenseless person would be paraded before a knot of angry people. Most times, the target was tethered in heavy handcuffs. Whoever dragged the victim into the circle of enraged faces pulled up on the chains to push the target's head down, making him or her bow to the mob over and over. Stirred by the speeches of party organizers, the crowd shouted at their prey. Louder and louder came the insults. Soon enough, the aroused pack began to rain blows on the defenseless person. To impress the Communist Party members and other villagers in the crowd, people vied to show their rage at the enemy on display before them. Feeding off each other, the mob became a storm of violence. Not all victims died, but many did.

In my mother's final hours, the people of her village beat her repeatedly. Next, they tied her to a tree. Some of them picked up stones. Closing in a tight circle around her, the local gang threw rocks and bricks at her. Finally, the mob moved so close they could beat her with the stones in their hands. Once their fury was spent, they left her bound to the tree to die a slow, painful death alone. In her last moments, no one in Lin Fong Lei lifted a finger to help my mother.

The most specific description of Mother's death came to me from a cousin of Joe, my sister Edith's husband. This cousin was known to us as Yee Deh, a respectful label for an older female close to the family. She lived in a village a short distance from Lin Fong Lei. Through family contacts and proximity to the scene, she knew the details of Mother's last days. Cousin Yee Deh shared the unspeakable facts with Edith and her family. Then, word of the tragedy spread to the rest of our family.

In talking about the past, I have no way to confirm this version of the tragedy. Word passed among all of Mother's children living in the United States, yet none of us discussed our mother's death. Our shock was too great.

As her children, we were haunted by the idea that we could not save our mother. None of Mother's immediate family had received any warning of the frightful suffering she faced. Because Mother could not read or write, communications from her would have been impossible if no one was there to assist her, a likely situation once her village had turned hostile. In the politics of the time, even had we known of Mother's fate, it is doubtful we could have done anything. Many families in China faced similar fates and could do nothing, even when not separated by an ocean, as we were.

For months after we learned the news, pain engulfed my brothers and sisters. The idea of enjoying anything in life seemed pointless. Grief crowded into my life with Charlie and the children. Charlie tried to shake me out of my sorrows. He reminded me of what Mother had done to bring all of us to safety.

"You escaped because of her plans and intervention. Always remember that," he said.

Faced with grief and regret, my brothers, sisters and I called upon our own techniques for survival. Silence was one defense. We said little to each other about what we had heard or even believed. I think we all faced the haunting reminder of how we had missed the opportunity to express to Mother our respect, reverence and love for her. Each of us knew the chance was now gone forever.

Mother had always promised us that we would return to the United States. She succeeded in getting each of us, one by one, back home to America. Yet in the end, she stood alone to face a terrible fate.

What I realized much later was that Mother probably knew the end was coming. She could see the growing hostilities all around her and realized she could do nothing to avoid the growing dangers. Even as she came to terms with fear, I suspect she called on her dignity, determination and will in the face of threats. She must have known self-assurance side by side with dread in a manner most of us never experience.

Years earlier, at my father's death, I learned how loss could come so unexpectedly. I discovered in losing my mother how a terrible death would shake me. I never was good with lessons. These were the hardest to take.

CHAPTER TWENTY-SEVEN

The Store:
Family and Identity

Over the course of many years, I learned a great deal about the grocery business by observing Charlie's operation of Wing Shing Grocery. Still, no matter how involved I was, the store was Charlie's business from top to bottom. He greeted shoppers, stocked the shelves, managed inventory and kept the books. Despite all the help he received from his family, Charlie was Wing Shing Grocery, and vice versa.

Little by little, I learned about the business of the store, but I never could match Charlie. At the end of most days, Charlie counted up the day's transactions with satisfaction. He kept impeccable records in his graceful Chinese characters and balanced his numbers daily. In analyzing the store's operations, his abacus clicked away late into the evening as he completed his accounting.

Even when our youngest customers came to shop, Charlie was all business. Wing Shing's large penny-candy counter attracted many little clients, carrying their change and pushing close to the glass for a look. Charlie waited on each one patiently as they picked out what they wanted. He never rushed them as they eyed the many choices before them. After they made their selections, he ensured they carefully counted out each item and then paid the full price. My husband treated them just like he did all his patrons—always giving them their money's worth, never more, never less. He felt even children ought to learn the real price of treats as well as the other things they wanted.

He was a businessman, first and foremost. He focused on quality and value for the customer. His attention to detail required long, often exhausting days in the store, followed by long nights completing his bookkeeping. Charlie had high standards, and he expected his children to live up to them as well. His discipline carried to the lessons they learned helping out with store operations. Thel, in particular, liked staying at the store until late. Many nights I remember the two of them working together, sweeping the floor and turning out the lights.

Our family learned how success at the store came from hard work, not luck. Wing Shing was open seven days a week, every day of the year, including Thanksgiving, Christmas and New Year's Day. Charlie opened the store at 10 A.M. and stayed until closing at 11 P.M., although we switched to 10 P.M. after the second robbery. The schedule required that all Wong family members put in long hours, year in and year out. Charlie's view was clear: success meant you had to work hard.

Not that Charlie didn't enjoy little intermissions during his day. I have a distant memory of him humming while he minded the store. Usually it was a song from one of his favorite Chinese operas. Other times, I heard him softly sing some American tune he liked. Most days, late in the afternoon, he would sit against the food freezer behind the counter, smoking a cigarette. He'd sip a Coke and listen to news on the old radio we kept in the store. News shows were the only stations he tuned on the dial. I never listened much, as the commentary taxed my English. To Charlie, news was important information, so he always tuned in.

For my husband, any chore could be transformed into family time. During the summer, after school let out, he often took the kids along on his rounds. They joined him at Montana Brand, of course, but also at the meat market or bank. Bill the butcher offered them hot dogs, and Agnes at the bank usually had suckers. Occasionally the bank deposit was accompanied by a song from one or all of the kids. Charlie often perched Nancy, about five or six at the time, on the counter. Sparked by a little prompting from a proud father, she would belt out "America the Beautiful" for

Charlie Wong in Wing Shing Grocery.

the bank staff and customers. At Christmas time, Charlie suggested that Nancy switch to "Silent Night" instead.

In his early days in Montana, Charlie developed a patriotic streak; he had a great devotion to his adopted country of America. And it stayed with him forever. One of his favorite singers was Kate Smith, and her version of "God Bless America" usually brought tears to his eyes.

During all our years together, Charlie continued to play an important role in Helena's Chinese community. His unofficial seat of operations for the Chinese community was the old, round table in the back room of our store. Here he sat and talked about all sorts of matters with a cluster of Chinese neighbors—all male, mostly men who lived, worked or owned businesses downtown. At Wing Shing, they found conversation and familiar Chinese goods. Charlie placed regular orders at Seattle's Chinatown for specialty items, such as herbs, spices, dried squid, unusual fish and canned goods.

Because Charlie could speak and read both Chinese and English, he often served as a translator for many of our Chinese neighbors. When a letter arrived from relatives in China, many families knew my husband enjoyed helping them decipher the intricate Chinese characters. For others, he assisted with documents in English that they could not decipher. Helena's Chinese population was fairly small at this time, so Charlie knew most of the faces pretty well. He enjoyed the requests—and the companionship.

From time to time, usually near the end of the evening, a smaller group might congregate. These gatherings, mostly the older Chinese men in town, drew the remnants of the Chinese bachelor community. Charlie had known many of them since his early days in Helena. The group might have been viewed as a gambling and drinking club. Yet, under my watchful eye, there was no heavy drinking or gambling. Instead, they conferred about their lives, changes back home in China and developments in Helena. Our back room was a comfortable, private setting. Some nights, they might gamble a little or drink a small shot or two of whisky. But mostly they talked. In many ways, this group reminded me of my father's assortment of male associates back in Lin Fong Lei. I knew from life with my own father that this was men's time and I should not intrude.

With the passage of time, the group became older and smaller as the Chinese population in Helena declined. Some men returned to China, while others passed away. For those going back to China, Charlie often helped them make their travel arrangements.

When someone of Chinese heritage died, Charlie often served another role: Assisting with the task of returning their remains to China. From his life and culture, Charlie understood the importance of a proper burial back in China so that one's memory could be honored by future generations of family. And he recognized the Chinese belief that anyone who dies without family to tend his or her grave becomes a wandering ghost, caught between heaven and earth. Working with local funeral homes, many of which appreciated these traditions, Charlie approached his reburial duties with sensibility and seriousness.

Some years later, Mrs. Elfreda Paulsen, spouse of a Helena funeral and cemetery operator, described various funeral customs in an interview. Her portrayal of funerals from the early 1900s combined some of the rituals I knew from China with her perspectives on American additions:

> The Chinese didn't believe in spending money on funerals. They used the Country Farm hearse—an old black thing. The hearse usually came first, going very fast. A Chinese man sat in the front with

the driver and threw out paper strips filled with tiny holes. This was to keep away the bad spirits from the deceased. The bad spirit had to crawl through the tiny holes. If enough holes were distributed, the bad spirit could not get through the holes and never catch up before the dead person is buried.

The Chinese held no ceremony at their funerals other than the passing of food to those attending the ceremony. Roast chicken was distributed and some kind of liquor in Chinese cups. Food and liquor in these cups were left at the burial site along with burning strips of punk. The earthly belongings such as clothing, bedding, etc. were burned at the funeral in an incinerator provided for this purpose at the cemetery. Even the clothing of a two-year-old was burned.

In her writing, Mrs. Paulsen also explained the later practice of unearthing remains so that they could be shipped back to family members in China for burial. She offered this depiction:

In the early forties, many of the bones of the Chinese were removed for reburial in China. A member of the Chinese Society came to Mr. Paulsen, presented his credentials and asked for permission to open graves of certain Chinese. This was done at the bearer's expense. The remains were packed in designated boxes, loaded in a large limousine to be taken to San Francisco and there transported to their native China.

Some people might view the task as grim. When he was called to help, Charlie sensed the person's safe return home was in his hands. He made sure the transfer was completed with dignity.

As I broadened my own set of skills, by the 1960s I began to take some of the load off Charlie at Wing Shing Grocery. And yet, I never came close to Charlie's talents at customer service and handling salesmen and suppliers. However, in one specific area of dealing with vendors, I excelled. Because we had our kitchen at the back of the store, I spent a lot of time there preparing meals and other treats. I could always be on call in case Charlie needed help. One of my specialties was doughnuts, deep fried and tasty. I also made cream puffs and Chinese meat-and-vegetable pastries known as *gai loong*. On very special occasions, I baked apple pies. Our salesmen learned to time their visits around my cooking schedule. When they could smell their favorite aroma from the kitchen, they met with Charlie at the counter, discussed their order quickly, then made their way straight to the back to see me. The kids complained loudly about how our business clients and visitors usually got first crack at the doughnuts and other goodies in my kitchen.

"All we get is the doughnut holes," was a common grievance from the Wong children.

Over the years, with Charlie as my teacher, I improved my cooking quite a bit. Most mornings, I fixed breakfasts of cold cereal, oatmeal or eggs. Because Charlie and I were strict about table manners, no one was allowed to leave the table until they finished all their food. Gloria, our fussiest eater, didn't like eggs, especially the yolks. I can remember some days when she sat at the table for what seemed like hours, eating all around the yolk without touching it. Finally, she sat and stared at the cold yolk in the center of her plate. After breakfast, one of the kids always had the duty to sweep the floor. Most mornings, someone swept while Gloria gazed at her egg. When she realized I wasn't going to let her leave the table, she stuck her fork in the yolk and gulped it down.

My family ate nearly every lunch and dinner in the kitchen at the back of the store. And because the store remained open most hours of the day, we juggled store operations with family meals. We monitored the store counter through the opening Charlie had made in the wall separating the back room and the sales counter. We could watch the front door without leaving the kitchen table; when someone came in, one of us would go out front. Typically one of the girls finished her meal first and would then go sit behind the cash register. Later, Charlie would take over. It never seemed like an intrusion on our dinners, but more like a regular part of life.

Our dinnertime supervision of the store did offer some interesting diversions. I remember several times when a neighbor kid ran through the door, grabbed a handful of candy or potato chips and dashed back out without paying. In response, the young Wong posse, spotting the theft from the back room, sprang into action. One or two of our kids headed out the front door in pursuit of the candy thief. At the same time, a couple of others ran out the back, hoping to surround the culprit. Finally, Charlie might get up from his meal to investigate. Most often, he would arrive only to discover that our band of enforcers had already rounded up the offender and retrieved the stolen loot.

Not only did we eat our meals there, but the children often used Wing Shing as their playground. The storage area between the store and the kitchen, filled mostly with cases of canned goods and empty boxes, became a favorite play area for our kids and their playmates. The kids moved and stacked the boxes to fashion a forest or a fort, whatever they could imagine.

For more than twenty years, the store played many roles for our family, and for our small community. Here was our business, our family room, the kids' playroom and our family center, much more than our house across the alley.

To Charlie, the store was even more. He saw it as his life and his connection to Helena's Chinese community. For nearly fifty years, Charlie thrived on the links he formed between his new hometown and his original homeland. Only his family was more important.

CHAPTER TWENTY-EIGHT

My Pathfinder Gone

The phone rang at the store just before noon on January 4, 1968.
As winter hit Helena that year, Charlie had seemed more fatigued. He had begun spending his days at the house while I tended the store. He confessed that he wasn't sure what his trouble was, but he didn't want to see a doctor. I worried, but I understood that pushing my husband to seek medical care would not change his mind. In recent days, Charlie had been lingering in our house, resting and warming himself by our small gas heater. As I left for the store that morning, he gave me no hint that he felt sick or any worse than usual. The weather on this morning was very cold.

At that moment, the caller on the line was our neighbor, Mrs. Oleson, the renter in our duplex. She heard a noise coming from our home and was afraid someone had fallen in our bathroom. Mrs. Oleson's alarm worried me so much that I ran across the alley to our door.

Checking the bathroom, I found Charlie slumped over on the floor. He did not respond to my voice, and his eyes were vacant. When I could not revive him, I went into something of a state of shock. I didn't know what to do. Before I could act, I heard a siren, and the ambulance emergency team came rushing in. Mrs. Oleson must have called for help. Quickly, the attendants lifted Charlie onto the stretcher and carried him to the ambulance. I climbed in the back, right beside him. Although I held Charlie and talked to him as the ambulance raced to St. Peter's Hospital, he did not respond at all.

By the time we arrived at the hospital and medical personnel began to examine Charlie, I believed he was already gone. Still, when the doctor confirmed my fears out loud, I fell to the floor. Irene and George Wong, Charlie's cousins who had been alerted to the crisis and were waiting at the hospital, helped me to a chair.

After I regained some composure, the doctor took me aside to say he thought Charlie's heart had failed. After explaining as much as he could, he asked if I wanted an autopsy to determine the cause of death. Throughout his life, Charlie detested the idea of surgery, so I told the doctor I could not approve such a procedure, no matter what it might tell us. He nodded and asked if there was any more he could do. Then he left me with George and Irene.

As soon as I recovered, I realized I had to get home to my children. They would be home from school shortly, and I had to be there to tell them about their father. George and Irene drove me to the house. On the way, I tried to compose my thoughts, but nothing I thought of seemed right.

As I entered the house, I knew I was too late. Their eyes told me they already knew. All I could do was gather my shattered family around me. We huddled together in our kitchen for a long time. I tried my best to explain what had occurred, but mostly I just cried. For days, the sadness swallowed us completely. Bess had to hear the news long distance. She was living in Chicago at the time, so I asked my sister Maymie to break the news to her.

Bringing focus to my thoughts was difficult in the following days, but I knew I had to arrange for the funeral. Fortunately, my family came to my aid. All my sisters as well as Kenneth traveled to Helena to support me. Friends also gathered for days at our house. I could barely speak most of the time. George and Irene Wong stepped in to help, too, contacting the funeral home and making most of the arrangements for Charlie's service.

On January 10, 1968, a bright and cold day, we buried Charlie. We laid him to rest in a grave not far from those of his son and his first wife. Despite the cold, no snow covered the ground. Charlie's funeral service was American, not typical Chinese. I arrived, dressed in black and followed by a long

Charlie Wong prior to his wedding.

procession of cars. Thinking back, I can remember only small bits of the day. A friend, PeeWee Weber, played Charlie's favorite song, "America, the Beautiful," on the organ. Frank Bishop, one of the salesmen who frequently visited Charlie, and a favorite of the kids, served as a pallbearer. Our kids had nicknamed him Mr. Kick-in-the-Shins, which sounded a little like the first name of the company he represented: Sheehan's Sundries. In turn, he called Charlie, "Wing," and me, "Shing," a twist on our store name.

At the funeral and in the days that followed, I limped along. Still in a daze, I fought against the heaviest blow of my life. It helped to have my family there. I had seen my brothers and sisters only sporadically since 1948, the year I came to the United States. Now, they came long distances to console me and my children. In death, as in life, Charlie helped bring my family together. Two decades earlier, before and after our wedding, he provided help to us in the money he sent. Now, we were together again. All but one. Only younger brother Robert could not make it to Helena.

In the years after my sisters, brothers and I arrived in America, we exchanged letters only occasionally. My sisters and I rarely called each other, as long-distance calls cost too much money in those days. Busy with work and children, each of us found little time to keep in touch. As the years passed, we mainly communicated by Christmas cards with short greetings. Mother's death, with its somberness, brought us together for a time, but then we seemed to lose touch again.

As I tried to come to grips with Charlie's death, having my family with me offered some of the relief I needed. In the Chinese way, we did not talk much about Charlie and his passing. Instead, we cooked, talked about our children and relived our past. Knowing that my family came from so far so quickly gave me a great sense of comfort. In private moments, however, out of sight of my children and family, my profound grief brought many tears. At times, the sense of loss overwhelmed me.

Once the funeral was over, I had to confront the question of what to do next. Here I was, alone, at age thirty-nine with five children and a long list of fears and reservations. How would I operate the grocery store? How would I finish raising the kids? How could I manage my budget and bills? All these anxieties grew until I felt completely overwhelmed. What I did sense was that I had grown immensely since my arrival from China. I had learned how to handle a new country, how to raise a family and how to make decisions on my own. My children, of course, offered all the assistance they could. But they were still young. Realistically, I knew the responsibilities fell to me.

What advice would Charlie give me now? As much as I liked to think of myself as self-reliant, I knew I was not one to strike out on my own, and I had always been able to rely on Charlie.

Memory took me back to my childhood in China, to a time when Maymie and I relied on our water buffalo for big jobs. A resilient buffalo that can pull the plow down a straight line is valuable. Now, like our water buffalo, I needed to show my own strengths. I would have to push and pull as never before.

Thinking back in time, I saw Mother with her careful judgment, character and energy. Those qualities, too, would help me, but I had to add my own measure of courage and self-sufficiency, I thought.

"You can't let your grief take over," I told myself. "Not now."

Getting back to the day-to-day operation of the store restored my balance in small measures. Still, words from a thoughtful customer with a simple offer of sympathy could be painful. "I'm sorry for your loss," they might say and I'd break into tears. For a time, the more customers or salesmen comforted me, the more I cried. Some days, handling my sadness and the store together was simply too much for me. I'd turn the counter over to one of the kids and take a break.

One afternoon, several weeks after Charlie's service, a good customer named Tom Nangle came into the store with his usual greeting, "Hi Flora, where's Charlie today?"

For a brief moment, I was silent. Then my sobs burst out. Mr. Nangle stood in the middle of the store in troubled bewilderment. I finally stopped crying long enough to explain why Charlie wasn't there. At once, he apologized several times, offered some kind words and departed.

When my kids arrived at the store after school, tears still ran down my cheeks. Perched on the counter were two-dozen long-stemmed red roses. Attached was Mr. Nangle's note of apology. Whenever I looked at his gift, I had another round of crying I could not control.

Still, like my work in China, the job running the store gave me purpose. The regular hours, the contact with customers and conversations with vendors helped me carry on. Having all my children there to assist was wonderful. All the kids pitched in to help as much as they could. I know this time challenged them as much as it did me.

As time passed, I settled into a family routine again, lifted up by the presence of all my kids. Without any prompting from me, they all found jobs and began looking to the future. Bess worked for the Helena school system and later for the federal road bureau. Gloria found a job at the Veteran's Administration at Fort Harrison. Thel worked for the State of Montana in several roles. All three helped out at Yat Son Noodle Parlor, the same place Charlie worked for years. After Charlie's death, my family spent more time with Fred Wong, the owner of Yat Son, and we enjoyed evenings at the restaurant watching as he served his special egg rolls and pork noodles.

As they grew older, Poy and Nancy also sandwiched jobs around school. Poy's favorite job was summer duty as a Forest Service firefighter. Nancy found a variety of jobs with the State of Montana.

How grateful I was for these dutiful children. I had worried all the time about how I would raise the kids in Charlie's absence. Yet they seemed to have some natural instinct to respond to our family needs. I feared my lack of experience in providing meaningful guidance would lead to problems. It never became an issue. Each of them enjoyed work. What was more, they brought their paychecks back to me, without a word from me. I deposited the checks in the bank, in accounts Charlie and I had opened in each of their names.

When the time came to go to college, they each paid their own way, never asking me for financial help. I was so proud of them.

But I was faced with another motherly test: how to handle my daughters' dating. I had not discussed relationships with my daughters for three very good reasons. Reason number one was that I really did not know what advice to offer. When my sisters and I were coming of age, Mother offered not one word about relations with boys. Nor had I ever talked about such matters with my own sisters or friends. Consequently, as my girls grew up, I had no idea where to start with any advice I might pass along. As my luck would have it, Carol Field, the daughter of the girls' piano teacher, often stayed for sleepovers. A few years older than my girls, she knew the "facts of life" and happily shared them.

Reason number two was that I had never dated, so I had no knowledge to share on the topic. With no facts at hand, I did what I thought was wise. I said nothing at all. Secretly, I tried different ploys to keep them at home as much as possible as each one grew up. Of course, that did not work. So I gave in to the natural course of events and hoped each would succeed on their own, as they had in work.

More complex was my third reason for avoiding recommendations. Many times in his life, Charlie insisted that he wanted his daughters to marry Chinese men. I respected Charlie's views on the matter, but, perhaps as a mother, I also realized times had changed. Disregarding their father's wishes was difficult for me because he and I grew up in an age when tradition and your family determined who and when you married. My daughters lived in a different culture, one where they were becoming accustomed to making their own choices on all manner of issues. As for practicality, Helena offered very few Chinese men appropriate for dating. The few remaining male members of the Chinese community were either too old or somehow related.

I had a judgment to make. Instead of telling my girls about Charlie's wishes, knowing they would feel pressure to do as he wanted, I kept his mandate to myself.

Soon the store became my biggest challenge. Simply keeping it open and running hung over me as a test. Business dropped off dramatically after Charlie's death. Competition was partly to blame, but Charlie's absence was a big factor. We still had many loyal customers, but they came in less frequently. In truth, Charlie himself was a large part of the draw of our store. People knew, liked and trusted him. Once he was gone, they slowly found other places to do business. Eventually, sales in the store dwindled to the point where I had difficulty finding enough money to stock our shelves adequately. The situation led to a downward spiral: fewer sales meant fewer items on the shelves. My smaller inventory, in turn, yielded still fewer sales. I remember many days when I reached into the box where I kept the store cash to make change for a customer, only to come up almost empty-handed. I faced another decision.

CHAPTER TWENTY-NINE

Homeward to Helena

In my struggle to keep our family business afloat after losing my husband, I found myself at a crossroads. I questioned whether I could ever get the store back on sound financial footing. I wondered, too, if I should move away to be closer to my other family members. I loved our community, but having my family together at Charlie's service had provided great comfort. My brothers and sisters were spread out east and west across the country. Should I uproot my family to have support close at hand? If so, where should I move?

These were difficult questions that my children could not help me answer. My sisters and brothers encouraged me to move. Each of them made a pitch about how much I would like living in his or her respective area. After weighing my options for several months, I decided the kids and I should look into the plan more seriously. So, we chose to take a family vacation as soon as the kids were out of school. For me, it would be more about research than relaxation. I vowed to examine each location carefully to see if it would make a suitable new home for my family.

When the school year ended in June 1968, our family journey began with a bus ride from Helena to Logan, Montana. There, we boarded a train to Chicago. On the train, a tall, elegant black man was our conductor. Dressed impeccably in his white jacket and hat, he took a liking to my clutch of kids. His close attention to our needs truly spoiled the children. Under his care, my uncertainties about the trip began to melt away. I relaxed and gazed at the scenery passing by our window. New adventures took shape on each leg of our journey, as my family had never taken a vacation together before.

While in Chicago, we spent several weeks with my sister Maymie, her husband, Mon, and their five children. Our kids had never met, but they got along right from the start. That left plenty of time for Maymie and me to catch up on our lives. We had spent very little time together since our days in China, so we had lots to talk about. Late nights were slumber party time for the kids, giving Maymie and me time to reminisce about the past and discuss what was to come. We also visited Chicago's Chinatown, where I tried escargot for the first time since China. As a small child, I ate snails a few times, but now their slippery texture bothered me. Maymie, however, swallowed the morsels easily.

Maymie and I had been very close as youngsters, but our lives had taken different courses. While I followed Mother's direction into marriage, Maymie, with a more independent mind than mine, went her own way. Six months after my departure from China, Mother put Maymie on a flight out of China. Arriving at the San Francisco airport on May 19, 1949, she cleared immigration and found Florence and her husband, Henry, outside. Also waiting for Maymie in San Francisco was a husband in an arranged marriage. Using her customary go-between in China, Mother set up Maymie's engagement to a young Chinese man whose name I never learned. The man's father, a U.S. soldier, and his mother operated a laundry. Working through Mother's matchmaker, the intended groom's family sent a ring to Maymie in China. Recalling the young man, Maymie confided to me that he did not speak English and had no formal education. As we sat in her Chicago home, Maymie spilled out her story. Not only did she reject this man, but she was determined to take charge of any marriage she might have on her own terms.

"I am the disobedient daughter," Maymie said.

"Even before I met him, I had a bad feeling about this marriage. Once I met him, all I could see ahead was a life in the laundry business. I actually got sick to my stomach thinking about such a future."

She continued, "I wrote to Mom and told her: 'It doesn't work this way for me.' I felt better right off. I returned the ring to the man's family and washed my hands of arranged marriages. I had to look out for myself. I came here alone, so I guessed I'd make my own way alone."

During her first month in San Francisco, Maymie stayed with Henry and Florence. Although they were still newlyweds, Henry gave up his half of their bed so that Maymie would not have to sleep on the floor of their small home.

"I knew I could not stay even though they were so kind to take me in. So early in their marriage and there I was, coming between them. I knew I had to move on."

Next, Maymie flew to Mississippi, where she stayed with Edith and her husband, Joe. After a short stopover, brother Kenneth took her on a tour to Chicago. There, Kenneth introduced her to Mon Ho. Mon's family also owned a laundry, but Maymie saw a much different future with Mon.

"Mon had a college degree, he spoke proper English and he had a quick wit. I liked his sense of humor. I think we hit it off right away. It helped that he was my choice rather than Mom's."

By the time of my 1968 visit, Maymie and Mon had been married for nearly twenty years.

From Chicago, Maymie and I drove my family south to Greenwood, Mississippi, where Kenneth lived with his wife, Joy. They had five kids and, like us, lived behind their grocery store. Their place felt a lot like home, and we stayed for nearly a month. Most evenings, the kids played cards while the adults gathered around the table for mahjongg. Summer in Mississippi was hot and muggy, weather that reminded me of southern China. Kenneth and Joy had a swimming pool in their yard, where I cooled off and the kids played with their cousins. The combination of the pool and the batch of new cousins was a great source of fun for my kids.

The new setting and latest batch of cousins kept my children so busy that I thought I could take some time to myself and call on a valued friend from my past. A cousin of Amy Wong, James Chow, learned I had come to Mississippi. Knowing how much Amy and I would enjoy visiting again, James came to Greenwood with his car and a plan. "How about a drive to see Amy?" he asked.

I answered immediately, "Let's go."

We drove to Baton Rouge, Louisiana, where I saw Amy for the first time in more than fifteen years. Ours was a wonderful reunion, as we chatted about our pasts and all that had occurred in the intervening years. More upheaval had come to Amy as well. After Sun You died of tuberculosis-related problems, Amy returned to the South, where she had family ties. In Baton Rouge, Amy had remarried. Her new husband, David Yang, was a professor at the university in Baton Rouge. With her two daughters, Letah and Lelan, she was enjoying her new life in Louisiana. When she told me how well she and her daughters were doing in their new home far from Montana, I became more encouraged that I might be up to the challenges of starting over somewhere else. As in the past, Amy helped me rebuild some feelings of assurance and self-confidence.

"You see," I told myself, "you can start over and make it work."

From Baton Rouge, I traveled to Arkansas, again with Amy's cousin James. This visit was short. Without my knowledge, the plan had been to set me up on something of a blind date in Arkansas. While I appreciated this effort at matchmaking, I knew I was not ready to contemplate a new life of that sort. I said "No" to the blind date and "No" to any further travel away from my family.

We turned the car in the direction of Greenwood, where I packed up the kids again and drove a short ten miles west to Itta Bena, Mississippi. A small town at the intersection of Highway 7 and Freedom Road, Itta Bena was home to Edith and Joe. They, too, owned and operated a small grocery store. Again, I felt we were on our home turf. Perhaps my mind got to thinking about the notion of freedom from the town's prominent avenue of the same name, because I started to sense the grocery business might not be my mission. It had been Charlie's life, but it had not been mine. Made a bit bolder by my late-night talks with Amy and Maymie, I was ready to try a new track.

With much to ponder, we loaded up the car again and drove north for about two hours to Memphis. Along the way, we detoured past Graceland, Elvis Presley's home on the south side of Memphis. My children, particularly the older ones, were hoping we might catch a glimpse of Elvis as we drove through his neighborhood. I knew little about the singer; I was more interested in Memphis for its airport. I wanted to keep moving.

There we caught a flight to Los Angeles, site of our next scheduled visit with my brother Robert and his family. By now, all the time on the road started to take its toll. Los Angeles was a blend of all the legs of the trip that preceded it, mixing family visits, food and fun. We visited my sister Joyce, her husband, Bill, and their two children at a large family dinner in Chinatown. With Robert and his family, we dug into more Chinese food, both home cooked and restaurant fare. In L.A.'s Chinatown, we saw several Chinese opera movies, which the kids and I agreed were odd. For me, they were a little reminder of Charlie, because he had been fond of Chinese opera, although in a different form than these movies. Next came Disneyland and Knott's Berry Farm. These diversions offered a whirlwind of fun, but they did nothing to settle my mind about the future.

Before departing, I had a talk with Robert.

"Sometimes I don't know where to turn. I almost feel like giving up," I said.

"You have a lot of options," he replied. "It might make sense to move here to be close to many families: mine, Florence's, Joyce's and Dorothy's."

"I just don't know which course to take," I said.

"A good answer will come to you. But you have to find it and you'll do it. You're stronger than you think."

In August, for our final stop, the kids and I flew north to San Francisco, home to my sister Dorothy, her husband, Wing, and their two children. This city's Chinatown, larger and very active, reminded me of my visits to Guangzhou many years ago. Its streets overflowed with Chinese goods and its restaurants served plenty of tasty Cantonese food. Dorothy and I enjoyed many conversations. Our kids got along flawlessly, something of a marvel because my children had been on the road for nearly the entire summer. From San Francisco, Dorothy and her husband drove us to San Jose to see my sister Florence. Florence, her usual boisterous self, happily introduced my family to her husband, Henry, and their four children.

After nearly three months of travel, the end to our trip was near. School for my kids would be starting soon, and the time had come to return to Helena. I had collected the information I needed in order to decide my family's future. Now I just had to make the decision. Somehow I felt I was ready to tackle the next phase of my life on my own.

Our final leg brought us home to Helena, where I knew I had to confront the question of whether it was time to move. I thoroughly enjoyed seeing my family again, and their concern for me and my family's future was reassuring. What was surprising—and had been largely forgotten to me for a time—was how much I liked the smells and foods of the Chinatowns we visited. Enjoying these scents again turned my mind to the parts of China I missed. Reconnecting to my Chinese heritage would mean moving closer to family. I knew I was facing a difficult choice.

Montanans often use the phrase "high, wide and handsome" to describe their state. The words suggest broad, open spaces and strikingly beautiful mountainous landscapes, visions I longed for all summer long. No matter where we went, I missed the open feel of Helena and its friendly people. I knew, too, that this was Charlie's home and that I really could not leave him. By the time we got off the plane in Helena, I had made up my mind—at least partially.

As we traveled the country, I realized that no matter where I went, my heartbreak and despair at losing Charlie followed me every day. Yet, I knew I could not, and would not, fall apart. As I gained enough of my own strength to handle this adversity, I learned, too, that I could lean more heavily on others. My children, though still in their teens, were strong enough that I could turn to them for help with my decisions. We were navigating tough times together, and their advice helped immeasurably. We were all a bit like the pines in Montana: bent by the wind and snow, but ready to bounce back from the harsh elements.

In the fall, after a few weeks back in Helena, I found renewed resilience and enthusiasm. No longer was I worried about how to keep going. Energy restored, I took on a fresh outlook, determined to tackle the changes I needed to make in my life.

Right away, family considerations framed my thinking. Gloria had started her senior year in high school. Moving her would be unfair. Soon after the school year began, I announced to the kids that we were staying put at least for a year. Next thing I knew, Gloria's final year concluded, but Thel was making plans for her senior year. Each fall, my dilemma looked the same. My kids were doing well in school and transferring them simply seemed unfair.

At the same time, I needed to determine the fate of the Wing Shing Grocery. In the end, the City of Helena made the choice for me. Before we set off on our cross-country trip, a city official had come by to discuss a development plan for downtown. Under a multi-million-dollar urban renewal plan for our part of town, city government had a new design for the neighborhood and a large section of downtown. Local officials had discussed the plan for some time, and I knew some buildings, including our store and duplex, were slated for demolition. Other older historic buildings were to be preserved. The plan called for part of Main Street, or Last Chance Gulch, to be converted into a pedestrian mall. Rolled into this strategy were new government buildings, a library and more shops. As we departed on our Wong family trip, I still considered the city's ideas to be talk, nothing concrete. But soon after we arrived home and just as I was thinking about my initial decision to remain in Helena, the same city official came back. The city was moving ahead, and we had to move. In the name of progress, both our store and our duplex would be torn down.

The City of Helena determined the value of various properties to be condemned, and offered owners of the houses, buildings and land in the urban renewal zone a settlement. Once the city determined its valuation of our store, duplex and land, I thought I had room for further talk or negotiations. I met with one man, who scratched out the details of a settlement on a yellow sheet of paper. Essentially he said I could take it or leave it, but here was the best offer we would see. He concluded by telling me we had to move out by a date in the not too distant future. What he proposed was the end of our store and home in no uncertain terms. I was very unhappy, but did not know if I had any other options. We had to close up the store, pack our things and be gone. Negotiating with the city for a better settlement did not occur to me. So we sold off our inventory and prepared to relocate.

In August 1970, we found a new home on the east side of town, just above the freeway on California Street.

In one of my last transactions at the store, I sold our 700-pound safe to Red Drennon. On a cold November day after we had closed Wing Shing Grocery, Red and a friend came to the store with his three-wheel all-terrain vehicle to move the safe. They maneuvered the heavy cargo onto a cart, hitched the cart to Red's scooter and drove north to his new shop location, about a half mile away at 821 North Main. Soon after Red took away the safe, I shut and locked up Wing Shing Grocery one last time.

As I closed our store that final time, I could think of nothing but

Charlie. Saying goodbye to this part of my life brought another round of tears, but I had no choice but to move on.

When the demolition crews destroyed my home and store, I could not bear to watch the spectacle. A small crowd gathered on the hill overlooking the site as a large crane swung its wrecking ball at our home. One strike of the ball took out most of the duplex. By the end of the day, all that remained was a heap of bricks and rubble. Some time later, the crew returned, and the store, along with other buildings on the block, became mounds of debris. Within a year, a new Lewis and Clark Library building stood next to where our store had been. The library parking lot covered the sites of the duplex and store Charlie and I had owned. Before the site was cleared completely, I retrieved from the debris a single brick. This reminder of a past life remains in my yard today.

Nearly thirty years later, I met a man at a retirement party for a friend. During our conversation, he asked my name. When I replied Flora Wong, he paused for a moment as if searching his memory.

"I think I tore down your store and house," he said.

"You did?" I asked. He looked so young that I couldn't believe his statement.

I hesitated, trying to think what more to say. For many years, the city's demolition of our store and home had been a sore spot for me. When the dust of destruction settled, the bulldozers and cranes had destroyed my physical ties to Charlie and our early days in Helena.

"You know, I didn't like that," I said. "You took my home and my history with your equipment."

"I was only doing my job. Please don't take it personally."

We talked some more in a very friendly exchange. He explained that he was a superintendent and equipment operator for the company hired by the city to complete the destruction of our neighborhood. By the time his crews finished, our neighborhood was gone. I told him where we moved, what I was doing and how I still enjoyed Helena.

After a bit, someone came by to take our picture. We smiled for the camera, turned to say goodbye to each other and walked away. Later, I realized he was correct. He was just doing his duty. And I was trying to move ahead with my life.

CHAPTER THIRTY

Time for a Job

A happy turning point in my life came when I landed a job as a sales clerk at McDonald's Department Store, Helena's largest store. Located downtown on Last Chance Gulch, just a few blocks from our South Main Street store, McDonald's (previously Fligelman's) had been a favorite stop for Charlie and the kids.

The location had a long retail history. The New York Store once sat at the same site at 44, 46 and 48 North Main Street. On July 16, 1928, fire severely damaged the New York Store. One year later, the brand-new Fligelman's Department Store opened at that spot. Known by its motto, "Helena's friendliest home store," Fligelman's was the prime shopping location on Main Street when I arrived twenty years later.

In 1958, the JM McDonald Company purchased Fligelman's. At some point in the transition, McDonald's added a large, two-story sign and covered the facade with metal sheathing. Although I never liked the new look of the store, I was happy to see that McDonald's retained one key Fligelman's practice: elaborate window displays. For my family, a shopping trip to the department store was always an adventure, and the window exhibits were usually the high point. In truth, we looked at the windows more than we shopped.

I started my McDonald's job in 1970. Right away, I enjoyed my work and my first boss, Gerald Homestead. He had plenty of experience in the retail field, which he was happy to share with his new hire. June Thompson, a friendly coworker, also showed me the ropes, including how to ring up sales, organize displays and greet customers.

But I had some immediate workplace challenges to overcome. What was an entry-level job taught me a number of important lessons.

First was my English. Despite years of effort, my vocabulary and pronunciations had hardly advanced. My Chinese tongue still could not wrap itself around many English words. To this day, I have trouble with the sounds for "th" and "r." The "th" becomes a "d" and the "r" simply disappears. Often, my customers used words that I did not know. I quickly learned to ask for clarification as soon as I misunderstood a word. Most customers were usually very patient and helpful with me as I explained the store's offerings in my halting way.

Another personal test was my lingering shyness. Over time at my job, I overcame my timidness, and I discovered great enjoyment in meeting new people and helping them find what they wanted. For many people, finding ease in welcoming new faces might sound like a small, simple step. For me, it was a big leap forward, one that required great effort.

In time, I became one of the top sales associates in the store. Lots of regular customers would come in and ask for me by name. If they couldn't remember my name, some would ask for me by my employee number: twenty-three.

As hard as I worked at my job and as frugal as I tried to be, money was still tight. We had a new house with two children at home and three in college. Yet, my McDonald's pay was so low, only $1.25 per hour, that we lived on a strict budget. On the plus side, McDonald's offered an employee discount on in-store purchases, a feature that my girls used to great advantage. Nearly all of my extra earnings went back to the store, largely for clothing for my kids.

Working full time in retail can be a grinding existence, I know, but I look back and think of McDonald's Department Store as my favorite job. Even the challenging customers were a source of pleasure and often merriment.

During my stint in the lingerie department, one of my favorite clients was a very large, heavy-set woman with a great sense of humor. One of her visits stands out as particularly memorable. She came to me in an urgent search for a new girdle. She needed it right away for a big affair—I think it was a family gathering. I set about finding just the right one for her, but I wasn't sure what would fit. After selecting an assortment of foundation garments for her to try, I sent her to the dressing room.

After struggling with several, she came back to me. Quietly, she bent her head next to mine.

"Not one of these works," she said. "They just don't do the job."

"Well, I think I showed you just about everything."

"Look again, because I have to find something. I have to look slimmer. And quick."

I searched our department again and came back with one final selection. Far and away, it was the largest girdle we carried.

For her final fitting, she asked me to follow her into the changing room to help with adjustments. As she struggled, I offered one last idea.

"You'll have to suck it in as you start," I said, a little afraid at how my girdling advice would be received.

"I will do the sucking in, if you will do the fastening," she said as she smiled.

I thought this strategy might work. It didn't. But rather than getting frustrated or angry, she found plenty of comedy in the whole episode. First, she started to laugh. Next, I started to giggle. Before long, we spilled out of the dressing room and into the hall, laughing to the point of tears. She left without a girdle but remained a good customer, a fact I attribute to her fine sense of wit.

Working at McDonald's offered me plenty: fun, a sense of accomplishment and improved skills at meeting people. My job there also helped me build a stronger sense of self-sufficiency as I faced my future.

In the spring of 1973, my working career took another turn. Financial demands forced me to begin thinking about leaving my job at McDonald's in search of a new opportunity. While visiting with Charlie's cousins George and Irene Wong, they brought up a business idea. They wanted to open a Chinese take-out restaurant, and they invited me in as a partner. For about twenty years, they had owned George's OK Café, an American-style restaurant on Main Street in Helena. The café served a menu of burgers, fries and shakes, made to order from scratch, plus homemade soups. We all thought George made the best chicken-fried steak in town. After years of hard work with a full-service menu, they decided they wanted a change of pace. The plan was a new restaurant with fewer menu items and shorter hours. That was the goal anyway. After taking a few days to think it over, I signed on as a partner.

On August 12, 1973, the three of us opened the Chinese Kitchen and Oriental Gift Shop on Euclid Avenue on the west side of Helena. When we opened, we were the first Chinese take-out in Helena. For our open house on the first day of business, we splurged on a full-page ad in the local newspaper. We even had a clown, played by a friend of George, to welcome guests. Right away, business took off. In our first week, we were running out of food before closing every night.

Lots of planning had gone into our new enterprise, and the facility turned out to be everything we expected it to be. Over a short span of time, we had acquired the site, designed a specific layout to fit our plans and finished construction. We split the duties. George prepared most of the ingredients. Irene supervised the front counter, provided customer service and did the books. I did the cooking, a responsibility I felt comfortable with after many years of cooking for my family. Our building was small, and we shoehorned all our necessities into its tight layout. At the entrance was a counter where customers placed and picked up orders. Adjacent to the serving counter was a small display area where we offered items such as dishes, teapots, chopsticks, lanterns and tea.

Running parallel to the service counter and back about six feet was a long steam table where we kept large trays of food piping hot. Our servers could work the front counter and turn to find the hot foods ready to go into take-out containers, all within easy reach. Farther back and off to one side behind the steam table were three gas burners, two for our large woks and one for soup.

Hours were Tuesday through Sunday from 3 to 9 P.M. Great hours, I thought at the beginning. Soon, I found myself at the restaurant each day before 10 A.M. in order to get ready. First, I helped with food inventory orders, then it was time to wash, chop and season the food. And I liked to have the woks going well before our 3 P.M. opening. We stayed an hour or more past closing to clean up and prepare for the next day. Despite the six-day work weeks and the long hours, I was happy churning out our specialty stir-fried meals.

Our food at the Chinese Kitchen acquired a reputation for being tasty, fresh and fast. I made it my goal to have the customers' broccoli-and-beef order fresh out of the wok in less time than it took a typical fast food joint to prepare a hamburger and fries. Of course, there were glitches. Because I improvised as I went, some menu descriptions did not match my meals precisely. Sometimes, due to the crush of business, we did not meet what I had set as our five-minute turnaround deadline. Customers rarely seemed to mind. Nonetheless, our kitchen crew and our band of servers worked together as a team, finding ways to improve. During our first week, we ran another ad in the paper explaining the circumstances of short delays and menu modifications.

For me, being a partner in the restaurant and doing the cooking brought equal measures of responsibility and creativity. But being a small business owner came with plenty of pressures and worries. When we took our annual vacation and shut the restaurant for two weeks in the summer, I always worried about whether our customers would return. At the grocery store, I wondered if I would ever learn Charlie's business sense and attention to detail. In the Chinese Kitchen, I knew I had.

My enjoyment in cooking took my mind off some of the business worries. I focused on simple Chinese dishes, ones I had mastered over the years after Charlie taught them to me. By insisting on the freshest ingredients and a spotless kitchen, we maintained high standards and found a good demand for our dishes. My kids helped out immensely in the restaurant's operations. Whenever they had the time, the girls came by after their jobs to help out at the steam table. Poy became an accomplished wok handler, while Gloria became an expert at carving pork legs for our barbecue dishes. At the end of those days, the scene looked like a big party as we finished the orders, had dinner together, cleaned up and closed for the night. And on the few occasions I was sick, Gloria and Poy filled in for me and cooked with great skill.

For any cook, the sustaining reward for your long time at the stove is satisfied customers. In terms of status in the cooking world, preparing take-out Chinese food in Helena, Montana, ranked low. I didn't care; I wasn't looking to make a name for myself. My satisfaction came from my customers; their enjoyment and encouragement brought me great happiness. My favorite customers included such regulars as Nellie Dean, Paul Paulsen and Joe Vantura.

Just as I can easily recall my favorite regulars, I remember my list of best dishes. Right at the top were my broccoli beef, almond chicken, pepper beef and egg foo young.

I knew the restaurant business would not be easy. It wasn't, but it worked out well. It gave me wonderful memories—of good food and the people we served.

In my work at the Chinese Kitchen and McDonald's, I learned many lessons with some common themes. If you are lucky, your days seldom will be filled with easy tasks and obvious answers to challenges. All I wanted to do at work was keep busy and develop new talents. Those wishes came true.

CHAPTER THIRTY-ONE

Lonely Hill

My return to Lin Fong Lei in 1990, after a forty-two-year absence, brought back the flash of memories I expected. As I looked around, I saw old mixed with new. As we traveled in Guangdong Province, I noticed electrical connections running to most houses, and many villagers told us they now had running water. Paved highways crossed much of the region, but dirt roads still connected many smaller towns. Earthy smells and the sounds of animals hung in the air, summoning memories of my first arrival more than fifty years ago.

Robert, Edith and Florence had visited Lin Fong Lei some years earlier, but I stayed away, mainly because of my pain at Mother's death. For the longest time, returning to the village held no interest for me. When Robert and Edith made plans for this second family trip, I wavered again. When I learned that all my sisters had signed on, I agreed to join them. My daughters Bess and Thel came too, along with Dorothy's daughter Lorraine and Robert's daughter Barbara. What a trip it was. Our first stops were in China's large cities, Beijing and Shanghai, with side trips to the Great Wall and Xian. As we turned farther south, we visited Guangzhou. There I retraced the steps Mother and I followed when we arranged passage out of the country many years ago.

Arriving in the fall, we were surprised by the heat and humidity, which felt more like summer. To reach Lin Fong Lei, we first climbed aboard a large bus. For the final ten miles, we transferred to a smaller van that barely held all of us, but only a smaller vehicle could navigate the narrow road. Soon we were off on what became a scary trip as our driver sped down a rutted road. As he dodged ox carts, we gripped our seats for balance in the tilting vehicle. Rounding a corner, we came to a dusty halt at a crossroads where a sign pointed out the village. We could barely make out the wording on the sign, but our driver turned down the left-hand fork.

Suddenly we came to an open field. In front of us stood our house, just as I remembered it, at the end of a row of houses. Villagers in the fields paused and stared as our van stopped.

A small gathering of people milled about next to Lin Fong Lei's assembly of houses. Our home and fields looked much the same, but some newer structures stood around the village. To the left of our house, the neighboring home had a new exterior of green tiles covering all of its walls. Walking up to our old front door, the family of one of our uncles, now the residents in the house, greeted us. We stepped inside and looked around. Off to one side was a downstairs bedroom, where pink ribbon trimmed the door jamb, a sign that a girl had just been born. Holding a tiny baby in her arms, a young woman stood in the center of the room. By tradition, the baby cannot be taken outside the house for its first month, so mother and daughter were still indoors.

As we explored the first and second floors after so many years, my sisters and I acted like the children we had been in these same rooms. We had lived there with no electricity, but now we noticed a single light bulb dangling from a thin wire in the ceiling in one room. On the floor next to the kitchen stood a large rice grinder similar to ours, its large wooden arm leaning on its pivot point with a large cement block at one end. Upstairs, the bedrooms looked bleak, with a few simple pieces of furniture, a metal folding chair and several wooden platform beds. Suspended above the beds were bundles of mosquito netting and clothing, hung there to keep away the insects, mice and rats. How my sisters and I had fit in our old bedroom was a question we pondered as we looked around.

One upstairs room was locked. The key, we were told, was in the hands of a woman from the family of Father's first wife. The contents of the room, she believed, were her share of the worth of the house.

Before we went downstairs, we inspected the family shrine, which occupied its precise spot above the hallway, with remembrances placed in the niches of our ancestors. I could not tell if offerings had been made recently, but I hoped so.

Back in the kitchen, I noticed a fire burning in the stove, the same burners Mother and Florence had used for our meals. A pile of sticks, dried grass and straw filled our wood storage spot. All that was missing was our pig burrowing into the heap.

From the time we stepped into the house, Mother's presence surrounded me. There in the kitchen, I kept thinking how Mother would be disappointed in its current condition. Her kitchen stove seemed dirty, the few shelves had a coating of dust and the floor needed sweeping. Our mother would not have rested in the face of such disorder in her home. I felt a force urging me to clean and scrub so that our home would again meet her standards. Reflecting on past New Year's house cleanings, I felt my sisters and I should sweep out all the dirt.

Another thought saddened me. Mother, once the driving force in our family and in my life, now existed only on the paper of old photographs, kept faraway in our homes in America. Her memory remained impressed on just a few, her daughters and sons.

As we looked around, more recollections crept into my mind. In many ways, my life in the village had been a bit of heaven and hell, family fun and togetherness on the one hand and hard work and malaria on the other. Toiling alongside my sister Maymie and my cousins in the fields offered me my first responsibilities and feelings of companionship. Returning as an adult, I could see how I first learned to cope with many of life's difficulties and conflicts based on early lessons in Lin Fong Lei. Traveling with my sisters again, I recalled those times and our regular routines that formed a structure and friendship in my life, stretching from Maymie to all my brothers and sisters. Would any of us want to go back to those days? Not at all. But we could look back and appreciate many of the lessons of our early years in the village; mainly that we survived many of life's challenges.

Although my purpose on this trip was to see my home and revisit my family's past, I thought, too, of Charlie and his family in nearby How Voy village. By this time, I had lost a number of people who were special to me. Still, Charlie's death was the most difficult for me to survive. Years earlier, I realized I would never get over the shock of his passing. Now, as we toured my old village, I thought back to when we lived together as newlyweds just a few hours' walk away.

My reflections turned to Father as well—a much more distant memory now. All of my family, I believe, had difficulty knowing what to make of Father. Mostly a mystery to us, he was aloof, stern, even unfair at times. His children were expected to follow his standards to the letter. The same was required of his wife. While I loved him, I realized now as an adult that I remembered him more as a figurehead, someone who passed along specific values I could describe, not so much as my father any longer. He was always there, always the same, but unapproachable and separate from his family. From him we learned to be quiet, obedient and loyal. All of these traits, still so important to me, echoed again as we walked around our village.

From the time our van arrived in Lin Fong Lei, I felt the pull of connection to the place. I knew I was tied to the fields, to the house, to the jumble of worn-out buildings. There was a feeling of peace as I gazed at the fields where Maymie and I worked, where Florence brought us lunch. My close bonds to my family and my past all originated here in this isolated spot.

What I also felt was sadness at my past fading away. The village, always very small, now looked even tinier than I remembered it. Somehow, the fields around the village, though still mostly rice paddies and vegetable patches, seemed like miniatures of what I recalled. The ground we dug, the fields our water buffalo plowed, the paths we followed, the world I knew years before must have been larger.

As we walked, I felt my family was retracing the steps of Mother and Father. Each path and alley marked the steps of my parents. I felt the presence of Mother and Father all around. In all the years since they went away, here was the first time I could visualize them again.

Yet, my generation of the family had all moved on. The people in this village no longer looked familiar. All that was left for us in Lin Fong Lei were the graves of Mother and Father, located beyond the fields, dirt paths and streams, on the hillside overlooking the small town.

By midmorning, we set off for the hike up to the resting places of our parents. Led by a few cousins and six or seven villagers, we wound past fields and smaller collections of rough houses. Although the day was slightly overcast, I felt the heat whenever the sun peeked out. Our trek linked us to ancient China. Annual visits to ancestral graves are a tradition, usually occurring during the Ch'ming Festival in early April. Some families call it *ta-ch'ing,* meaning "stepping on the green." Others call it *pai-fen,* "bowing before the grave." On these memorial days, processions of families returning to the burial places of their ancestors were a common sight. Here, I suppose, were the teachings of Confucius in clear view: remembering the debt owed by the living to their deceased and revered ancestors. Often during these cemetery visits, a feast is prepared and carried to the grave. The men clean the gravesite and plant new trees. Women in the family prepare the feast and show devotion in worship services for the dead.

On the day for our hike, several villagers lugged a whole pig on a platform attached to poles they balanced on their shoulders. Others carried offerings in baskets. We brought whisky, oranges and bowls of rice.

As we neared Father's grave, Robert took the lead, the role dictated by tradition for the oldest son. He brought us to Father's burial site, where we made our offerings of whisky and food, burned paper money and lit punks of incense. Robert spoke of our respect for Father. The solemn event ended with fireworks.

Then, we walked a short distance and slightly higher up the hill to Mother's grave, as the villagers followed behind carrying the pig and their baskets. My mother's resting place had no marker, but our cousins knew the site. Again, we laid our offerings around the gravesite, including more whisky and food. We lit our money and incense and concluded again with fireworks. Thinking we were finished, the villagers hoisted the pig for the journey back down the hill to the village, where we planned to hold a feast with relatives.

As everyone turned to leave, I faltered in my stance. If I haven't got a perfectly clear image of the day's events and my Mother's solitary grave above the village, the fault is not entirely my own. The countryside presented few fixed images. The rice fields, rows of vegetables and earthen walls we passed seemed identical. The low hills projected no striking landmarks to give directions and bearings. Arriving at her grave on this small rise with a view of the valley, I was surprised at first by the vista. Situated near the crest of a low ridge, the site offered a trace of a view of the lowlands below and our home village. If it were not Mother's resting place, I might have called the outlook pleasing. Abruptly it occurred to me how lonely I felt, how isolated the location seemed.

I tried to steady myself amid a rush of emotions and gloom. I was shaken by the notion that the people standing atop this rise were the only carriers of Mother's memory. Yet, day by day those memories would fade from existence if we didn't strive to pass them along to our children with the accuracy and meaning they deserved.

Again, my regrets tormented me. Why didn't Mother try to flee China and return to the United States? Why did she not try to reach out for help? She saved each one of us; why couldn't she have saved herself? But we only know to ask these questions as we look back in time.

In that moment many years before, no one could have anticipated what would happen to Mother. She could not have guessed what horrible fate awaited her back in our village. Estimates are that millions of innocent men and women were persecuted mercilessly in China's land reform and prison camps. No one knew the rage and violence that was coming. Mother, for her own reasons, chose to go back to Lin Fong Lei. We will never know why exactly.

Silently, I reasoned with myself: To think this way does no good.

For a long time, I stood gazing at the landscape, my family group and Mother's grave. After departing from my village four decades earlier as an eighteen-year-old about to marry, I had returned for the first time to stand at Mother's grave. In many ways, this spot and the gathering closed the complete circle of my travels. Part of me longed to go back in time to 1948 so I could be by her side in life again, to stand with her to face the anger of the villagers and the consuming drive of China's new government to punish landowners. I know my brothers and sisters would have done the same.

Misery swept over me. We wanted to comfort Mother, but we knew she was beyond our reach. Falling to my knees at Mother's grave, I began to sob. Soon, many other family members were in tears as well. After a time, we consoled each other enough so that we could make our final offerings to Mother's memory. From the top of the hill, we looked down again at Lin Fong Lei. The low angle of the sun alerted us that it was time to retrace our path down to the valley. A somber mood settled over us, one that endured through our late afternoon feast in the village.

Later, as our driver took us away from the village, I considered our trip. We had traveled nearly 7,000 miles, returned to our family home, walked in the footsteps of my childhood and stood at my parents' graves. These were powerful, moving experiences. I couldn't shake the longing I had felt to protect Mother.

I thought about how she is buried higher up the hill, slightly off to the side of the valley from our father's grave. She is by herself in that spot. On the drive to our hotel and later on the flight home, I kept telling myself over and over, "She shouldn't be alone, all by herself on that distant hill."

Because of Mother, her decisions and her actions, I have enjoyed a wonderful husband, a fine family and a full life in America. She gave these things to me. Her choices made me who I am.

You Can Do It

Helena, Montana, is not my birthplace, but I feel like it should have been. For more than sixty years, I have lived in this distinctive place—first in its historic downtown and later on the east side. I have experienced it as a town of 17,000 people and later as a city of nearly 40,000. Even now, in its more modern form, Helena retains its Western character, its friendliness and its beauty. For me, it has offered anxieties and challenges, opportunities and support. I travel but always come home to stay.

Helena's YMCA, always a part of my family's life, got me going in organized workouts years ago. My "Y time" started when I took my two youngest there for swimming lessons. Watching them in the water, I began to wonder if I could learn to swim. To myself, I said: "I want to do that, too."

Thinking I could teach myself to swim, one day I returned to the pool on my own. How I thought I could teach myself, I don't know, but since I was approaching my late thirties, I thought I should try. That day at the pool, I stood for a long time at the edge, too afraid to take that first step. But I wasn't ready to give up either, so I slowly climbed down into the three-foot depth and retreated to the corner of the pool. There I was: out of the way of other swimmers and safely surrounded on both sides by the crook of concrete. I stood for a very long time.

After thinking about my situation for quite a while as I stood in that corner, I concluded that this was a foolish idea and I should get out of the pool. Just then, two kindly and sympathetic female swimmers approached me.

"We can see you haven't made much progress so far this morning. Do you need some help here?" one said, in something of an understatement.

I offered an enthusiastic "yes." With that, the two kind women set to work teaching me to swim.

"We'll have you float on your back. That is an easy way to begin," said the second woman.

"Okay," I said. To say otherwise would be to quit.

"Here is what you can do to start," said the first woman. "You lean back into my hands, settle down on your back and lift your feet off the bottom. We'll steady you."

"Are you sure about this?" I asked. They seemed to know what they were doing, so I tilted back into their hands and got in as deep as my ears. Trusting their judgment, I lifted my feet up off the pool bottom. Before I knew it, I was balanced just fine. Then they let go. Immediately, I was sputtering water, gasping for air and jumping back to my feet.

They apologized quickly for letting me sink. Just keep trying, they assured me, and you will soon improve.

"I am not sure about this. Do you really think I can do it?"

"Of course," they said.

My two instructors encouraged me to try again. Soon, they had me floating on my back. I gazed at the ceiling, kicked my feet tentatively and fluttered my hands at my side. Shortly, I was smiling a bit foolishly and kicking my way across the width of the pool. They seemed pleased with their work.

What a joy it was to kick and float from corner to corner in the pool. Still, I wasn't sure that this first lesson would sink in, so I did not get my swimming hopes up right away.

But with my usual steady, stubborn approach to most anything, I kept coming back to the Y almost daily that first week. Before long, with the help of other swimmers, I flipped over on my stomach and took a few tentative freestyle strokes. As my next step, I swam the width of the pool without touching bottom. I realized my time to venture to the deep end was at hand.

For this undertaking, I recruited June Ketron, a familiar face at the pool. I asked her to give me pointers and monitor my progress as I left the shallow end behind. Coached by June and other swimmers, I progressed from short swims to longer laps. In a matter of weeks, I became a regular in the Y pool.

Over the next year, my confidence in the water improved noticeably and my swimming helped me get in better shape. About this time, Poy and Nancy joined a synchronized swimming team, and they talked me into joining them for a few competitions. We did a trio swim together.

Out of my determination to swim—first to learn and then to make it a regular habit—I found my first competitive fire. But other concerns intervened, forcing a long break in my swimming and other athletic pursuits. Later, Charlie's illness and death diverted my attention to the business and my children.

When I returned to athletics early in the 1980s, running caught my interest. I got my start by watching my kids jog, then began running on my own for fun, working on my mileage until I was ready to enter a race. My initial running event came in 1982, at the Governor's Cup in Helena. Although the Cup is a large race, with plenty of serious competitors, I ran purely for fun. I tackled the 5K race alongside Bess. Cheers from the crowd boosted my adrenaline, and I knew I was hooked. My children, always more active than I, provided added inspiration.

Next year, I was back at the Governor's Cup, this time running the 10K race with Thel. For both of us, the event was more about exercise and enjoyment and less about our time at the finish. Both of us struggled to complete the run. A bad knee slowed Thel, and I was not sure this longer distance was right for me. Running was a great way to get fit, I thought, but other exercise was worth a look as well.

In 1985, my children presented me with a gift of a Helena YMCA membership. Right away, I made plans to get back to my swimming, this time with an eye on better technique. Getting back in the water after so many years was a little frightening. I started with an organized water aerobics class. Soon, I adjusted so easily to the routine I got bored. Maybe if I had stayed with the aerobics, I might have enjoyed it, but my mind moved on to other pursuits. I decided to swim a lap, then another and another. Before long, whenever I came to the pool I was swimming length after length. Plenty of people say swimming laps is a bore, but I like it. To keep it interesting, I count my laps in Chinese.

By this time, my life was turning a new corner. Between 1948 and 1985, I cared for my family—cooking, cleaning and sewing. Then I went to work, although I really did not consider the grocery store, McDonald's Department Store and the Chinese Kitchen as careers. As I neared age fifty-five, I found a little more time for myself. At first, I was not sure what to do to keep busy. Soon, I discovered that a combination of running, swimming and dancing was just right for me.

As a youngster, my daughter Thel had taken dance lessons from Blanche Judge. Remembering Thel's descriptions of her experiences, I signed up for tap dancing in my sixties. A bit later, I joined another dance group of five men and ten women organized by Shirley Cummings.

At the urging of son Poy in 1989, I registered for Montana's Big Sky State Games in Billings. I have been back almost every year since. My first race was the 5K run. By 1991, I competed in swimming events at both the Big Sky State Games and the Montana Senior Olympics, winning my first gold medals.

Over the years, the more I succeeded, the more I felt a competitive fire. I set more and more goals for myself. New activities tested my old muscles, but I pushed to keep improving. The more time I spent around these athletic events, the more they grabbed me. When my youngest daughter Nancy ran the Portland Marathon in 1991, I determined that I, too, wanted to try this longer distance. By 1994, I thought my swimming endurance would carry me through a 26.2-mile run.

Well managed and relatively flat, the Portland Marathon is ideal for first-time marathoners. The trouble was I didn't train beyond my regular swimming schedule. I just happened to be in Portland in early October, realized the race was taking place the next day and, on the spur of the moment, showed up at the starting line at 7 A.M. Joining me were my four daughters and son-in-law Rick. Just under eight hours later, I completed my first 26.2-mile event. Slow, I thought, but not bad for someone age sixty-six. The weather that day, fortunately, was cool. The course, true to reputation, was relatively easy, except for the approach to the St. Johns

Bridge. Walking at a good pace the whole route, I finished pretty much as I'd planned, in less than eight hours. Good thing, too, as the course marshals closed the route right after I crossed the finish line. My time did not discourage me in the least. I enjoyed the event so much I immediately planned my return.

My next goal: To return and improve my performance. For eight months prior to the event, I followed a much more rigorous training schedule, exercising along with my sister Maymie on vacations. Adding to my excitement was the fact that the 1995 marathon was to become something of a family reunion. All my kids, one son-in-law and several of Maymie's kids joined in the run. Also on hand were my sisters Edith, Florence, Maymie and Dorothy and brother Robert. My grandchildren, Maymie's husband, Mon, and some of their grandchildren participated in the shorter fun run. Training paid off, and I shaved some time off my previous effort, finishing in six hours. I had so much fun that I returned in 1997 and 2000—always with lots of family for support.

Starting in 2003, I turned to a shorter distance, the half marathon at the Montana Governor's Cup in Helena. Gloria Lambertz, a good friend, training partner and coach, helped me prepare. Over the years, we completed more than a half dozen of these runs.

Along the way, my schedule began to fill with other regular events. Favorites have included the half marathon at the Montana Governor's Cup, the Montana Women's Mother's Day 8K in Billings and the Mount Helena Run. Also in Montana, I always try to make it to the Big Sky State Games, the Prickly Pear Run, the Race for the Cure, the Ice Breaker and the Grizzly 10K run.

Outside my home state, I make dates for the Wyoming Senior Olympics, the Idaho Senior Games, the Bay to Breakers 12K Run in San Francisco, the Bloomsday 12K in Spokane, the California Senior Games, the Nevada Senior Games, the Huntsman Games in Utah and perhaps the Chicago Marathon's 5K race. My swimming times have qualified me for participation in national and world competitions for seniors. I have traveled to four nationals and one world games in New Zealand. In my last national swim meet in California, I came home with five medals. Although none was a gold, I was proud of my five silvers.

With all of these competitions and the necessary travel, my calendar

Flora at National Senior Games, August 2009.

fills up quickly. My timetable prevents me from seeing my family as much as I would like. We have found the perfect remedy, however. Many of them continue to join me at competitions and events throughout the year.

For its scenery and fun, the 12K Bay to Breaker's Run remains one of my favorites. Each year, the race is part family reunion and part circus. My daughter Thel and sister Dorothy open their homes and hospitality to a large group of extended Wong family members. We eat, talk and drink too much to prepare for the event, celebrating so much it is easy to forget that we are in San Francisco for a long run from downtown to Golden Gate Park. The pre-race fun comes back to haunt us when we come to the Hayes Street hill, a steep climb early in the race.

But the bands, the incredible costumes on runners and walkers and the complete lack of costumes—or any clothing at all—on others make up for any pain. I usually walk the course, but my daughters have noticed my pace picks up just after the start in downtown San Francisco. It is the scenery, I say. But my daughters accuse me of trying to keep up with a group of naked runners.

Count the Huntsman World Senior Games in St. George, Utah as another highlight of my annual athletic calendar. Again, I usually attend with a large number of family and friends, so the event is part reunion, part track and swimming meet. I love accumulating medals, so I push myself to enter the maximum allowed number of events. A normal week in St. George sees me entering the 200-, 400-, 800-, and 1500-meter running events. In swimming, I try for the 50-, 100-, 200-, 400- and 800-yard freestyle events, the 50-, 100- and 200-yard backstroke races and the 100-yard individual medley.

As good fortune would have it, my birthday usually falls in the midst of the Huntsman Games action. In the tight schedule of athletic events, we set aside time for a birthday party, organized by Bess with help from other family members in attendance. The fun includes a large number of friends from around the country who return each year for the games. How better to spend your time than with athletic events and a grand party surrounded by good friends and family.

During one year at the Huntsman Games, we had so many family members in attendance that we formed five triathlon teams. Maymie and Robert teamed up with me. Daughters Thel, Bess and Gloria formed another group. Kevin Ho, Maymie's son, teamed up with a good friend of his from Chicago. Damon Ho, another of Maymie's sons, linked up with Poy and Gloria Lambertz. Rounding out our contingent was my nephew Larry and his team of friends. Best of all, my team won gold in our age bracket.

When I am home, my regular routine consists of swimming 2,000 yards daily, nearly every week, usually at the Helena YMCA. If the weather allows, I try to walk between two and five miles once or twice each week. As a big event approaches, I try to step up that training pace slightly. The biggest payoff has been that, as a woman in my eighties, I enjoy robust health.

In terms of athletic stature in sports, my events rank near the bottom. Very few titles at the games I attend merit much mention in the media, not even in the hometown papers of the many participants. But I can assure you senior athletes approach each race with keenness and preparation that ranks alongside many better-known athletes. And I would wager that we are happier with our performances, no matter the outcome, than most of the famous athletes you hear about regularly.

Our finishes rate lots of cheers from small crowds. Our fellow competitors are always delightful, the cities we visit are almost always charming, the thrill of competition is constant. One of the pleasures of competition is the knowledge that you will celebrate the events with people you enjoy. We always seem to have a great party or two. We look forward to the conversations and diversions, which are part of all these games.

At the close of each meet, I am happy to be heading off to the next competition on my calendar. You could argue, I suppose, just as some of my family members might try, that this pace is too much for someone in her eighties. Be assured I will tell them when I am ready to stay home.

My philosophy in sports is simple: Do what you love and love what you do. And keep at it. You can do it. Don't beat yourself up over a bad performance and don't listen to the naysayers. For me, a win is whenever I am doing my best. I know my viewpoint isn't unique or revolutionary, but it works for me.

Another formula for success in sports is to enjoy the people you meet. Sure, I remember the medals along the way, but the people I meet make the competition so valuable. These many friendships have made all the difference in my enjoyment of events. Your fellow athletes are a source of tips and encouragement. Believe me, even if we don't admit it to ourselves, we all need that encouragement. In my sporting life, my grandchildren—Melissa Snyder, Mackynze Snyder, Krissy Wong and Nik Wong—are among my best supporters, proving to me again and again how sports bring people together.

Years ago, at the beginning of my athletic endeavors, I did not think much about the medals. Now, I must admit I am proud of the mass of them I have accumulated. Further, I have to admit I really do like the gold ones better than any others. Since getting serious about competition in 1991, I have won about 565 medals. But it takes work. As I write this, my swimming log shows that I have covered 4,660 miles in the water in about thirty years. As a youngster, I never felt a competitive streak, but I see that element of my personality has changed. When the games start up, so do I.

Now, in my third decade of competition, I remain just a little disappointed if I don't take home a gold medal in each of my events. And, I admit, I do enjoy the modest recognition that comes my way. In 1999, good friend Gloria Lambertz nominated me as Big Sky State Games Female Athlete of the Year. What an honor when I won and carried the torch around the track, passing it off to Olympic Gold Medalist Trent Dimas. Ten years later, another friend and fellow competitor, Terry Dagenais, nominated me to be included in the Helena Sports Hall of Fame. In 2009, I received the award at a large banquet, but the highlight of my day was a parade around downtown Helena on the back of an old fire engine. With my fellow inductees on board, we made two laps around the city, waving and laughing.

The way I see it, we have three reasons to enjoy sports, and life for that matter. First, sports are a chance to test yourself against your past performances. Yes, one could say that it's time at this stage of life to slow down, but that is not my goal.

Second, you are alive. That you are able to stand up and get moving, even if the pace is slower, is something to celebrate each day. I try to live by that notion, and it keeps me going. Sure, the time will come when I have to slow down. But even if my pace slows, I trust it will remain steady.

Third, I know that if I quit, I lose. By contrast, when I keep moving I am never unhappy. In fairness, that simple recipe does not mean you won't be discouraged, won't wonder sometimes how you will cope, won't have feelings of despair. Still, my life has taught me that the resilience of the human spirit can be wondrous beyond belief. And even when you don't hit life's highest points every time, you will find, by pushing ahead, by resolving to make the most of your time and talents, you will make each day of your life so much more pleasant. To me, the determined outlook of athletes is inspiring. When I compete, I recognize my need to temper my pace as I continue to test my limits. Sports remind me you can't quit when you are tired; you quit only when the job is done. Through athletics, I again learned you can overcome your fears. I discovered this lesson in other ways early in China, whether dealing with war, hard labor or saying goodbye.